FALANGE

FALANGE

The Axis Secret Army
in the Americas

By

ALLAN CHASE

G. P. PUTNAM'S SONS
NEW YORK

TO MARTHA

**WITHOUT WHOSE AID
THIS BOOK COULD NOT
HAVE BEEN WRITTEN**

"Spain is the key to two continents."
—HERMANN GOERING, 1936

"The great unity of the Axis includes Nazis, Fascists, and Spanish Falangistas. There is no longer any distinction between Fascism, Nazism, and Falangismo."
—BENITO MUSSOLINI, September 30, 1942

"Many thanks to you and the German peoples. May your arms triumph in the glorious undertaking of freeing Europe from the Bolshevik terror."
—FRANCISCO FRANCO to Adolf Hitler, December 7, 1942

This book is made possible by the work of hundreds of brave, selfless, devoted men and women in Latin America, the United States, North Africa, and Axis Spain. Many of them are my friends. Many of them I know only by their efforts. Many of them are anonymous soldiers in the ranks of the republican Spanish People's Army, scattered, without uniform, throughout the world.

There are times when a writer can gratefully acknowledge by name the persons who helped him most in the creation of a book. There are other times when such acknowledgments would be like a kiss of death. Such are the times we know today: a time which sees the armies of the Axis alive and intact. To reveal the names of many of the brave people who helped me—to reveal their names while Hitler sits in Berlin as a ruler rather than as a prisoner in a death cell—would be to betray them to the mercies of Axis killers everywhere.

I am thinking particularly of people like the girl Josefina, whose hair turned gray in twelve hours during a Nazi assault on Cartagena in 1937, and who today is making the invaders of her native land pay a fantastic price for their crimes. Or General X, whose loyalty to the republic he served wavered with neither defeat nor poverty. Or the former scholar, Esteban.

Esteban is a proud, fearless Spaniard. When Hitler's legions invaded Spain in 1936, Esteban was a graduate student in philosophy at a Spanish university. His family was among the first to be killed by the bombs which fell from the black bellies of the Axis planes. His books were destroyed, his classroom became a snipers' nest, his college became a front-line trench of World War II.

Esteban gave up his books for the war. He has not picked them up since 1936; for Esteban, like so many others of his generation, has long since learned that freedom of thought is impossible in a Fascist world. Without heroics, and after 1939 without uniform, Esteban has been a soldier of democracy in the war against fascism. From dawn to dawn, seven days of each week, Esteban has waged the good fight. Whether in Spain, in France, in North Africa, in Latin America—the front remained.

He is merely one of many who never surrendered—like the Spanish Republican Army which took to the hills in the Asturias in 1939 and has been killing Nazis ever since. Like the Spanish Republican veterans now in the armies of the United States and England, Esteban goes on fighting the butchers of Guernica, of Warsaw, of Lidice. For the war which started in Spain has since spread all over the world.

We met in a café somewhere between Key Largo and Buenos Aires. Josefina, who had made the arrangements, had warned me to make a tight fist while shaking hands with Esteban. As I sat down after so greeting him, there was a paper-covered roll of microfilm in my right fist; negatives of documents taken from a supposedly secret vault the Falange maintained in the Western Hemisphere.

It was a very plain café, its open front looking out on an ancient cobbled square, a brooding massive cathedral, a stall with a white and pink quarter of beef hanging in the sun. The square and the cathedral had been built by Spaniards who died hundreds of years ago.

We might have been sitting in Spain itself, I thought; and, as if to heighten this fancy, an old woman wound the antique gramophone under the yellowing lithograph of a Madrid bull-fight on the far wall and put a scratchy disk under the blunted needle. "Flamenco," Esteban said wearily. "Gypsy music."

The record played through to the end, and then the old woman played a dozen others. They were mainly flamenco records; and listening to them under the steady flow of Esteban's words I thought of what an old friend had said about flamenco songs—that they are all rituals before death. I remembered these words and thought of Spain's ordeal as Esteban spoke and flamenco followed flamenco.

Esteban's long fingers tore the hard crust of a *flauto;* and, because he had grown used to hunger as a way of life, he automatically brushed up the crumbs and flipped them into his soup. "It was perhaps an imperfect republic," he said, "but it was a good one. Man, too, is imperfect; but man is fundamentally good." He spoke about the school the Republic had opened in a small Andalusian village in 1932, and of the girl who had gone from Madrid to teach the children of illiterate peasants how to read. He spoke of a clinic in Madrid, an agricultural institute in Valencia, a momentous session of the Cortes in 1936. He spoke of the law which put windows into the rooms of the slums in Barcelona and of the prize fighter who had carried Pablo Casals on his shoulders from the concert hall to the hotel after a great recital. "It was a republic of hope," he said.

He spoke of the fascists, too. Of the Falangistas who shot the poet Federico Garcia Lorca. Of the vulgarian Quiepo de Llano and his pornographic radio speeches to the women of the Republic. Of the Italian Colonel at Guadalajara, the day it rained and the Republic for once had enough *aviones,* and the Italians ran like sheep: the Blackshirt Colonel tore off his uniform and picked up a spade, and stood in the field turning the soil and shouting in Spanish, "I'm just a poor peasant," until Esteban's commander personally sent a stream of machine-gun bullets through the coward's eyes. "He was a small creature," Esteban said of the Colonel. "A small creature without dignity."

We finished our coffee, and Esteban said "no" to another rum. The old woman was changing another record when Esteban said *it.* I don't remember the words that came first, but I recall them as being quite natural and easy. "I know what I'm doing," Esteban said softly. "I know why I'm doing it, and I'm not afraid." The words read like bad theater, but he spoke them like a man talking about the weather. They were a casual answer to a question I had framed without speaking.

"Because I am a Spaniard," he concluded, as simply and

as softly as he had spoken when telling about that village school.

"And now," he said, rising to his feet, "I must go."

We both stood up, and he embraced me and pounded my back and laughed. I tried to think of something to tell him, something that would not sound banal. "Because," I said, "because I am an American . . ." And then I stopped, a little self-conscious, and more than a little afraid to make Esteban feel I was mocking him.

We were supposed to meet again that week. But the next day Esteban was already on the high seas, bound for Spain and the republican underground on a boat that had once flown the colors of the Spanish Republic.

Because I am an American, Esteban—this book.

ALLAN CHASE

April 19, 1943

Contents

CHAPTER ONE

Der Auslands Falange Is Born

EARLY IN 1934, Adolf Hitler summoned General Wilhelm von Faupel to the Chancellory in Berlin. Their conference lasted for nearly a full day. When he left, von Faupel's bulging brief case was thicker by one sheet of paper, a paper that was to affect the destinies of scores of nations, millions of people.

The paper, signed by Hitler, was Wilhelm von Faupel's appointment as chief of the Ibero-American Institute of Berlin.

On the surface, there was nothing sinister in this appointment. The Institute had been formed in 1930 by Dr. Otto Boelitz, a German scholar. Its assets had included some 150,-000 volumes collected by German universities, donated by Latin-American institutions, and willed by individual German and South American pedants. It had acted as a cultural clearinghouse between intellectuals in Germany and their colleagues in Latin America, and had added materially to its collection of books since its inception. Then, a week or so before von Faupel met with Hitler, Boelitz suddenly found himself in disgrace. He was booted out of his post and disappeared from sight.

General Wilhelm von Faupel was not a scholar. A slight, graying aristocrat, he peered at the world from under the archest, bushiest eyebrows in all Europe. His fellow officers of the old *Reichswehr* generally tried to avoid him; he had a nasty manner of mocking their inner weaknesses with his cobra eyes. Behind his back, they called him "Colonel Eyebrows" and "Field Marshal Ears"—the latter in deference to his huge teddy-bear ears. But they never openly treated him with disrespect.

There were many reasons for this cautious politeness; perhaps the foremost was von Faupel's known standing as an "I. G. general." His fellow officers were no fools. They knew that the I. G. Farben chemical trust and the heavy-industry crowd led by Thyssen were the real powers behind Hitler. For at least a year prior to von Faupel's appointment the Berlin grapevines had been heavy with rumors about a key post being created for the general by I. G. Yet none but a handful of key men had even an inkling of what this post would entail.

The man had many talents. During the First World War, von Faupel had distinguished himself at the Western Front. He spoke French, Russian, Spanish, Portuguese, Chinese, and other languages with fluency. He was a great military theorist. He had served as Inspector General of the Peruvian Army.

The fabulous career of the tight-lipped General offered many keys to the mystery of his new assignment. As a young Imperial Staff Officer, von Faupel traveled to China in 1900 to serve on the Kaiser's military legation. From China, he had moved to a similar job in Moscow. In 1904, fresh from his stay in Moscow, he was rushed to German East Africa, where he served as an officer in the punitive expeditions which came close to touching off the First World War a decade ahead of its time. Then, in 1911, Wilhelm von Faupel made the most important move of his career: he accepted an offer to join the staff of the Argentine War College in Buenos Aires.

Wilhelm von Faupel left Argentina when the war broke out in 1914, but in 1921 he returned to Buenos Aires as military counselor to the Inspector General of the Argentine Army. The von Faupel who returned to Argentina, however, was a completely changed man. Not a trace remained of the youngish, soft-spoken military specialist who had relished native wines and Viennese waltzes in the gay years before the war. His soft, almost gentle voice had hardened into a perfect instrument for the tempered steel trap that was now his mind. Germany's defeat had seared von Faupel's soul with its bitterest of acids.

The new von Faupel started counseling the Argentine military leaders on more than merely army procedure. Day after day, as he drilled the Republic's troops, von Faupel drilled into the heads of the influential upper-class Argentinians the doctrine of total war on the "mob-beast of democracy." It was this "mob-beast"—the common man of Germany—whom Wilhelm von Faupel held primarily responsible for the victory of the Allies and the collapse of the German home front.

For five years von Faupel held his important post in Argentina. He brought over many of his German officer friends, found assignments for them as specialists in the Army. He made many friends among the wealthy landowning Argentinians who controlled the political life of the nation. In 1926 he left Buenos Aires to accept a high military post in the Brazilian Army. Here, again, he assumed the dual role of military expert and anti-democracy agitator.

The embittered Prussian general's fame as an army builder spread throughout the continent. It became so imposing that the Peruvian Government invited him to assume the job of Inspector General of Peru's armed forces. Von Faupel took this command in 1927. Not until he was certain that the Nazis would get control of the Fatherland did von Faupel resign this post. He left it for an amazing mission in China which ended when Hitler called him to Berlin to take over the Ibero-American Institute.

During all of his years of self-imposed exile in South America, Wilhelm von Faupel had maintained close ties with German enemies of democracy—men like Fritz Thyssen, the banker Baron von Schroeder, Franz von Papen, and I. G. Farben's Georg von Schnitzler. He knew of their plans to destroy the Weimar Republic through the Nazi "revolution" they were financing and guiding. And he knew of their plans to create a German world empire once their man Hitler assumed the mantle of Germany's chosen leader.

Wilhelm von Faupel lived only for the day when he could play his part in this coming drive for empire. Carefully he worked out a theory of his own, a theory of German world conquest. Bit by bit he put together the jig-sawed pieces of a flawless plan.

"I am prepared to conquer all of Latin America," he blandly informed von Schnitzler when he returned to Germany in 1934. His plans were minutely detailed in a fat thesis typed at least a year before the Reichstag Fire.

The idea of a German conquest of Latin America was far from a new one in *Reichswehr* circles. During the First World War, the Germans had tried to win over Mexico and other Latin-American governments. That they failed von Faupel ascribed to the stupidity of the Imperial Staff's approach to the problem. His two decades of intimate contact with Latin America had brought him face to face with what he became convinced was the key to the domination of twenty nations. That key was—Spain.

In nearly every country south of the United States borders, von Faupel had made contact with the landed Spanish aristocracy. The great bulk of these people, many of them first- or second-generation Spanish by birth, still recognized no allegiance other than the one they bore to monarchist Spain. Immensely powerful in the economic and political life of the Latin-American countries, these Spanish concentrations looked forward to the day when the victories of the armies of Bolivar, San Martin, O'Higgins, Sucre, and the United States—victories which drove Imperial Spain out of the New World and the Philippines—would be wiped out. They talked morosely, mystically, but *seriously*, of the glorious day when the Spanish Empire would again come into its own.

The canny von Faupel always made a point of agreeing with such sentiments whenever he heard them expressed. A realist to the bitter core, he had nothing but contempt for the uprooted Spanish aristocrats who worshiped a monarchist Spain as decadent and as futile as that of Alfonso. He kept his contempt discreetly hidden, however, and formulated what in the beginning seemed even to him hopeless dreams of an imposing imperialist Spain revived and controlled by the coming new German World Order.

The events of April 12, 1931—when the Spanish monarchy was bloodlessly overthrown by the "mob-beast" at the ballot boxes—seemed to write *finis* to von Faupel's maturing dream. For it was clear to the fact-facing Prussian militarist that the great majority of Spaniards in Spain itself entertained none of the mystical notions of empire common among the Spanish aristocrats of the New World. Alfonso XIII's inglorious abdication and retreat to the Monte Carlo gambling pavilions, the Constitution of the New Spanish Republic—patterned so closely after the Constitution of the United States—were frontal attacks on the very spine of Wilhelm von Faupel's master plan. Without a hope of a Spanish empire, with a new Spain committed to travel in the democratic path of the despised "Jew-Protestant Colossus of Washington," the spiritual ties which bound the overseas aristocrats with the mother country were doomed to wither and die.

To von Faupel's joy, he discovered that the men who were financing Hitler had no intention of letting such technicalities as the Spanish general elections of 1931 stand in the way of the German drive toward empire. To be sure, the Thyssens and the von Schnitzlers had somewhat overlooked the spiritual ties which bound noble Spaniards abroad to the Bourbon throne. They had not, however, overlooked the tungsten, mercury, iron, olive oil, citrus, copper, tin, lead, and potassium riches of the young Iberian Republic.

Nor had the tacticians and military geographers of the finance-*Reichswehr*-industry cabal behind Hitler ignored Spain's strategic position as the key to the Mediterranean, the gateway to the Atlantic, and the flank supreme against France.

"Spain," Hermann Goering declared while studying the maps of Europe and South America, "is the key to two continents."

The Berlin gossip mills hummed overtime when Wilhelm von Faupel was appointed head of the Ibero-American Institute. While tongues wagged, the General himself set about quietly changing the course of world history.

His first move, in 1934, was to reorganize the Institute itself. He broke it up into five main divisions, each directly controlled by himself. Section I covered Argentina, Uruguay, and Paraguay. Its executive was Professor Freiberg, director of the Asunción (Paraguay) Botanical Gardens. His assistant was Frau Simons Erwin Hoene, a German aristocrat.

Section II, which consisted of Brazil only, was headed by Professor Otto Quelle—editor of the *Ibero-Amerikanisches Archiv,* published in Berlin. Doctor Richert was appointed Quelle's liason with the huge German colony of Brazil.

Section III covered Chile and Bolivia. Fritz Berndt, Berlin correspondent for a number of Bolivian newspapers and principal of a Berlin high school, headed this division. His liaison in Bolivia was Federico Nielsen-Reyes, one-time secretary of the Bolivian Legation in Berlin.

Section IV was responsible for Peru, Ecuador, Colombia, and Venezuela. This section was placed in charge of one of the most extraordinary women in Germany, Dr. Edith von Faupel. Many years the junior of her husband, "Peter," as she was called by her intimates, not only performed her own sectional duties but also roamed the length and breath of Latin America as her husband's inspector general.

Section V, Panama, Central America, and Mexico, was placed in charge of Dr. Hagen and a Nazi spy named Bock.

The primary function of these sections was to organize the first- and second-generation German populations of Latin America. Through this block of some six million expatriates, General von Faupel planned to organize widespread espionage and fighting machines in all of the twenty nations below our borders. These were to be the Third Reich's shock troops in the coming battle for world empire.

Since they were Germans, these shock troops could not hope to consolidate the power they might ultimately seize. General von Faupel knew that the consolidation of Nazi power in Latin America depended heavily on the concentrations of Spanish aristocrats in each of the countries. These Spaniards—controlling as they did so much of the economic life of Latin America—were earmarked for the role of Germany's most powerful allies. Themselves tied spiritually and economically to Spain, they were potentially capable of performing great service for Germany if these services were demanded in the name of Spain. But to win them over, the Spanish Republic had to be crushed and replaced with a German-controlled Spain which would appeal to the aristocrats.

Destruction of democratic Spain called for huge funds and extraordinary powers. The men behind the creation of Hitler saw to it that Wilhelm von Faupel lacked nothing in the way of money or authority. In fact, I. G. Farben loaned one of its most trusted agents to the Institute to work directly under von Faupel.

This agent, Eberhard von Stohrer, spoke Spanish fluently. It was the least of his qualifications for the job. During the First World War, Stohrer had served in the German Embassy in Madrid as military attaché. In this post he had made firm and lasting friendships with the pro-German cliques of the swollen Spanish military hierarchy. He had also made a few clumsy diplomatic blunders. The chief of these was the organization of a military ring designed to force Spain into the war on the side of Germany. Allied Intelligence agents exposed this plot so devastatingly that the Spanish Government was forced to expel von Stohrer from the country.

An older and wiser von Stohrer was determined to make up for his old mistakes in Spain. While the furniture was being moved into the newly organized Ibero-American Institute in Berlin, von Stohrer boarded a plane for Lisbon, where he made a beeline for a quiet villa at exclusive Estoril Beach. The master of the villa was a chubby little dandy whose talents with wine and women had made von Stohrer's years in Madrid more pleasant than they might have been. His name was General José Sanjurjo.

This time von Stohrer's desires to see his old friend had little to do with past pleasures. Herr von Stohrer was on a mission, a quite official mission. He was charged with the responsibility of bringing Sanjurjo back to Berlin.

Two years earlier, on August 10, 1932, Sanjurjo had led a monarchist uprising against the year-old Spanish Republic. The *putsch* had been squelched in less than a day, its leader captured at the Portuguese border while fleeing the country. In their anger the Republic's officials had sentenced Sanjurjo to death; but within a few days, with the characteristic Christian generosity which was later to spell their own doom, they had commuted Sanjurjo's sentence to life imprisonment.

Sanjurjo was jailed in the Santa Catalina fortress in Cadiz. In prison the old monarchist general held court like an Eastern potentate. He was visited daily by Maria Caballe, the Madrid music-hall entertainer he subsequently married. Monarchist officers made his cell their Mecca.

Then, in 1934, the liberal government gave way to the CEDA coalition headed by Gil Robles. One of the first acts of the new government was the declaration of a general amnesty freeing all the imprisoned leaders of the 1932 uprising. Sanjurjo was exiled to Portugal and given a government pension of 10,000 *escudos* a month.

Gil Robles knew exactly what he was doing when he freed Sanjurjo. For Robles, like the men behind him, hated the Republic and wanted it overthrown. He looked upon Sanjurjo as the strong military leader chosen by destiny to restore the monarchy. Before long, the old general's Portuguese villa had become a regular port of call for enemies of the Republic like Juan March, the sinister ex-smuggler who rose to become one of Spain's wealthiest financiers; the coal and oil magnate Goizueta; and ranking officers of the old Army.

All this was known to von Faupel when he sent von Stohrer to Lisbon to fetch Sanjurjo. Other agents of the Third Reich were already conspiring with officers of the Spanish Army in Madrid—particularly with Colonels Kindelan and Gallarza, Major Haya, and Julio Ruiz de Alda.

The exiled Sanjurjo greeted von Stohrer with undisguised joy, and after a brief conference gaily consented to return to

Berlin with his old German monarchist carousing companion.

In the Nazi capital, Sanjurjo was granted an immediate audience with General von Faupel. The old dandy gave von Faupel a prepared list of officers still in the Army of the Republic who would most certainly be willing to lead a "monarchist revolt" against the government they had given their oath to uphold. Before the conference ended, it was also arranged to place Sanjurjo on the Nazi pay roll.

Within a few months of this 1934 meeting, Sanjurjo made a series of visits between Lisbon and Berlin. In Lisbon, he met secretly with Generals Mola, Goded, and Fanjul, all of them then in the service of the Republic. General Francisco Franco, at that time chief of the Spanish General Staff, never attended these meetings in person. Mola was his secret representative at these sessions.

By the end of the year von Faupel had formulated a complete set of plans for the Spanish "revolt." He appointed Sanjurjo "chief" and approved of Sanjurjo's choices of Goded and Fanjul as assistant chiefs. Privately, through German agents in Madrid, von Faupel advised Franco that, once the shooting began, Germany would look with great favor on the pudgy little traitor's own soaring ambitions. Franco, in turn, promised and sent hand-picked young Fascist officers to Germany for training in total warfare.

General von Faupel played his cards like a master. He knew that the language of monarchy was the most potent one within the ranks of the old Spanish generals. (Under Alfonso, there were 859 generals and 27,000 commissioned officers in the standing army of considerably less than a million troops.) He also knew that it would be a domestic political blunder inside Nazi Germany if it became known that the Nazi New Order Saviors were backing a Royalist rising in Spain. For German home consumption, a more congenial ideological tie had to be invented.

The shaping of this ideological cipher became von Faupel's next problem. A survey of the existing possibilities in Spain turned up little that looked promising. There were three main anti-Republican groups: the Monarchists, the CEDA (Confederation of Spanish Rightist Parties), and the Falange.

The Monarchists were out of the question for obvious National Socialist reasons. The creators of the Nazi movement had cleverly designed it to play on the anti-monarchist sentiments of the German people—who could never forget the horrors of the war brought on their heads by their Kaiser. The pseudo-socialism of the Nazi platform was meant to win over the great anti-monarchist majority of Germans. Were the Nazis to back an openly monarchist movement in Spain, they would have weakened their psychological grip on thousands of their followers at home.

The CEDA, led by Gil Robles, was the most powerful of the anti-Republican groupings. But Gil Robles was well known throughout Germany as the Jesuit political leader of Spain, and the CEDA was too openly recognized as the Catholic political arm. The danger of backing the Church in Spain while attacking it at home was too great for a totalitarian super-state with an avowed ideology of the future.

This left only the Falange, organized and led by young José Antonio Primo de Rivera, son of the late Spanish dictator. Openly Fascist in politics, the Falange was ignored politically by Spain's most powerful Fascists themselves.

Even von Faupel, by 1935 accustomed to the brawling Brown Shirts, threw up his hands in sheer disgust when he discovered the composition of the Spanish Falange. It was nothing but a vast employment agency for the scum of the underworld in Spain's larger cities. The rank and file of the Falange consisted of paid mercenaries almost down to the last man—hired sluggers and killers who, for a price, performed acts of fatal and nonfatal violence for all of the parties in the anti-Republican opposition. No idealistic convictions about throne, or empire, or Church kept them in the Falange—unless the creed of cash paid for bloody services rendered can be called a political or moral code.

General von Faupel grew progressively more anxious

about the ideological end of his Spanish venture as the zero hour neared. For what was needed was more than a political package suitable for German home consumption. The new Spanish puppet state had to be endowed with a political façade that would shine in the eyes of the monarchist Spaniards in Latin America and the Philippines as the streamlined hub of a dynamic empire.

In sheer panic, von Faupel deposited his ideological problem squarely in the arms of the high priest of Nazi philosophy, Alfred Rosenberg. Hitler's court metaphysician retired to his study and emerged in due time after a serious session of Aryan soul-searching. Rosenberg decided in favor of the Falange. The decision was passed on to Hitler, who in turn ordered Goebbels to start building up the Falange as a true sister Fascist party.

In due time, Berlin gave the Falange a set of appropriate principles. These "Twenty-Seven Points" have not exactly been kept under a bushel since 1936. They have been published by Falangistas in many parts of the world and in many languages. The English version issued by the Falange in San Juan, Puerto Rico, in 1936, is the one quoted verbatim below. Whether in Spanish or English, the heavy German accent of this program is apparent at once. Point by point, the program of the Falange Española Tradicionalista de la J. O. N. S. (Juntas Ofensivas Nacional-Sindicalista) is just about carbon copy of the program of the Deutscher Nazional Socialistiche Arbeiter Partei.

Here is the full program of the Falange, exactly as it appears in the official text, original spelling, punctuation and all, published by Falangist agent de la Torre in Puerto Rico. The italics, however, are mine. The Falange's own English translation is used for reasons of accuracy—and because in this translation it captures the same type of semi literate banality that characterizes the original Spanish. Like the writings of the Nazis and the Italians, the official literature of the Falange is an accurate reflection of its cultural level.

Tradicionalist Spanish Phalanx of the J.O.N.S.

NATIONAL SYNDICALISM
PROGRAM
NATION, UNITY, EMPIRE.

1. We believe in the supreme reality of Spain. The urgent task before all Spaniards is to strengthen and rise Spain to her old glory. To do this, all individuals, groups, classes and communities pledge themselves above everything else.

2. Spain is a unit of Destiny in the Universe. Any conspiracy against this unit is repulsive. All separatism is an unforgiveable crime. The present [democratic] Constitution stimulates separatism, attemps, conspires, against the unit of destiny that is Spain. Which explains why we demand the immediate annulment of the Constitution now in force.

3. *We have the will of an Empire and assert that the historic legacy of Spain is the Empire*. We demand a place of prominence among the European nations for Spain. We won't tolerate neither the isolation of our country neither foreign intervention.

Regarding the Latin American countries we intend to tighten the links of culture, economic interests and of power. Spain claims to be the *spiritual axel of the Spanish World* as a recognition of her universal enterprises.

4. Our land, air and naval forces shall be as great and powerful and numerous as the complete independence, the preeminence of Spain and the national security demands.

We shall restore to our land, naval and air forces the prestige which it deserves and shall model Spanish life along military lines.

5. Spain will again find her glory of old and her riches in ocean paths. Spain shall be again a great maritime power that it was in trade and war. We demand equality for our country, on the air, the seas and land.

STATE, INDIVIDUAL, LIBERTY.

6. *Our state will be a totalitarian instrument* at the service of the country. All spaniards will have a share in it through domestic municipal or syndical activities. No one shall participate through political parties. Party lines shall be ruthlessly wiped,

no matter what it costs, with their party representation, suffrage and the Parliament.

7. Human dignity and the integrity and liberty of man, are eternal and intangible assets. But only he who forms part of a free and powerful nation is a free man. Nobody shall have right to use his liberty against the unity, strength and liberty of his country. A strict discipline shall prevent all atempt to poison the national mind, to desintegrate the Spanish nation or conspire against the destiny of Spain.

8. The national syndicalist state shall foster all initiative of a private nature which is compatible with the collective interests and shall help along and protect those initiatives which prove beneficial.

9. From the economic standpoint we figure Spain as a gigantic producers' syndicate. We shall orgaize corporatively Spanish society by means of a system of syndicates, according to fields of production, syndicates which will be at the service of national economic integrity.

10. *We repudiate the Capitalist system* which overlooks the needs of the masses and dehumanizes private property to the extent of reducing workingmen to an amorphous mass with only misery and hunger as their heritage.

We also repudiate Marxism and will guide the energies of the workers, mislead by Marxism, into the right paths and will demand their share of participation in the great task of keeping the national unit.

11. The National syndicalist state will not evade the economic struggle between men nor shall have a grandstand seat to look complacently at the struggle between the powerful against the weak. The national syndicalist regime will make class conflict impossible, because all those who contribute to make government possible and cooperate in the production constitute part of the national unit.

We shall repudiate and not tolerate abuses from certain particular interests against others and will avoid anarchy among the working classes.

12. The main purpose of richness—and thus the State will contend is to promote welfare and the standard of living of those who from the nation. It is intolerable that great masses shall live deprived of their most elementary needs while a few enjoy luxuries and leissure lives.

13. The State shall acknowledge private property as licit means to meet personal, domestic and social needs and shall protect private property against the claws of great financial interests and powerfull speculators and professional loaners.

14. We contend that banks be nationalized and so shall be nationalized other public utilities.

15. Every Spanish citizen has a right to work and the State shall see that unemployment it conjured or that public enterprise provide bread and butter for those who can't find work. While the main objective of a great national structure is being attained we shall see that workers derive the most benefits from teh social legislation enacted.

16. All Spanish citizens have the duty to work, so the National syndicalist State will have no consideration for those who do not fulfill their duty when they are able to do so and when they try to live at the expense of others who are doing their part.

THE LAND.

17. We must, at all costs, raise the standard of living of the rural classes which are the seed of the Spanish nation. Towards attaining that goal we have pledged ourselves to carry on and without excuses the economic and social reform in the rural districts.

18. We shall enrich the agricultural production through the following means:

Insuring a minimum price for all products of the land.

Demanding that great part of what the city absorves today in payment for intelectual and commercial services to the peasantry, be returned to the country.

Organizing a true Agricultural Center, which, when it may lend money to the peasant, with the warranty of it harvests and lands, may deliver him from the clutches of usurers.

Teaching the peasants all about modern farm methods.

Decreeing the use of lands according to their conditions and the chances of marketting the products.

Enacting the tariffary laws protecting the agricultural products an dairy products.

Speeding up hydroelectric projects.

Suppressing great properties of land as well as very small lots, by means of an equal distribution of fields.

19. We shall socially organize agriculture through the following methods.

Redistributing tillable land, thus instituing the domestic property and stimulating the syndication of peasants and laborers.
Delivering from misery those poor classes who nowadays give the best of their energies to make baren land produce.
Transporting these humble and willing workers to more fertile regions.

20. We shall start a camping por [campaign for] cattle repopulation of the land as well as reforestation and shall deal mercilessly with those who hamper this work. Even if the whole of Spanish youth has to be mobilize to attain this objective we must tackle the job of reconstructing the natural riches of the land.

21. The state shall have right to expropriate without payment of indemnity all property that has been acquired ilegally or used without right to do so.

22. The State shall pay immediate attention to the reconstruction of property in city and country.

NATIONAL EDUCATION

23. Through a very strict discipline in education, the state to build up the one and only strong national spirit and make future generations feel the joy and pride of the Spanish nation.

All men shall have premilitary education which will prepare them for the honor of becoming a soldier or officer of the National Army of Spain.

24. Culture shall be so organized that no talent or genius shall be lost because of means of development, for lack or resources. All those who deserves, it, shall have free access even to superior education.

25. Our movement incarnates a Catholic sense of life—the glorious and predominant tradition in Spain—and shall incorporate it to national reconstruction. The Clergy and the State shall work together in harmony without either one invading the other's field in a way that it may bring about discord or be detrimental to the national dignity, and integrity.

NATIONAL REVOLUTION.

26. The Traditionalist Spanish Phalanx of the **J.O.N.S.** fights for a new order, summarized in the principles enunciated before. *To establish it against the existent government, it resorts to revolution.* Its style shall be direct, passionate and active. Life is struggle and shall be lived with a sense of sacrifice.

27. We struggle to achieve our aims only with those forces under our control and discipline. We shall make few negociations. Only in the final push in the conquest of the State shall our command talk terms and only when our terms are the ones to be discussed.

Like the Nazi and Fascist programs, the Falange's program promises all things to all men. With the exception of the point about the Catholic sense of life—included for obvious reasons—the entire program of the Falange is patently a crude rehash of the standard Fascist programs of Germany, Italy, and Portugal.

To peasants, Falingismo promises the breaking up of large estates and the redistribution of lands. To large landowners, it guarantees the rights of private property. To radicals, it promises the abolition of the capitalist system. To capitalists, it promises war on Marxism.

The Ninth of the Twenty-Seven Points is a bow in the direction of the powerful anarcho-syndicalist movement of the Latin countries—a movement which preached the doctrine of a state controlled by workers' syndicates (or unions.) The Nazi architects of the Falange neatly combined this theory with the corporate-state fascisms of Italy and Portugal. To make the Falangist creed more acceptable to anti-Fascists, the Nazis (who for similar reasons called their fascism "national socialism") dubbed Falange fascism "national syndicalism."

In the hands of a master like von Faupel, this program was just the key Germany had long needed—the key to the hearts of the Spanish aristocrats in the New World and the Philippines. His agents, working out of the many branch offices of the Ibero-American Institute, were able to con-

vince the wealthy expatriates that the provisions of the
Falange program which called for the redistribution of the
land and the repudiation of capitalism were as completely
meaningless as the similar provisions of the official programs
of Fascist Italy and Nazi Germany.

Over fragrant little cups of coffee in the private board
rooms of Havana and Buenos Aires, during the afternoon
quiet in the great countinghouses of Manila, von Faupel's
emissaries explained to Spaniards how to read the program
of the Falange. The points about Spain's will to empire,
about this new empire's tightening her links with Spanish
America, about Spain's becoming a totalitarian state—these
were couched in a language the wealthy expatriates welcomed and understood. Nor, when they learned that National Socialist Hitler was backing National Syndicalist
Sanjurjo, did the Spanish aristocrats in Spain or abroad have
any fears about the syndicalism of the New Spain.

To the most realistic of the Spanish aristocrats abroad,
von Faupel's agents even discreetly boasted of the thousands
of trained *Reichswehr* troops who were quietly shipped to
Italy and Spanish Morocco as tourists between April and
July 1936. These husky tourists carried German-Spanish
dictionaries in their pockets; arms and German army uniforms in their trunks. They were the advance troops of the
Condor Legions, organized by von Faupel to "rise Spain to
her old glory" and to "repudiate the Capitalist system which
overlooks the needs of the masses" in Spain.

These Condor Legionaires, quartered in hotels in Rome,
Milan, Turin, and other Italian cities as nonpaying guests of
the Italian Government, had an official marching song
which became quite a hit in Italian army circles.

> *We whistle high and low,*
> *And the world may praise or blame us.*
> *We care not what they think*
> *Or what they'll one day name us.*

It was the kind of a song bound to appeal to all Fascist
officers, expressing as it did their philosophy of arms and

men. Every ranking Fascist sang it—that is, every ranking Fascist in Italy except Il Duce.

What Mussolini actually had to say about the Condor Legion in 1936 is still a deep secret—but no secret is the fact that these cocky Nazi warriors were living evidence of one of Mussolini's latest mistakes. With characteristic judgment—or luck—Il Duce had chosen to back the wrong Fascist party in Spain. As dictator of a Catholic country, Mussolini had seen fit to support the CEDA of Gil Robles. Now, in 1936, the Father of Fascism was learning that backing the wrong Fascist cliques of other countries was a luxury he could not afford.

Hitler pointed out to Mussolini how to atone for this earlier stupidity—a stupidity that had begun some years before the Nazis took over Germany. The plan was simple: Italy was to pour tens of thousands of troops into Spain when the Germans began their big push. In return, Hitler was to throw open some Spanish *Lebensraum* for good Black-Shirt families who balked at emigrating to Ethiopia. Mussolini agreed to this plan with jackal's alacrity. It promised him a cheap, swift, and painless military victory, some land, and perhaps even a few Spanish mineral resources the Germans might care to throw in after the final victory.

Der Tag, for von Faupel, came on July 17, 1936. By that date, however, Franco and Goded were no longer in Spain. The Gil Robles government had been replaced by the Popular Front government, which "exiled" the two generals to army commands in the Canaries and Majorca, although it had already accumulated enough evidence against both men to warrant shooting them as traitors.

General José Sanjurjo, wearing a peacock's dream of a uniform—the London-made gift of Adolf Hitler—boarded a Junkers plane in Lisbon and ordered his pilot, Captain Ansaldo, to take off for a secret landing field in Spain. But on July 17 the old general was actually headed for another landing field his Nazi comrades had chosen without his knowledge.

A few remarks he had let slip to intimate friends in Estoril earlier that year had, unknown to Sanjurjo, reached certain Berlin ears. On April 13, 1936, for instance, Sanjurjo had complained, "They want me to start a revolution to serve the bankers and the speculators, but I won't do it." Two weeks after saying this, he made another trip to Berlin. He remained in Germany for only a few days, and on his return he went to work in earnest on his plans for the pending revolt. What happened in Berlin while Sanjurjo conferred with von Faupel is of little moment now. His fate had already been sealed before the visit.

Very shortly after Sanjurjo's plane took off from Lisbon, a German time bomb planted in the baggage compartment exploded. The blazing fragments of the Junkers monoplane became the pyre of the Anointed Chief of the Spanish Revolution. José Sanjurjo had the dubious honor of being the first of the Nazis' million victims of the Spanish War.

General Goded was a bit more fortunate. The plane which was assigned to carry him from Majorca to Barcelona got through without incident. He took command of the uprising there within an hour of the time General Fanjul led his end of the *putsch* in Madrid's Montana Barracks.

The events of the next few days sent chills down the steel spine of Wilhelm von Faupel. Again his hatred of the "mob-beast of democracy" had led him to underestimate this low-born creature's tenacity. For within three days the armed citizens and loyal soldiers of both Spanish cities had put down both the Goded and the Fanjul rebellions, and the two German-owned generals were in the death cells of the aroused Republic.

From Berlin, von Faupel sent word to Franco in the Canary Islands; the round little man was to fly at once to Spanish Morocco. There, supervised by Nazi staff officers and financed with German money, Francisco Franco y Bahamonde was to organize an army of Moors and Spanish Foreign Legionaires to be flown to Spain in German army transports piloted by Nazi officers. By default, Franco was becoming the Number One man of the puppet general staff.

A few hours after these orders reached Franco, Hitler dispatched von Faupel to the shores of the Mediterranean as the head of a secret military mission. *Spain is a unit of Destiny in the Universe*. General von Faupel's campaign for Latin America had finally reached the shooting stage.

The conquest of Spain took a little longer than von Faupel had expected. The General planned on a three-months campaign; it was three years before the weary soldiers of the Republic finally yielded—as much to sheer exhaustion and treachery as to the power and weight of German and Italian arms.

It was the strangest, cruelest, dirtiest military campaign in history. In their fury at the embattled Republicans who refused to surrender, the Nazis repeatedly drove themselves to militarily useless horrors like the blotting out of peaceful Almería from the sea and the pulverizing of rural Guernica from the air.

The Nazis were more successful in London, Paris, and Washington than they were in Spain. For in that unhappy land, they were bitterly opposed by a brave, united people. Outside of Spain, aided to no mean extent by a favorable world press which accepted the von Faupel line that the war in Spain was a civil conflict between "Nationalists and Reds," the Nazis early in the war won the greatest of all diplomatic battles of the Spanish tragedy. Hitler himself could not have drawn up two more favorable pieces of aid-to-Germany legislation than the Non-intervention Agreement of London and its American corollary, the Arms Embargo Act of 1936.

The Non-intervention Agreement pledged all nations of Europe not to send arms to either side in Spain. The American Embargo forbade the shipment of arms to any warring nation. The Non-intervention Agreement, to which Italy and Germany were signatories, was observed scrupulously by England and France in regard to both sides. The Axis countries, of course, limited their observance of the agreement to only one side.

Even more favorable to the Nazis was the American Embargo—since the State Department, while recognizing the legally constituted Republic of Spain as a belligerent, refused to recognize the fact that Germany and Italy had invaded Spain. Thus, according to the law, the Spanish Republic was unable to buy either the arms or the raw materials of self-defense from the United States, while at the same time German and Italian commissions were openly buying war materials in the United States and transferring them to their Spanish front.

Only two countries, Mexico and the Soviet Union, recognized Spain's right as a sovereign nation to buy arms for her own defense. Whenever Soviet freighters got through the sub-infested Mediterranean, the speedy little fighter planes they brought as cargo would soon be clearing the Spanish skies of Axis aviation. But all the sea approaches to Spain were patrolled by Italian and German submarines, which attacked, without partiality, English-owned food ships, Greek-owned medical ships, and Soviet-owned munitions ships bound for Republican ports.

Of course, Germany and Italy denied that the mysterious "pirate submarines" were from their fleets. In fact, at the suggestion of the British, the Germans and the Italians joined in the international patrol which hunted these "pirates." To the surprise of nobody, this international patrol never found a single pirate.

In vain, day after day, the bleeding Republic appealed to the statesmen of the world for simple, elementary justice—for the mere right to purchase, for gold, arms with which to defend itself. The Republic chose as its earliest battle cry: "Make Madrid the Tomb of Fascism!" But the statesmen of Europe, at that time, were individuals named Chamberlain, Daladier, Blum, Hoare, Laval, Halifax.

Madrid, which was to have been and could have been the tomb of world fascism, became instead its womb. A new battle cry rang out in Spain, a cry first uttered by Dolores Ibarruri, who became known to the world as La Pasionaria.

"Far better to die fighting on your feet than to live on your knees!" cried La Pasionaria.

The Spanish Republic, battered and betrayed, died fighting on her feet in April 1939. By September 1939 the Nazis were ready for the second round of their campaign for the world. Germany launched the march on Poland, the Lowlands, France.

Neither the sudden loss of Goded, Fanjul, and other Spanish military leaders, nor the unexpected toughness of the Republic, which refused to yield, seriously delayed the plans drawn up by von Faupel. The creation of the Falange Exterior—the Spanish-speaking division of the Auslands Organization of the German Nazi Party—was not delayed for more than ten minutes by the master mind of Hitler's campaign for the Iberian Peninsula and Latin America.

The Falange Exterior got under way just in time to make the best use of a sudden gift from the Loyalists—the gift of a commodity every Fascist movement needs. The Spanish Republic, acting through a legal tribunal in Alicante on November 18, 1936, gave the Falange a genuine, full-blown martyr. The Republic was kind and generous; rather than an obscure procurer like Horst Wessel, they gave the Falange a martyr of real prominence when they condemned to a traitor's death José Antonio Primo de Rivera y Saez de Heredia, the founder of the Falange Española. Young Primo, who had been arrested for treason in May, suffered the personal misfortune of being tried after his countrymen had already learned that the only cure for fascism is a hail of bullets. He went to his grave unmourned by the Germans, who had begun to suspect him of feeling too big for his breeches. In death, however, they gave him the homage he had long wanted.

With Martyr de Rivera and Leader Franco on its standards, the Falange Exterior was aggressively entered into the export business, concentrating primarily on Latin America and the Philippines. A universally believed rumor—originating in the Continental gossip mills—had the world believe that Serrano Suner, Franco's brother-in-law, was in charge of the export division of the Falange.

A legend sprang up to the effect that Suner was fervently pro-Nazi and that Franco, who hated the Nazis, had made poor Suner chief of the Falange in order to keep him from doing any real harm. This fantastic story is still believed in many quarters. In Berlin and Madrid, however, people knew better. They knew that the Nazis would never place the direction of the Falange Exterior in the hands of a Suner on the grounds of sheer efficiency alone.

The Falange Exterior was placed in charge of a group of anonymous German-trained Spaniards acting directly under the orders of von Faupel. The ruling body of this export division was the National Delegation of the Exterior Service, of which the Secretary General of the Falange Española, Raimundo Fernandez Cuesta, was a member. José del Castano, a veteran Falange leader, was the nominal head of this National Delegation.

In German hands from the start, the Falange Exterior was at once more successful in many ways than the Spanish Falange had ever been. The Spanish élite of the New World and the Philippines flocked to its banners at once; money poured into its many foreign coffers; and the members of the various exterior branches were able to strut about in their uniforms without facing the certain mayhem which would have befallen a Falangista strutting around Spain in the organization's blue shirt before the Germans arrived in force.

By October 1938 the Falange Exterior had spread over the world. It had functioning branches in over twenty foreign countries. It boasted of upwards of a million fanatical members outside of Spain—more than twenty times the number of Falangistas in Spain itself in 1936. It did so well that the National Delegation of the Exterior Service published a 56-page handbook, filled to the brim with interesting photographs and facts. This book, printed in Santander in 1938, was immediately suppressed by the flabbergasted Nazis—but not until a few copies had already been sent to Latin America via the Portuguese diplomatic pouches.

This rare little book, *La Falange Exterior*, is at once a source of information and an explanation of von Faupel's reluctance to entrust Spanish Falangistas with posts of great responsibility. According to the German, they boast too much in the wrong places.

On page 24 of *La Falange Exterior*, for example, there is a list of official publications of the Falange in various foreign cities. Notice that tiny United States-owned Puerto Rico is credited with two official Falange organs. Notice, too, that Manila is included on this list:

ARRIBA	Buenos Aires
ARRIBA	Sullana (Peru)
ARRIBA ESPAÑA	Havana
ARRIBA ESPAÑA	La Paz
ARRIBA ESPAÑA	Parana (Argentina)
ARRIBA ESPAÑA	Panama
ARRIBA ESPAÑA	San José, Costa Rica
AMANECER	Ciudad Trujillo, Dominican Republic
AMANECER	Guatemala
AVANCE	San Juan, Puerto Rico
CARA AL SOL	Ponce, Puerto Rico
ESPAÑA	Colon
GUION	San Salvador
NUEVA ESPAÑA	Guayaquil
UNIDAD	Lima
YUGO	Manila
JERARQUIA	Bogota (Columbia)

On page 25 of the book the Nazis did not quite succeed in suppressing, the chiefs of the Falange Exterior boast that between August 1, 1937, and October 30, 1938, they distributed to "members, private parties, foreign sympathizers, libraries and universities in Europe, the Americas, Asia, Africa and Australia" some 954,000 pieces of Falange propaganda. This included some 17,000 pieces printed in English and distributed in the United States.

Page 33 is captioned, "Decalogue for the Comrades Abroad." The Decalogue runs:

1. Feel the Motherland at all hours. Above time and distances, above classes and interests.
2. Defend without compromise the union of all Spaniards all over the world, under the traditional and revolutionary symbol of the yoke and arrows.
3. Obey the Caudillo [Franco], leader of our people in war and peace.
4. Maintain the brotherhood of the Falange and behave always as National-Syndicalists with justice, sacrifice, and discipline.
5. Fight with faith, for the triumph of Hispanidad.
6. Give all acts the decorous morality and austerity expected of Spaniards and Falangistas.
7. Love the country in which you live. Respect its laws and flag and contribute a generous effort to its growth, uniting in a communion of joy and sorrow with the peoples with whom you share work and daily bread.
8. Overcome, by the idea of Spain and Falange, any regional, local or personal differences.
9. Feel the eternal presence and the voice of blood of those who fell to make Spain, to maintain her and to raise her across history.
10. Pay perpetual homage to the memory of José Antonio. This decalogue remains synthesized in the permanent and vigorous cry: *Arriba España!*"

Upwards of a million Spaniards in Latin America take this seriously. If point 7 seems familiar, it should. It is quite similar to the language used in the oath of the German-American Bund, and is inserted merely as window dressing for point 5. Twentieth-century Hispanidad is one of the many brain children of Wilhelm von Faupel: in essence, it is a properly mystic creed devoted to proving that all that was once Spanish shall revert to the empire again.

The basic creed of the Falange Exterior is further expounded in some curious paragraphs on pages 10, 11, and 12 of *La Falange Exterior:*

The Nationalist-Syndicalist doctrine cannot accept classifications into classes among Spaniards, nor can it allow their spiritual separation from the Motherland. That is why it had to create organs of unity and and cohesion for expatriated Spaniards, *called to collaborate in different spheres with the actions of our diplomatic and Consular agents.** . . . These organs were to be the Exterior Falanges, since our movement . . . was bound to reach across the sea and frontiers.

From this it must not be inferred, however, that the Falange leaders of the various countries take their orders from the Spanish legations. On the contrary. General von Faupel arranged for the Territorial Chiefs of the Falange Exterior to have the highest Spanish power in the countries to which they are assigned.

Sometimes old-line Spanish diplomats balked at taking orders from the Berlin- and Hamburg-trained young Falange chiefs. Sometimes, when diplomats in the New World refused to take orders from Falange leaders, angry letters traveled across the ocean via trusted couriers. And generally, after an exchange of these letters, a country found itself going through a change of Spanish ministers.

Letters like the ones that passed between Luis Roldan Moreno, provincial secretary of the Falange in Colombia, and Antonio Valverde, its chief, are a case in point. It is necessary only to cite Valverde's letter of September 13, 1939.

This letter, written in San Sebastian on the letterhead of the National Delegation of the Exterior Service of the Falange, said, among other things:

* The italics are mine.

. . . I have learned of the incident which occurred with the Minister. I suppose that the reply that the National Secretary of this Service sent in Official Letter Number 84 of the 5th has already reached you. To this I want to add . . . and underscore the following: The Provisional Chief, which you are *pro tempore* in my absence, represents in the political aspect the National Chief of the Movement, who is El Caudillo [Franco]. Consequently, your office cannot under any circumstances admit interferences alien to its function and in its charge, regardless of what their source is, unless orders to the contrary are received from the only superior authority—which in this case is the National Delegation of the Falange Exterior.

The ideal thing would be to have the diplomatic representatives realize that Falange is Spain and that it is their duty to support and protect her in the Exterior and to strengthen the activities of the [Falange] authorities in the Exterior, contributing in a discreet form but without vacillations to establish the true unity within the heart of the Falange. But if some diplomat, ignoring the doctrine of the organization of the Falange that is Spain, and unacquainted with its function, tries to boycott or interfere with its responsible authorities . . . in that case the [Falange] Provincial Chief cannot under any circumstances limp along or much less submit to the arbitrariness or maneuvers of said diplomat. . . .

As there are many complaints received from all parts because of the lamentable actions of certain diplomats, measures are being prepared by the high authorities directed toward correcting these actions. Falange is Spain! . . .

Such quarrels, however, were merely the expressions of the growing pains of any monster. The diplomats were soon made completely subservient to the Falange or replaced by Falangistas chosen personally by von Faupel. By 1940, the Falange Exterior was so well intrenched that Berlin was prepared to give it the acid test of genuine service to the Axis. Gestapo Chief Heinrich Himmler made a special trip to Madrid in the summer of that year for a personal survey of the Falange situation.

After Himmler departed, von Faupel created a new body in Madrid, the Council of Hispanidad. This was presented to the Falange as a revival of the Council of the Indies, created by the Spanish Throne during the sixteenth century as the supreme body charged with directing the destinies of Spain's colonies in the Americas.

The Council of Hispanidad was officially formed by a decree of the Spanish State on November 7, 1940. The decree declared:

ARTICLE I: With the aim which it has of helping to fulfill the obligations it has of watching over the well being and interest of our spirit in the Spanish World, an advisory organization is created, under the Ministry of Foreign Affairs, which will be called the Council of Hispanidad, and will be the director of that policy destined to assure the continuation and efficiency of the ideas and works of the Spanish genius.

ARTICLE II: The responsibility of all the activities that tend to unification of the culture and economic interests and power related to the Spanish World, shall be the responsibility of this Council.

ARTICLE III: The Minister of Foreign Affairs will supervise the Council, make its rules, and name its members. In the course of a month, the Council will elaborate the organic rules that will precede its functioning.

ARTICLE IV: The Minister of Foreign Affairs is authorized to suppress, fuse, and modify and in general regulate the associations, organisms, and other entities of the Spanish public interest that have as a sole and principal aim the fomenting and the cultivation of relations between Spain and the nations of America and the Philippines.

If this decree had about it the distinct odor of the somber tracts the Nazis had earlier issued about the blood-ties between the Third Reich and the Germans abroad in places like the Sudeten territory of Czechoslovakia, the coincidence was far from accidental. The preamble to the decree establishing the Council of Hispanidad included a few sentences which bring to mind Hitler's oft-repeated disclaimers of designs on any territory outside of Germany. Said the preamble:

Spain is not moved by the desire for lands or riches. She asks nothing nor does she reclaim anything, only wishing to return to Hispanidad the unitarian conscience, being present in America with the intelligence, the love, the virtues that always preceeded her work of expansion in the world as was ordered by the Catholic Queen in her day.

The Council of Hispanidad became merely another weapon in the arsenal of the Falange Exterior.

On the surface, von Faupel had—in the Falange Exterior—delivered to the Third Reich a remarkable network, extending from Havana to Buenos Aires, from Lima to Manila. This network, according to its creator, was capable of concerted espionage, political diversion, arms smuggling, and anything that any other Fifth Column in history had accomplished.

It remained only for the *Wehrmacht* to give von Faupel's instrument the tests which would determine whether the Auslands Falange had been worth all the trouble its organization had entailed. The answer was soon provided by a number of Falangistas—among them one José del Castano.

Falange Es España, or What Really Happened in Manila?

IN AUGUST 1938 a lead editorial appeared in all seventeen of the Falange Exterior publications, from *Yugo* in Manila to *Arriba* in Buenos Aires. It was called "Falange es España," and appeared under the byline of José del Castano.

This editorial addressed itself in gentle terms to those Spaniards abroad who had not yet joined the Falange, and went on to say:

> The Falange Exterior has been constituted precisely to establish the bond with our compatriots who live away from our frontiers while we in Spain are fighting to win the war against International Marxism and the creation of a new state based on the twenty-seven points that constitute our Doctrine . . .

Up to this point the editorial was merely explanatory, although it must be remembered that at least three of the points of the doctrine to which del Castano referred had to do with the restoration of Spain's old empire—a restoration that could only be done at the expense of other nations, including the United States.

However, after modestly stating that "death for the Falangista is no more than the strict fulfillment of the greatest and most honorable of his duties," del Castano got to the real point of his editorial. It was a veiled threat to those Spaniards who had not yet joined the Falange Exterior.

> The Spaniards who live away from the Motherland [he warned], should not . . . wait to join for the moment when the war has ended . . . because when those happy days arrive we will have the right to refuse to admit those who in the days of uncertainty and sacrifices looked upon us with skepticism and doubted us.

This editorial, signed by the chief of the National Delegation of the Falange Exterior, became a weapon in the hands of agents all over the world. They used it to force employees of Spanish business houses—young clerks, drivers, and secretaries who were in many cases anti-Fascist at heart—to join the local branch of the Falange Exterior without further delay. It was not so much what the article said—it was the name of the man who wrote it. The name bears repetition. It was—José del Castano.

In November 1940 *Arriba*, official organ of the Falange in Madrid, described certain diplomatic appointments in these words: "Two good comrades are going to take their places as warriors in lands where our flag flew until recently."

The *Arriba* story went on to say that Genaro Riestra had been appointed Consul General to Cuba, and that José del Castano had been made Consul General to the Philippines.

At that time the official papers in Spain had been engaged in the anti-American campaign which has been conducted six days a week since April 1939; most Spanish papers are not published on Mondays. The Madrid newspaper *Informaciones*, devoting a full page to the subject of "the difficult and glorious hour of our expansion," flatly stated:

Let us not forget the Philippines. Japan will impose a new order. Yankee domination can never cast out from the Archipelago what our forefathers sowed to last forever.

Manila was a particular target of heavy Falange fire. Scarcely a week went by but one of the Falange papers in Spain would print a blast at the "Jew-Washington-Masonic" administration of the "Catholic Philippines"—an attack which would generally be reprinted in most of the many Falange organs abroad.

In this manner an article like the Madrid *Arriba's* "Manila, Outpost of Hispanidad," found its way into the December 15, 1939, issue of *Avance,* official organ of the Falange Exterior in San Juan, Puerto Rico. This article dealt with the visit to Madrid of Father Silvestre Sancho, Rector of the University of Santo Tomás of Manila.

In the Orient [runs the story] is our love the Philippines. . . . Three thousand islands. Enormous riches. The North Americans went there as International Brigades, to separate us Spaniards and Filipinos. They have not yet left the islands. They are the ones who rule. . . .

But in the Philippines three centuries of Spanish civilization have remained forever . . . in this University of Santo Tomás, nailed as an advanced bulwark in the Orient, a worry to the world today . . . is Father Silvestre Sancho, with the faculty of teachers, giving daily battle in defense of Castillian and Catholicism. Perpetually fighting, without dismay, and without rest for Spain.

The flowery article then goes on to tell how Father Sancho arrived in Madrid "as a recruiter" to find a professor for "the chair of Hispanidad" at the university, "the first in the world." Also, that the rector wanted to set up the machinery for the exchange of students and professors. The article wound up with a characteristic mystical quotation by Falange leader Rafael Sanchez Mazas about times having changed so that now Spaniards looked at a new horizon. "And the horizon," concluded the *Arriba* author, "is the Empire."

Shortly after *Arriba* revealed this new horizon, Rector Sancho appointed a new honorary rector of Santo Tomás, the oldest university in the American world. The new rector's name was Generalissimo Francisco Franco, and in the verbiage that went with the honor Sancho got in a few rousing licks about the approaching glorious day when the Generalissimo would rule over a revived Spanish Empire which would embrace Manila.

Franco's appointment as Honorary Rector of Santo Tomás failed to stir a ripple in official Washington, where editorials about the Philippines in the Spanish press were dismissed as mere pep talks designed for home consumption. Therefore, the appointment of José del Castano, chief of the National Delegation of the Falange Exterior, to the post of Spain's Consul General to Manila raised no eyebrows among the members of the State Department. Apparently it was never even questioned by Washington.

The day after del Castano was appointed to the diplomatic post, he was called to a conference in Madrid with General von Faupel and some Nazi officials he had never met before. When the conference ended, von Faupel appointed Del Castano regional chief of the Falange Exterior for the Philippines. This appointment was duly reported in the Madrid press.

Big things were lurking under the surface in Madrid. The reports from von Faupel's agents on the reception of the initial propaganda splurges of the Council of Hispanidad had given the General some new ideas. To accelerate the drive on the Philippines and the Americas, von Faupel now opened a new institution—La Casa de América—in Madrid, and decided to send the most trustworthy and the ablest Falange leaders abroad to where they could do the Axis cause the most good. The Axis, at this time, was concentrating Falangist efforts on Cuba and the Philippines— hence the new assignments of such important figures as Riestra and del Castano.

José del Castano had long been intimate with the problems of the Falange Exterior in the Philippines. As the head of the National Delegation of the Auslands Falange, del Castano had been directly responsible for the Manila Falange from its very inception. While Madrid remained in the hands of the Republic, del Castano had made his headquarters in Burgos and later in Salamanca. To these headquarters, the Falangist chiefs of the Philippines made their reports. From them, they received their orders.

During the Spanish War, not all of del Castano's letters reached him. One highly important letter, mailed to him by Martin Pou, then a leader of the Philippine Falange, on January 20, 1938, fell into the hands of a Republican counter-espionage officer while it was en route to Salamanca.

It was an amazing letter. Although it is devoted exclusively to an internal quarrel in the Fascist ranks in Manila, it inadvertently described the whole Falange organization of the Philippines in the process of making its point. Pou set out to prove to del Castano that Enrique Zobel and Andres Soriano—his chief enemies—had taken complete control of the Falange and the Fascist movement in the Philippines.

Zobel and Soriano were no small-time agitators. They were two of the wealthiest Spanish businessmen in Manila. Zobel, who held the post of "consul" of the Franco regime, claimed to be Franco's personal representative in Manila. His nephew, Soriano, owned Manila's largest brewery and held the Philippine agency for a giant American tobacco company.

Early in the course of the Spanish War, these two had taken over the Franco movement in the Philippines. When Pou arrived on the scene and started giving orders, he ran into difficulties almost at once. Zobel, according to his letter, had then arranged for Pou to be recalled to Spain. Pou objected to this order.

I went to his [Zobel's] house [Pou wrote], and he showed me Mugiro's order asking me to indicate the date of departure, although it was irregular—I would have to get this data from the [Falange] authorities. I told him not to be an imbecile, and as he insisted, I offered to throw him out of the window— a thing which made for a notable difference in his attitude and very frightened of his own skin. He proposed that I take this to the chief of the Falange in the Headquarters . . . and that on the other hand he would not show anyone the order that I had to leave. . . .

He began to give circulars to the consular agents of Germany, Portugal, Italy and Japan to gain the attention of the Spaniards whom he had seen in my company and generally treating me more or less like a monster.

Note this reference to the Axis diplomats. The Falange was and is so subservient to the Axis authorities that, in order to destroy a Falangista, it was considered necessary to denounce him before the German, Italian, and Japanese authorities. Pou continued:

I did not do anything more than to cite him before the Military Tribunal, following which I notified you so that you could check his telegrams from the 24, 25, and 26. In the interim the [Spanish] Colony has come to my side and against him. The parade of the Spaniards to my home was constant and continuous, offering themselves to me for any job and requesting instructions from me. Having sent my telegram, I did not want to do anything more. After many [telegrams] had gone to Salamanca [then seat of the Franco regime], Zobel became scared and began to say that he had not asked for my deportation, that he was not an enemy of the Falange, that he recognized me as a great patriot. . . .

The official Spanish Chamber of Commerce drafted a petition for the expulsion of Zobel . . . the petition won by a great majority. Thereafter, Zobel began to phone Spaniards telling them that he represented Franco and that to go against him meant going against the Caudillo. . . .

After complaining that Soriano, on his trips to Salamanca, acted differently than he did in Manila, Pou suggested that "the new Falangist chief should come from Spain. He should be a man of arms, and he should reside in the consulate."

Then, to drive home his point, Pou listed the heads of the Falange and the Franco offices in the Philippines, and next to each name showed the ties between the officers and the two Spaniards who opposed Pou. According to Pou, Garcia Alonzo and a man named Lizarraga were associates of Zobel and Soriano. Pou's own description of the Falange Exterior organization in Manila reads:

Chief: La Vara (employee of Garcia Alonzo)
Administrator: Fernandez (employee of Lizarraga)

Press & Propaganda: Martinez Gil (employee of Soriano)
Information: Castelvi (Soriano's secretary)
Secretary: Beaumont (employee of Soriano)

These were the official Falange Exterior officers. Pou
went on to describe the other Franco officials as:

Representative of the Spanish State: Soriano, and in his ab-
sence, Antonio Roxas, his cousin.
Consul: Zobel (uncle of Soriano and of Roxas)
President of Chamber: Zobel
President of School Board: Zobel
Secretary of School: Beaumont (employee of Soriano and
vice-chancellor of consulate)
Secretary of Casino: Castelvi (Soriano's secretary)

Even though this particular letter never reached del
Castano, he already knew that, in the Philippines, the Falange Exterior had made tremendous strides. As the quarrel
between Pou and the Soriano crowd continued, del Castano solved it by removing Pou. Neither Wilhelm von Faupel nor José del Castano cared to antagonize the wealthiest
Spaniards in Manila.

The Manila to which José del Castano sailed in the winter of 1940 was in many ways more fervently Falangist
than Madrid itself. In Madrid, as the new Consul General
would have been the first to admit, popularity had never
been one of the Falange's characteristics prior to the glorious
victory of the Nazis, the Italians, and the Caudillo.

To the utter amazement of the new Regional Chief, the
five branches of the Philippines Falange Exterior put on a
show for him that could not have been duplicated for sheer
numbers in Madrid in 1936. The affair took place in December 1940 at a Manila stadium—secured at a nominal
rental from the Spanish businessman who owned it.

First, to start the festivities, the five- and six-year-old
youngsters in uniform lined up in military formation and
started to march across the field to the music of a brass

band. They wore uniforms, these little fellows—blue shirts
and shorts and Sam Browne belts like the Exploradores
(Boy Scouts). But they were not Exploradores, they were
Jovenes Flechas (Young Arrows) de Falange. The uniforms
were, for the time being, somewhat alike. In the beginning,
the Jovenes Flechas were taught how to march, how to
sing *Cara al Sol*, the Falange hymn, and how to give the
brazo en alto (upraised arm) salute when they shouted
"Franco! Franco! Franco!" Later, they would learn how
to shoot, like the older ones.

Following the little fellows came the Sección Femenina
de la Falange de Manila. This contingent was an utter
surprise to del Castano. It embraced everything from five-
year-old preschool girls to nurses in their teens to matrons
built along the lines of assault tanks—all of them in im-
maculate blue uniforms, marching behind the banners of
the Falange and Imperial Spain, saluting smartly with the
approved stiff arm, carrying themselves like women fit to
grace the beds and the kitchens of the new conquistadores.

The feminine section was followed by an older group
of Flechas—these ran from eight to about fourteen. They
also wore short pants, but they marched with the precision
of soldiers. After the Flechas retired, a large color guard—
youths of fourteen to twenty—paraded smartly with the
flags of Spain and the Falange. They wore the Blue Shirts
(*Camisas Azules*) of the *Movimiento*—the glorious *Camisa
Azul* of José Antonio, *El Apóstol*.

In a long letter he wrote to Madrid that night, del Castano admitted that the sight of these smart young men way
out there in the Orient brought tears to his eyes. So thick
were the tears, he wrote, that he could scarcely see the
tremendous Falange emblems sewn on the jerseys of the
two soccer teams that played a rousing game in his honor
to bring the ceremonies at the Manila stadium to a magnificent climax.

During the first week that del Castano was in Manila,
he had dinner with a certain Spaniard residing in the Philippines who might have been one of the glamorous figures

of the Spanish State. This individual (his name is known
to the American authorities) had amassed a huge fortune,
primarily as agent in the Philippines for American manu-
facturers. He was one of the men on whom von Faupel's
agents had originally tested the program of the Falange—
and his reaction had been a bit too positive. "Permit me,"
he had said, "to finance the entire *movimiento*." When the
Nazis invaded Spain without this caballero's backing, he
was offended. But he was soon brought around to the New
Order, and he became a great patron of the Philippine
Falange.

This man was typical of the wealthy Spaniards who
formed the core of the Franco crowd in the Philippines.
Sons of wealthy Spanish planters and colonial traders, they
had, as boys or youths, emotionally or physically fought to
keep the Archipelago within the Spanish Empire during the
Spanish-American War. Trained from childhood to hate
the freedom of peoples, the freedom of religions, and the
freedom of education, they had within their own lifetime
seen all three freedoms develop in the Philippines. The
peoples of the Philippines, chattels under the Spanish Empire, had had their lot improved under the Americans. It
had been no Paradise, to be sure; but the form of the gesture had been one of democracy.

And then, the Spaniards complained, without too great
a struggle the Washington Idiots had signed a paper actually giving the Filipino savages the right to govern their
own destinies.

Under the monarchy, the One True Faith had made
great headway among the savages. Now, with the separation of Church and State—for which the Protestant Masonic
Bankers of Boston were responsible—paganism was again
rife.

In the days of the Empire, education was controlled by
the Church. It was a privilege, accorded to those worthy
of it. Now, thanks to the American devils, secular education was free and universal. And it was education of Satan's
own design, with pagan Protestant teachers permitted to

expound upon heresies like birth control, the French Revolution, and the New Deal of the Jew Roosevelt.

The wealthy Spaniards who spoke and thought in these terms did what they could to keep their wives, their children, and themselves from the contamination of this new society. They published their own newspapers, ran their own private schools for their heirs, subsidized colleges—maintained whatever links they could with the Spanish monarchy. When the monarchy rotted away of historical gangrene in 1931, the caballeros refused to believe that the corpse was more than merely sleeping. When the Falange thrust its five arrows over the horizon, the rich Spaniards in the Philippines saw in them the pointers to the type of Spanish Empire their fathers had really known.

In addition to being rich, these Spaniards were also realistic men. By 1940 they knew that Imperial Spain was part of the same Axis as Imperial Japan. It was no secret that Japan had a design or two on the Philippines herself, as well as a few nationals here and there on the Archipelago. Nothing serious, of course, and nothing to get excited about, but nevertheless a problem that was growing acute by the time Don José reached Manila.

"Don José," they asked del Castano, "is it really true that the little brown Japanese monkeys will restore our Empire?"

"Our Fascist brothers in Japan," the Consul General would answer sternly, "are united with us in the common struggle. When they strike, we must help them. When we strike, they will help us."

Del Castano must have repeated this answer a hundred times during his first week in Manila, each time using the exact words he used when he had rehearsed the few sentences for General von Faupel and those strange Nazi luminaries back in Madrid.

The Consul General was very careful to say nothing which would make his set speech on Spain's Fascist brothers in Japan sound in the least bit false. When not discussing the Japanese, del Castano spent much of his time in the first

weeks studying the scripts of the radio shows the Spanish
groups put on regularly, speaking at dinners, bolstering the
spirits of the local Falange chiefs, and, in his spare moments,
attending to his diplomatic duties.

These radio programs were amazing. At the time del
Castano arrived in Manila, for example, the Ateneo de Manila, one of the exclusive Spanish private schools, was doing
a series on the ideal corporate state of Portugal's Salazar.
This was the familiar clerico-Fascist line of all good Axis
propagandists in Catholic countries. Within time, del Castano was to hear programs contrasting the American pioneers and the Spanish conquistadores so cleverly that the
listeners gained the impression that the pioneers who ex-
plored with Boone were drunken desperadoes while the
soldiers who pillaged with Pizarro were hymn-singing ab-
stainers.

As regional Falange chief and as Spanish Consul General,
del Castano was in supreme command of all anti-American
Spanish activities, from radio programs to downright espionage. The scope of del Castano's work as a propagandist,
the seriousness of his results, can be gathered in the open
alarm expressed by two officers of the Philippine Military
Academy, Major José M. Hernandez and Lieutenant Ricardo C. Galang, who, a few months before Pearl Harbor,
prepared an emergency manual on counter-propaganda for
their government (*What Every Filipino Should Know
about Propaganda*).

Two bitter sections of their slim publication speak volumes about what the Falange accomplished on the propaganda front alone in the Philippines:

Transfer is a device by which the propagandist carries over
the authority, sanction, and prestige of something that we
respect and revere to something he would have us accept. For
instance, in our country, the people have a very high regard
for the Church because our people are essentially religious. If
some foreign power succeeds in getting the Church to sponsor
a movement, it is very likely that our people will be won over.
We should not be surprised if Generalissimo Franco of Spain

finds a way to influence the Catholic Church to win over some influential Filipinos to a cause that would be inimical to the democratic ideals of our people. Filipinos must remember that even from the pulpit, propaganda, aside from religious, may be sold to our masses. . . .

There is another type of subtle propaganda being used in the Philippines. It is the Spanish propaganda. Fellowships have been offered to Filipinos so that they may study in Spanish universities courses in medicine and social science. Everybody knows that the most outstanding, the most famous, the most scholarly authorities in medicine and social science are *not* in Spain. Why are we being enticed to study medicine there? Because it is earnestly desired that we see present-day Spain with our own eyes, so that we might be convinced of the power and strength of the Franco government, a totalitarian government that maintains views radically different from a purely democratic ideology and inimical to it. Franco has come out in the open in defense of the Berlin-Rome Axis and, therefore, against all democracies, including America and the Philippines.

Why have professors and students of certain educational institutions been persuaded to contribute money to the cause of the Franco government? Why have publications been issued for the perpetuation of Spanish culture in the Philippines? These are instances of pure and simple propaganda for Spain, by overzealous Spaniards seemingly unappreciative of their privileges to live on the bounty and hospitality of Filipinos.

For an official government publication, circulated openly, these were strong words—even though they came much too late. The story they tell is clear enough. Not only had Rector Sancho's dream of exchanging students with Spanish universities worked out since 1939, but, once the plan got under way, it was put to more than cultural uses by the New Spain. More than one of the Spanish students sent to Manila in exchange for a Filipino scholar turned out to be a little old, a little military, and a little lackadaisical in his studies—but not at all backward in his real duty: espionage.

Under del Castano's expert guidance, the conditions the two Philippine officers described in their book grew in intensity. The Falange membership increased, and many of the more influential Spaniards in the local colony began to drink toasts to the imminent return of the good old days of the Empire.

Then, on June 18, 1941, the Spanish colony of the Philippines—which had long wondered why so important a Falange official as José del Castano had been assigned to a post as far from Madrid as Manila—was suddenly made aware of del Castano's real importance. A brusque official announcement from Washington suddenly explained del Castano's real status. The President of the United States had given the governments of Germany, Italy, and Japan until July 10 to close their consulates on United States soil and territories—which, on July 11, would make José del Castano the ranking Axis diplomat on the Archipelago.

This announcement was followed, in a day, by the word that Señor del Castano would temporarily take over the consular duties of all three closing consulates in Manila.

Not publicly announced, but nevertheless just as official, was José del Castano's appointment after July 18, 1941, to the most important Axis espionage post in the Philippines. The Falange chief was made the top liaison agent of all Axis undercover work in the Islands. His consulate-general offices became headquarters, post office, and clearing house for the entire Axis spy network. His real mission—the mission for which he had been personally picked by General von Faupel—had begun.

Now del Castano really got down to work. He organized his liaison duties, memorized new codes, and tapped some of the most reliable of his Falange *militantes* for service as agents in the Axis intelligence. But del Castano was too big a man to be wasted in a simple liaison job.

It was a matter of days before the new sealed orders, in code, arrived from Madrid. José del Castano decoded the message, read it twice, and then slowly burned the small strip of microfilm on which the message had come and the sheet of paper on which he had translated it. The General was after major stakes this time, and as del Castano scattered the ashes of the message he began to feel the nearness of the big push von Faupel had hinted at back in Madrid. Yet the message said nothing about any of the things von Faupel had discussed then. It merely said that del Castano was to detail every Falangista to join the ranks of the Philippine Civilian Emergency Administration; and that, once there were enough Falangistas in the C. E. A., del Castano would receive further orders.

José del Castano was no fool. He could have given orders to all Falangistas to sign up as air-raid wardens at once. The orders would have been obeyed—but with murmurs. So instead of issuing these orders by virtue of his supreme authority as provincial chief of the Falange Exterior, del Castano started to hold a series of informal conferences with prominent leaders of the Spanish colony. He told them that the C. E. A., as it was then developing, was becoming the nucleus of an anti-Spanish, anti-Catholic civilian force. Del Castano let his confidants suggest to him that the Falange should counter by quietly infiltrating the C. E. A. ranks and gaining control. It was the type of maneuver which vindicated von Faupel's earlier judgment.

Within a month of the day von Faupel's sealed orders had reached del Castano, practically every Falange member in the Philippines was enrolled as a worker in the Civilian Emergency Administration. The total number of Falange members in the Philippines is known to very few—a trustworthy estimate places it at close to 10,000.

Had only half of the estimated ten thousand calculating Falangistas moved in on the civilian defense organization, the Axis purpose would have been accomplished. The Falangistas who went into civilian defense work all received special training from Falange chiefs close to del Castano himself. They were no average citizens, amiably going through routine drills for air raids and emergencies they never quite believed would come. The Falangistas in the Philippine Civilian Emergency Administration were a trained Axis Fifth Column army, ordered to their posts by the Nazi general who sat as *Gauleiter* of Spain, and directly responsible to the chief liaison man for all Axis espionage in the Archipelago.

As the international crisis mounted, the Falangistas in the civilian defence worked like Trojans at their tasks. They were particularly keen about distributing the posters and cards containing the ten "Emergency Pointers for the Citizens" which the C. E. A. had printed. The first two points were:

1. Beware of rumors. Be guided by truth and nothing but the truth. Get your facts straight from C.E.A. officials and organizations.
2. Keep calm. Avoid hysteria and prevent panic. Have faith in your C.E.A. leaders.

The Regional Chief of the Falange Exterior ordered all Falangistas in civilian defense to become well known to all their neighbors as C. E. A. workers and officials. The Falangistas in the C. E. A. carried out these orders to the letter.

Toward the end of November, José del Castano made a thorough check-up on the work of the Falange Exterior in the Philippines. He sent a coded report to Madrid, via courier, in which he expressed himself as satisfied with the preparations taken by his Falanges.

On December 7, Spain's Japanese Axis partner bombed Hawaii and the Philippines.

The official Madrid newspaper, *Informaciones*, bluntly editorialized:

Japan has reached the limit of her patience. She could no longer tolerate the interference and the opposition of the United States. . . . We hope Manila will be saved for Christianity.

In Manila, after the shock of the first attack, the people looked to the government, to the Army, to the Civilian Emergency Administration, for guidance. In most cases, the average Filipino turned to the C. E. A.—under ordinary circumstances the proper thing to do. But on December 7, 1941, the C. E. A. was so shot through with Falangistas as to be the foundation of the Axis Fifth Column in the city.

For three weeks the Falangistas in the C. E. A. lay low. They performed their defense tasks diligently—on orders from their Falange leaders—and concentrated on winning the confidence of citizens in all walks of life in the great city.

On December 29 the Japanese air forces staged their first great raid over the city of Manila. For three hours the Jap planes rained bombs on the forts along the bay, the docks, and the homes of the poorer Filipinos.

Then the planes flew off. But something had happened during the bombardment. The civilian defense organizations seemed to have broken down completely.

Wardens were receiving orders to be everywhere except the places where they were needed most. Stretcher-bearers were dropping like flies with bullets in their backs. Streams of confusing and conflicting orders had most C. E. A. workers running around in crazy circles.

Wild rumors spread like hurricanes through the city— rumors the character of which had already become familiar in all lands invaded by the Nazis in Europe: MacArthur had fled to Washington. Quezon had gone over to the Japs. The entire American Air Force had been destroyed. The American Army had received orders to shoot all Catholics and imprison all Filipinos. Henry Morgenthau had personally requisitioned all the funds in the Philippine National Treasury. *Ad infinitum.*

There was something official about these rumors, something had been added that made even level-headed citizens give them credence. For these rumors were not being spread by obscure Japanese spies: they originated directly from Civilian Emergency Headquarters, from the lips of the hard-working air-raid wardens who had been so diligent about tacking up the posters bearing the ten emergency pointers for the citizen. "Get your facts straight from C. E. A. . . ."

Modern total war is the war of the organized rear. Civilian defense organizations may not be as vital as armies, but they are necessities. Manila taught the world what a menace a city's civilian defense organization becomes when it falls into the hands of the enemy.

All the details of what happened in Manila during the next thirty-six hours are today in the army archives in Washington. Some day, perhaps, they will be revealed in full. Then it will become painfully clear why, thirty-six hours after the first big Jap air raid on December 29, the military authorities in Manila were forced to break off all relations with the civilian defense organizations.

Thanks to the Falange—and its regional chief, Spanish Consul General José del Castano—the rear had been completely disrupted. The civilian defense organizations, created to bolster civilian morale and to counter the effects of enemy air raids, were accomplishing just the opposite.

At three o'clock on the afternoon of January 2, 1942, the Japanese marched into Manila, their military tasks having been lightened a thousandfold by the effective Fifth Column job within the city itself.

The freedom-loving world was stunned. But in Madrid, *Arriba*, official organ of the Falange, hailed the Japanese successes in these words:

The ancient and renowned culture of the magnificent Oriental Empire, and its exceptional human values, are shown in the important victories of the first days—victories that have won for Japan the admiration of the world.

In New York, in London, in Moscow free men and free women mourned the tragedy that had befallen Manila. But in Granada, Spain, on January 5, 1942, there was a joyous Falange celebration. Pilar Primo de Rivera, the psychopathic sister of young Primo and the chief of the feminine section of the Falange, brought the crowd screaming to its feet. In the name of the Philippine Section of the Falange Española

Tradicionalista de la J. O. N. S., Pilar Primo de Rivera accepted a formal decoration from the Japanese Government —a decoration awarded to the Philippine Falange for its priceless undercover aid to the Imperial Japanese Government in the capture of Manila and for a host of other services. Among the latter were the fleets of trucks and busses the Falange had ready and waiting for the Japanese invasion troops at Lingayen, Lamon, and other points.

The cheers in Granada had hardly died when the Archbishop of Manila issued a pastoral letter calling upon all Catholics in the Philippines to stop their anti-Japanese activities and to co-operate with the Japanese in their noble efforts to pacify the Archipelago.

Whatever doubts the Nazi High Command may have entertained about the value of the Falange Exterior to the Axis cause vanished with the fall of Manila. They now knew that General von Faupel had not been wasting his time.

José del Castano is still Spanish Consul General to the Philippines, still regional chief of the Philippines Section of the Falange Exterior.

Sometimes, when del Castano rides around Manila in his new American car, he passes the ancient University of Santo Tomás, founded in 1611 by Spaniards. His Caudillo, Francisco Franco, is still honorary rector of Santo Tomás. Perhaps, when del Castano passes this ancient seat of learning, he thinks that Franco's title should be changed to "honorary warden."

For at present Santo Tomás is not a university. Today Santo Tomás is the Japanese Government's concentration camp for American nationals who were trapped in Manila by Falange treachery and Japanese arms.

Del Castano's old colleague Andres Soriano is no longer in Manila. The wealthy Manila businessman who served as representative of the Spanish state and so dominated the Falange and the Franco organizations of the Philippines, no longer gives the *brazo en alto* salute while standing alongside Falangist leaders at Manila demonstrations. Soriano, who felt the fury of Axis terror on Corregidor, is very far from Manila.

Andres Soriano is at present in Washington. He has a new job, too. He is the Secretary of the Treasury in Manuel Quezon's Philippine government-in-exile.

He has to get around Washington quite a bit. Sometimes he has to pass the Spanish Embassy. When he does, perhaps he pauses to read the sign which went up on the white gates of the Embassy after Pearl Harbor. It is a simple sign bearing the words:

SPANISH EMBASSY
IN CHARGE OF JAPANESE INTERESTS

It would be interesting to know how this sign affects Andres Soriano.

CHAPTER THREE

Cuba: Pattern and Center of Falangist America

THE GRAY, pencil-slim edifice of the Spanish Legation on Havana's Oficios Street overlooks the fine harbor. From its windows one can see all the shipping that enters and leaves Havana. At night, the soft green moon that shines only over Havana and over no other city in the world plays thousands of weird shadow-tricks on the stone façade. Cubans say that these nights the Havana moon traces the outlines of Hitler's face in the shadows on the front of the Spanish Legation. They say, too, that the Nazi Führer's face looks pained and troubled.

This, of course, may be merely a legend. The Havana moon does make many people see many things. But there is nothing mythical about the inside apartment of the Spanish consulate—the apartment on the second floor. In this apartment, a few paces to the left of the stairs, there is a heavy steel door in the wall, a door with a shuttle lock made by an excellent German locksmith. This door opens on a steel and concrete vault.

When one knows how to operate this steel door, it opens on a wealth of reports, secret documents, special codes, and exhaustive lists of people in every Western Hemisphere country from Canada to Argentina, from the United States to Paraguay and Chile. The entire contents of this vault are one of General von Faupel's most closely guarded secrets. They are the records of the Falange Española Tradicionalista in the New World, and they are most complete.

It is no accident that these records should be cached in the Spanish Legation in Havana. From the very beginning of the Falange Exterior offensive in the Western World, Cuba has been the chief advance base of all Falange activities on the American side of the Atlantic. The director of all

Falangist activities in North and South America, appointed personally by General von Faupel, has always made his headquarters in Havana. From the Cuban capital, Falangistas in the twenty Latin-American nations have re-received their orders—relayed from Madrid. Similarly, when Falangist chiefs of other countries need guidance and answers to pressing problems, it is to the ranking Falange chief in Cuba to whom they write via secret courier.

The Falange-versus-the-democracies pattern of Cuba, Falange center of the Americas, is the basic pattern of every land south of our borders. Without an understanding of what this pattern is like, the success of the Falange Exterior looks like a triumph of racial mysticism. Actually, the racial ties which bind the Falanges of Latin America to the Madrid-Berlin core are very much overtouted by casual investigators who blitz their way through the Latin countries. There was nothing racial about the support Spaniards in Latin America gave to the Nazis and the Italians who spent the years between July 1936 and April 1939 in the slaughter of over a million racially pure Spaniards in Republican Spain.

Rare and talented American diplomats like Spruille Braden and Claude Bowers understand this pattern very well, but they form so small a minority in the councils of our State Department as to be all but voiceless.

The Falange network of Cuba will be described in detail in these chapters. But first—because it will help explain the strength of the Falange in Latin America—it is important to examine the soil from which Falangismo receives its greatest nourishment in the Americas.

As a colony of the Spanish Empire, Cuba had an economy completely dependent on the mother country. It could trade only with Spain, exporting the products of its soil and receiving its imports of manufactured goods only via Spanish ships. Absentee owners in Spain shared the ownership of the vast agricultural estates with Spanish colonial planters. A small, compact set of Spanish colonials controlled all the mercantile business of the island.

The Indians whom Columbus had discovered on the island were enslaved and ultimately killed off by the new Spanish masters. In the sixteenth century slaves from Africa were brought over to replace the native Indians. The island raised cattle for Spanish ships plying the Spanish Main, and sent to the mother country the hides, tobacco, sugar, molasses, and other products of the vast *haciendas*.

The Seven Years' War Spain waged with Britain a decade before the American Revolution gave Cuba its real start as a nation. For during this war Britain seized and held the port city of Havana for one full year. It was a year of amazing prosperity for the island, a prosperity directly due to the fact that Britain had made Havana a free port. Ships of all nations were allowed to trade with Cuba on even terms. The price structures of the Spanish monopoly were ignored by the Cubans—who during Havana's year as a free port sold their exports to the highest bidders and bought their imports from the most reasonable traders.

Spain recaptured Havana in 1762. But now the Empire had to compete with British "pirates" for the commerce of the Antilles. An increasing number of colonial planters had become Cuban *independistas* who chose to risk the hazards of free trade in quest of higher returns for their products.

Under the Spaniards, imports became the chief mercantile trade of the island. Spaniards and Spanish firms in Cuba, protected by Spanish sea power, built great fortunes by acting as agents for Spanish products. In many cases the colonial traders became so wealthy that they were able to buy controlling interests in the Spanish firms from which they bought their wares.

The importers became the leading mercantile factors in Cuban economic life. Because they always had ready cash, they often took control of the banks originally dominated by the large planters. In time, they began to buy into the control of the agricultural estates of the colony.

In the nineteenth century, when the Cuban independence movements began to grow, one of the rallying cries of the *independistas* was a demand for native industries which would free Cubans from dependence on Spanish imports.

For this reason the colonial mercantilists were the first to send their sons into the ranks of the "Voluntarios," the dreaded and despised *guerrilleros* of the Spanish captain-generals. The Voluntarios were the storm troops of the monarchy in Hispanic America whose ugly terrorism against the leaders of the movements for Cuban Independence did so much to win the *independistas* the support of the entire civilized world.

The Spanish-American War of 1898 shook this mercantile class to its very roots. Only the most powerful of its members survived the dawn of Cuban independence, even such independence as Cuba enjoyed in its early years as a free nation. These individuals united to form the Lonja del Comercio, and, if possible, to resume business as usual. Despite the competition from American interests, the Lonja crowd managed to get along pretty well.

The Lonja soon became the center of all Spanish business on the island. Its members invested in real estate, shipping bottoms, sugar lands, tobacco lands, wholesale and retail trade. For the main part, most of them retained their Spanish citizenship and continued their centuries-old practice of siphoning off generous portions of their Cuban profits for Spanish investments.

In politics the Lonja crowd backed Cubans who could guarantee them the highest possible profits at the lowest possible capital outlay. At the same time the Spanish businessmen in Cuba had very good economic reasons for keeping their fingers on the political pulse of Madrid. Their financial stake in Spanish reaction was often as great as their stake in Cuban tyranny.

To the Spaniards in Latin America, the birth of the Spanish Republic in 1931 meant only one thing: a higher standard of living for the people of Spain. This higher standard of living meant living wages, and living wages meant smaller returns on investments in Spanish enterprises. For decades, wealthy Spaniards of Latin America had talked in colorful and mystic terms about restoration of the empire of Ferdinand and Isabella. Beneath all of this fine racist gibberish lurked a genuine and quite materialistic concern over large-scale business ventures in the Holy Motherland. (Few non-Spaniards realized this better than Wilhelm von Faupel.)

The chief spokesman for this Spanish business crowd has always been the *Diario de la Marina,* Havana's oldest daily newspaper. Founded in 1832, *La Marina* was always more monarchist than the monarch. Its ties to the Spanish Empire were of the strongest. They have never been broken.

The Voluntarios had their heart and life's blood in the columns of *La Marina* until Cuba won her independence from Spain. In these columns Cubans were exhorted to join the Voluntarios, to fight for king and colonialism, and to destroy all attempts to organize groups dedicated to Cuban freedom.

Today, in Cuba, there are hundreds of monuments to José Marti, the revered leader of Cuba's great struggle for independence. The *Diario de la Marina* pays its employees in paper pesos that bear Marti's picture; the cell in which Marti languished as a prisoner of the King's is a national shrine in Havana. But during Cuba's three wars for independence—the wars of 1868-78, 1890, and 1895-98—*La Marina* denounced José Marti as a "foolish dreamer." Maximo Gómez and Antonio Maceo, the military leaders of Marti's forces of liberation, were described simply as "bandits" by the paper. And when, a few years before the Spanish shackles were finally torn from Cuba's heart, José Marti died on the field of battle, the *Diario de la Marina* editorialized that now, thank God, there would be an end to the stupid troubles Marti had caused.

Loudest of the *Diario de la Marina*'s loud voices against Cuban independence was the voice of Don Nicolas Rivero. As a young partisan of the Carlists in Spain, Rivero had run into the sort of political trouble which caused Europeans to flee their countries in the '70's. He settled in Cuba, where he won his spurs as a journalist, and soon made his peace with the Bourbon dynasty. He rose to become editor and part owner of the *Diario de la Marina,* where his decades of molding Cuban opinion were of such nature that, in 1919, he was made a Spanish count by King Alfonso. As an editor and a publicist, Don Nicolas gave no quarter in his savage campaign to keep the Spanish Empire in business. He penned the most violent of the attacks on José Marti and the other tireless leaders of the Cuban independence movement. He made many speeches, chose to back the anti-democratic wing of any dispute that arose in Cuba after 1898, fathered two sons, and died in bed after the end of the First World War—a soldier of the Spanish Empire to the end.

Count Nicolas Rivero, eldest of Don Nicolas's sons, showed little talent for journalism or controversy. He is now Cuba's envoy to the Vatican. The second son, José Ignacio —or Pepin, as everyone calls him today—showed more talent and ambitions for the calling of the old Don. He was brought into the paper while still a young man and soon became director and publisher of the venerable organ of the Spanish colony.

During Pepin Rivero's early days as a journalist, *La Marina* went through its worst crisis since 1898. In April 1917 the *Diario de la Marina* ran a ringing editorial entitled, "Gold! Gold! Gold!" The editorial explained that the real reasons for America's entry into the war against Germany were commercial—only the Yankee lust for gold was behind the war declaration. The American Government promptly dispatched a one-man board of economic warfare to Havana, with instructions to tell the paper's management in simple but stiff words that one more manifestation of such sentiments would find the *Diario de la Marina* suffering from an acute shortage of newsprint sources.

This experience taught Pepin the lesson of caution. Only the birth of fascism in Europe led Pepin to throw caution to the winds so soon after learning its value. Long before Hitler had even aspired to meet men like General von Faupel socially, Pepin was admiring Benito Mussolini in column after column of the *Diario de la Marina*. His favorite device in those days was to sigh that the world was running recklessly toward revolution and ruin, and that in

Fascism, at least, good sober folks had the sane and modern antidote to Bolshevism.

When Hitler invaded Spain in 1936, Pepin—who reflected perfectly the sentiments and interests of the tightly-knit Spanish crowd in the Lonja del Comercio—quickly made the *Diario de la Marina* the most completely pro-rebel paper in the Caribbean. All the Franco forces of Cuba rallied around the paper, and Pepin became one of their most popular spokesmen both in print and on the public platforms.

Shortly after the start of the Spanish War, Pepin made a trip to Europe. One of his first stops was Berlin. Here, in a rousing speech delivered over the Nazi radio, Pepin wound up with a prayer for the success of Adolf Hitler, "the great man of humanity. God save the Führer," he said.

From Berlin, Pepin went to that section of Spain then in the hands of the Nazis. He donned the uniform of the Requetes and sent pictures of himself in Fascist uniform back to his paper. (Old Count Rivero would have been stirred by these pictures; the Requetes were the uniformed Carlists of 1936. They were incorporated into the Falange as a body in 1937.) Pepin participated as an honored guest and speaker in official ceremonies, met the important Falange chiefs, and returned to Cuba convinced that Hitler was guaranteeing the Spanish investments of every good Lonja member in the Spanish set.

Pepin was very busy as a public figure when he returned in triumph from Spain. Fortunately, he had been able to find just the man he needed actually to run the paper in the person of young Raoul Maestri.

Scion of a wealthy, socialite Havana family, Raoul Maestri had started his career in the most amazing manner. This was back in the mid-'20's, while he was still a student at Havana University. Although he shudders to think of it today, Maestri made his initial impression on Havana as a firebrand dilettante in radicalism. Many a Habanero today remembers vividly the scarlet era when young Maestri delivered fulsome lectures on Marxism.

Maestri's family snatched him from the arms of Karl Marx

and sent him abroad to absorb some *Kultur* in German universities. He studied hard and he studied long, and one of the end results was a weighty book published in Madrid in 1932—a book called *German National Socialism*. In this book Maestri expounded an interesting thesis: capitalism and communism having failed, only National Socialism remained as the hope of suffering humanity.

This and many other writings in a similar vein impressed Pepin, who watched Maestri grow up to become one of the intellectual leaders of the Fascist-minded circles of Havana. Maestri was invited to join the staff of *La Marina*, and quickly rose to the position of sub-editor, second in command only to Pepin himself.

The editors of *Diario de la Marina* receive much sage advice from the inner council of the paper, a council composed primarily of heavy stockholders. This inner council includes men like José Maria Bouza, millionaire and violently pro-Falange official of the powerful Gallego Regional Society. Bouza is the father-in-law of Segundo Casteleiro, also a millionaire. Casteleiro owns a cord factory in Matanzas where, in the spring of 1942, the Cuban Secret Police arrested five of his employees who happened to be Nazi spies. Until July 10, 1941, a Nazi agent named Clemens Ladmann was Casteleiro's partner in this Matanzas venture. But Ladmann also happened to have been the German consul in Matanzas and was expelled from Cuba when Batista followed Roosevelt's lead in closing down the German, Italian, and Japanese consulates.

Within hours of the moment the first Nazi bomb dropped on Spanish soil in 1936, Havana's Spanish aristocracy rushed to form the Comite Nacionalista Español de Cuba. This committee immediately started to raise funds for the protectors of their Spanish investments.

Senator Elicio Arguelles, one of Cuba's most prominent political figures, became president of the committee. The Lonja del Comercio was well represented on the board; Lonja directors Federico Casteleiro, Facundo Graell, and

Florentino Suarez became leaders of the Comite Nacionalista Español, too.

The Marquesa de Tiedra, immensely wealthy and member of a prominent Spanish clan, became head of the family
commission of the Comite. Nena Velasco de Gonzalez Gordon, wife of a wealthy Havana entrepreneur, became the
new organization's treasurer.

In the Comite Nacionalista Español, the Spanish set of
Cuba was putting its best foot forward. No rough stuff, no
spying, no riff-raff and rabble. Its members were all drawn
from the best social circles. Pepin Rivero was honorary
president.

The Comite collected its funds in the names of widows,
orphans, and simple Christian charity. Typical of the
Comite's own financial statement is the one issued on July
18, 1938:

RESUME OF THE CONTRIBUTIONS MADE TO THE NEW SPAIN

To the Spanish State	$303,541.68
To the Requetes	5,000.00
To the Falange	5,000.00
To the Falange's Auxilio Social	1,000.00
To Hospitals	3,000.00
To Auxiliary of the Nationalist Navy	22,664.00
TOTAL:	$340,205.68

The Comite, which from this report was obviously raising
funds not for war sufferers but for the Spanish Fascists
to use as they best saw fit, also shipped vast quantities of
Havana cigars and Cuban rum to Nazi Spain during the
three years of the Republic's agony. With the above report,
the Comite and Senator Arguelles addressed a letter to all
contributors:

Under the destinies of the Caudillo Franco, genius of the
Movement of Salvation, we look to the future of the new Spain
with full confidence and racial pride. Franco, while reconquer-
ing Spain, returns her again to the moral and material grandeur

of Isabella and Ferdinand and gives her models of maximum humanity and Christianity, helping the fallen and bringing extermination to hatred and class differences. FRANCO! FRANCO! FRANCO!

Continuously we receive messages from the real Spain, grateful for the moral and material aid that reaches her from Cuba. To you, co-operators of the new Crusaders, they are addressed and to you we transfer them. *VIVA CUBA! ARRIBA ESPAÑA!*

While the bluebloods were organizing the Comite Nacionalista Español, a Cuban manufacturer, Alfonso Serrano Villarino, hastily formed the Falange Española Filial de la República de Cuba. This Falange was organized into cells. The head of cell R-1 was José Ignacio (Pepin) Rivero. Elicio Arguelles headed cell A-1.

This was in July 1936. But Villarino was something of an amateur. He made the mistake of admitting to the inner councils of his Falange some very ambitious men, among them one Capitan Jorge de Vera. The hot-blooded Capitan wanted to be the Caudillo; failing in this desire, he split the young Falange in two by walking out and forming the J. O. N. S. de la Falange Española en Cuba.

This state of chaos in the Falange movement went on for a whole winter. In the spring of 1937, a courier brought a sealed packet to Cuba from Burgos, then seat of the Franco-von Faupel government. The packet was for Juan Adriensens, the Franco "consul" in Camaguey. In the packet were some books on Falangismo and a series of directives on the organization of the Falange movement in Cuba. The packet was followed by a small commission of Burgos agents headed by Francisco Alvarez Garcia.

Adriensens brought about a measure of peace in the movement. Jorge de Vera came sheepishly back to the fold, and one great Falange Española Tradicionalista de la J. O. N. S. en Cuba was organized—with Francisco Alvarez Garcia as its Caudillo. But just as things began moving smoothly, someone stepped on Jorge de Vera's sensitive toes again. The result was a new de Vera rump organization—the Falange de España en Cuba.

At this point, General von Faupel, who had already decided that Cuba was to be his main advance base in the Americas, ceased to be amused. In 1938 he appointed Alejandro Villanueva to the post of Inspector General of the Falange Exterior in all the Americas, and shipped him off to Cuba with orders to get down to serious business.

Villanueva, a sharp-faced organizer with a fantastic memory and a vile temper, was given extraordinary powers. He was ordered to act as von Faupel's personal representative in the Falange Exterior organizations from Montreal to Buenos Aires. He was to make Cuba the hemispheric center of all Falange activities. He was to consolidate the Spanish control of all commerce. He was to organize all Spanish activities in the New World under the single banner of the Falange. Most important of all, Alejandro Villanueva was to place the Falanges in the hemisphere on a complete military footing. In this last task Villanueva was to work under the direction of Nazi agents assigned by Berlin to guide him.

The Axis could not have chosen a better man for the job. The new Inspector General worshiped Adolf Hitler as a god. He saw in Hitler the genius of a new and lasting era of world fascism—and therefore based all of his actions on the simple theory that, if Hitlerism conquered the world, Villanueva would have nothing to worry about. Villanueva played only on this basis. The results are evident in the vault on the second floor of the Spanish legation in Havana: only a man completely convinced that he was on the winning side could have been so open, so reckless, and so thorough in his entire campaign.

In the beginning, Villanueva concentrated on helping Francisco Alvarez Garcia build the Cuban Falange into a great, disciplined, fanatical army. They soon had it up to a membership of 30,000 fanatics organized into a military structure familiar to any student of the Nazi state in Germany.

The chief of the Cuban Falange, Alvarez Garcia, was all-powerful. His second in command—another Burgos export named Sergio Cifuentes—was the second most powerful man in the Falange. Alvarez Garcia, of course, took orders only from Villanueva—who, in turn, took his orders only from General von Faupel.

The members of the Falange wore stock Fascist uniforms and developed the muscles of their right arms by frequent use of the raised arm (*brazo en alto*) Fascist salute. Once a week, the average Falangista of military age joined members of his cell on the country estate of some Falangist aristocrat for military drill—often under the supervision of German Army instructors. Not all of the military instructors of the Falange in Cuba were *Reichswehr* officers, however. There were a few Spaniards and also, on occasions, men like former Czarist Naval Officer Golowchenko, of whom more later.

From the very start, Falangistas had been trained to carry out routine espionage duties for the Axis. Even under the leadership of Villarino, the Cuban Falange's original leader, all Falangistas had to fill out a form called *Cuestionario Confidencial*. This was a simple questionnaire which called for answers to, among others, the following: "What languages do you speak? Have you had military instruction? What rank? Do you know how to handle firearms? What arms? Can you drive a car? Do you have a car? Do you know radio telegraphy?"

When Inspector General Villanueva appeared on the scene, the military and espionage aspects of Falangismo were given a thorough overhauling. For with Villanueva came the Germans. And the Germans made such stern demands that more than one simple fellow who signed up with the Falange because his boss or his friends or his priest told him it was the thing to do, started to develop cold feet.

The files of the Ministry of Justice in Havana are crammed with letters from just such simple Spaniards. There are, for instance such letters as that of Antonio del Valle, dated November 30, 1941. Señor del Valle, in his letter to the Ministry of Justice, reveals that he had no idea what was in store for him when he joined the Falange. He charges that most Falangistas are compelled to commit many acts detrimental to Cuba, "such as photographing U. S. Naval Bases in Cuba" and turning the photos over to a German individual employed by a commercial aviation company. "And this German individual reproduces the photos for shipment abroad."

While the military effectiveness of the Falange was being developed, the propaganda and money-raising activities of the von Faupel column were not ignored. Scarcely a week passed but the Falange held some big meeting or dinner in one of Cuba's cities, or celebrated some special Mass in one of Cuba's churches.

The relations the Falange enjoyed with most of the Hierarchy of the Church in Cuba were similar to those they enjoyed with Spanish businessmen. The reasons for this *entente cordiale* were quite similar. The Hierarchy had funds invested in Spain. It was no secret, for instance, that the Church had great holdings in the Barcelona tenements and the Valencia orange groves. Under the monarchy, the Church had also had a monopoly on education. The free schools established by the newly born Spanish Republic in 1931 cut deeply into the Church's revenue. The social laws passed by the Republic—laws which called for certain needed but costly housing improvements and higher wages for orange workers—also affected Church revenues.

The Nazis were able to exploit these conditions most effectively. On the one hand, they were able to win much Church support for their Falange by promising to repeal all social legislation of the Republic and closing the free public schools. On the other hand, our old friend Eberhard von Stohrer—who succeeded von Faupel as German Ambassador to Spain in 1937—promised the fanatical Fascists of Germany and Spain that the "destiny of the Falange is to eliminate the power of the Catholic Church in Spain."

In Cuba, Villanueva was able to keep most of the Hierarchy very much on the Falange side. When Cuba's faithful found Nazis and Italian Black Shirts sharing the dais under massed Falange, Swastika, and Italian Fascist banners at most Falange affairs, the majority of them balked at following the Hierarchy politically.

Typical of these public manifestations was the *Plato Unico* (Single Dish) banquet held in honor of and for the financial benefit of the Fascist armies in Spain. The dinner was held in Havana on February 19, 1939. With Swastika banners flying overhead, the seven speakers of the evening took their places at the main table. The following week *Arriba España*, official organ of the Falange Exterior in Cuba, carried all seven speeches. The speakers were: Dr. José Ignacio Rivero; Camarada Alejandro Villanueva, Inspector Extraordinario; Camarada Miguel Espinos, Franco's "Ambassador" to Cuba; Camarada Miguel Gil Ramirez, (nominal) Jefe Territorial en Cuba; Camarada Salvador Ruiz de Luna, Jefe Territorial de Intercambia y Propaganda; and Their Excellencies, the Ministers of Italy and Germany, Giovanni Persico and Hermann Woelckers.

Pepin began his speech with a glowing tribute to the diplomats.

Señor Representatives of the glorious nations of Germany and Italy [he began]. Señor Representatives of the only Spain recognized by all the persons of good will in the world, Comrades of the Falange Española, and I call you comrades because, although I am not inscribed in that glorious institution, I am with it in spirit . . .

According to the records of the Falange Exterior and the files of the Cuban Secret Police, Pepin's ties to the Falange were more than merely those of the spirit.

At the time these seven speeches were broadcast over the Cuban radio, the Falange Exterior was going through its first of three phases. In this phase, the role of the Falange was merely one of building an organization, an Axis machine. The military drills, the bits of espionage, the public manifestations were merely preparations for the second phase. Just as the war then going on in Spain was merely the first round of Hitler's military struggle for world domination, so—during the Spanish War—was the Falange Exterior maintained merely to make this Spanish triumph of German might all the more complete.

In April 1939 the Republic of 1931 succumbed to German arms. For the time being Spain was Germany's. And between April and September, while Spain buried its dead, the Falange Exterior was mobilized as part of the world offensive the Nazis were to launch in Poland.

The day after the Republic fell, Washington, London, and Paris hastened to recognize Francisco Franco as the head of the Spanish State. Cuba, which, like most of Latin America, follows Washington's lead in diplomatic affairs, also recognized Franco Spain. Now the Nazis had one of their basic objectives—a "neutral" diplomatic network all over the world. The Spanish legation was quickly staffed with trained Fascists. The hectic second phase of the Falange Exterior was on.

The main Falange headquarters were established in the Spanish consulate on Oficios Street, and here, with a brashness that made patient Cuban Secret Police officials like General Manuel Benitez and Lieutenant Francisco Padrone shudder, Nazi agents called regularly to supervise the real work of the Falange.

There were six thousand members of the German Nazi Party in Cuba at this time. Their chief was Eugenio Hoppe, who operated a razor factory in Regla. Their main headquarters were at Copinar Beach, near Guanabacoa.

Hoppe, a favorite of Havana society, presided over a complete Nazi world in Cuba. There was the National Socialist German Workers Party, the Winter Hilfe Fund, the Death Fund, the Hitler Jugend, and all the standard Nazi foreign organizations. These were allied with the Falange in all of its Axis war tasks.

The Italian Fascists and the Japanese were also tied to the Falange. Prince Camillio Ruspoli, Chief of the Black

Shirts in the Americas, controlled about three thousand Italian Fascists. Their front was the Societa Italiana di Assistenza, whose offices were in the Casa D'Italia on Havana's Prado. Ruspoli, a wealthy aristocrat who owned vast orange plantations near Camaguey, acted as president of this society. Like the Falangistas, the Italian Black Shirts were a uniformed Fascist group. At their meetings, the Falange and Swastika banners were displayed as prominently as the Fasces.

Although they had only 700 agents in Cuba, the Japanese were in many ways the best organized of the Axis groups on the island. They were the first subjects of totalitarian nations to be organized as a complete espionage organization in Cuba. Organized into small circles, under military leadership, the Japanese were there for only one purpose: to prepare for the eventual Japanese war against the United States. All of their efforts in Cuba were directed toward this objective.

The primary task of the Japanese was carried on by Tokio naval officers. This was a continuing study of the Gulf currents—a work in which they were later joined by the Nazis. The importance of the Gulf Stream as a U-boat path is immeasurable. Because of the Gulf Stream and other more obvious factors, Cuba is the naval key to the Gulf and the Panama Canal.

Aided no little by the fact that smart Cuban society leaders felt naked without Japanese servants, the Tokio espionage ring in Cuba did yeoman service for the Axis cause. Despite the fantastic, storybook sound of the statement, it is nevertheless true that most of the Japanese servants in Cuban aristocratic homes were trained agents, officers of the Japanese armed forces.

The Japanese concentrated their efforts for years in the north of Cuba and on the Isle of Pines. It is known that the humble and self-effacing Nipponese forwarded hundreds of reports to Tokio on the politics, the economics, and the geography of Cuba. Tokio was deeply interested in backing anti-American movements in Cuba, and groups like the

Falange were made to order for the purposes of the Japanese High Command, which was to eventually order the bombing of Pearl Harbor—and Manila.

Of all the Axis concentrations in Cuba, the Falange was the greatest. The Germans, in April 1939, went to work at the task of making it the most efficient.

The formal outbreak of the war, in September 1939, found the Falange at the peak of its efficiency. It had come through its second phase with flying colors.

The third phase of the Falange Exterior in Cuba—and throughout Latin America—was carefully blueprinted by General von Faupel.

The Nazi general's plans for the Falange Exterior at this point were clear: as long as the Axis was able to maintain its legations in the New World, the Falange was to continue more or less as usual. It was to make propaganda for Germany, commit acts of sabotage and espionage, and stand by for the inevitable day when Germany, Italy, and Japan would be compelled to close up diplomatic shop. At that point, the Falange Exterior was to take over as the diplomatic front for all Axis Fifth Column activities and to supply the cadres for most of these actions.

It was in line with these plans that José del Castano and Genaro Riestra were sent abroad by von Faupel in the fall of 1940.

Riestra reached Havana in November 1940. Affairs were not going too smoothly for the Falange. For one thing, the Cuban Government, the year before, had made the Falange an illegal organization.

This was no secret to Riestra, for he had been in Havana in 1939 when the Cuban Government acted. Twice, before being appointed consul general in 1940, Riestra had quietly visited Havana on Falange business. A violent and most undiplomatic young government official, Riestra had long been a storm center in Latin-American affairs. The Mexican Government had seen fit to expel him for abusing its hospitality, and Alejandro Villanueva looked upon him as an interloper. For his part, Riestra looked upon the Falange Inspector General for the Americas as a serious rival, and on his earlier visits to Cuba he had tried to increase the power of Francisco Alvarez Garcia, Chief of the Cuban Falange, at the expense of Villanueva.

After the Cuban Government cracked down on the Falange in 1939, Riestra had arranged for Alvarez Garcia to establish his office in the Spanish consulate in Havana. At that time, still smarting from his insults, Riestra held a minor post in the consulate. But he had played his cards cleverly.

He set an example for all Falangist officials by the way he held together the most minute ties of the organization, and when he returned to Spain, early in 1940, he carried in his trunks a complete file of documentary evidence proving that he had successfully circumvented the action of the Cuban Government. Among his exhibits was a letter dated February 5, 1940, a letter from the Rector of the Escuelas Pais—a religious school—in Pinar del Rio. The letter said:

This college feels great gratitude toward the generous gesture of the Falange Española Tradicionalista, and towards you particularly, for having thought of us, Spanish scholars, when distributing college scholarships.

You cannot imagine the happiness we felt upon receiving your letter . . . asking about our school pensions. In answer, I give you the rates we will assign to students recommended by the Falange Española.

The letter then went on to quote special tuition rates and to bless Riestra. It was signed by Antonio Ribernat, the rector. Its significance becomes clear when it is recalled that at the time the letter was written the Falange was illegal in Cuba. Wily Genaro Riestra was able to use this and similar letters as proof that he had been able to keep the Falange going in Cuba despite the Cuban Government's laws.

Riestra's files impressed von Faupel, and he was rewarded with the post of Consul General. He took over his duties at the same time that José del Castano took command in Manila.

The new Consul General started out like a house on fire. Blithely ignoring the laws and the dignity of the Cuban Government, Riestra began a whirlwind drive to organize all Spanish activities under the banner of the Falange. He concentrated primarily on the Spanish Regional Societies, the social welfare organizations to which most Spaniards in Cuba had belonged for years.

Cayetano Garcia Lago, then head of the Centro Gallego —one of the largest of these societies—was Riestra's chief lieutenant in the drive to make all Spanish societies part of the Falange. For a few months, the campaign hummed along like a Stuka on a bombing mission over unprotected territory.

Then, shortly after the new year began, Senator Augustin Cruz arose in the senate and made a ringing speech. Brandishing documentary evidences of Riestra's contempt for Cuban law, Senator Cruz demanded that the fiery diplomat be given his walking papers.

The Cuban Government took action. For the second time in his hectic career as an Axis agent Riestra was expelled from a Latin-American nation.

Not content to stop with the expulsion of Riestra, the Cuban Government began to take action against the entire Falange. Ace Cuban investigators like Benitez, Padrone, and Captain Faget started to make raids on the secret headquarters of the Falange. These raids uncovered thousands of sensational documents. In the raid on the headquarters in a macaroni factory in Guanabacoa—a coup pulled by the Cuban police in the summer of 1941—fantastic evidences of the ties between the Nazi war and propaganda machines were seized. (This raid took place after the German, Italian, and Japanese legations had been closed.)

Vast amounts of Nazi propaganda, in Spanish and in English, were taken. A whole series of letters from Post Office Box IPL 244, Hamburg, Germany, were transferred from the Falange strongboxes to the files of the Cuban police.

These letters dealt extensively with Falange fueling bases in Latin America for Nazi surface raiders off the coast of Brazil and German submarines in and around Cuban territorial waters.

The police found forged passports of Britain and the United States, vast quantities of Cuban Government stationery printed in Leipzig, and hundreds of strategic maps and photographs of electrical, industrial, and war installations in the Antilles.

But the most amazing document seized in this raid was a complete and detailed set of military orders for a secret army evidently in existence on Cuban soil. This army consisted of:

An infantry regiment of 120 officers and 3100 men.
An artillery battalion of 25 officers and 725 men.
A cavalry squadron of 15 officers and 332 men.
An engineers company of 4 officers and 250 men.
An aviation squadron of 22 officers and 179 men.
A sanitary company of 6 officers and 100 men.

The communication which described this skeleton secret army was in the same file as a letter requesting (1) artillery, antiaircraft guns, field radio telephones, motorcycles, and other war materials and (2) the arming of three fast merchant ships evidently owned by the Cuban Falange.

The Cuban police then raided the homes and business establishments of a large number of known Falangistas. In raid after raid, they discovered caches of rifles and small arms, bullets, and other materials of real armies.

This sudden toughness of the no-longer-tolerant Cuban Government gave the Falange and its leaders a fine case of jitters. Alejandro Villanueva simply disappeared. Some Cubans, intimate with the inner workings of the Falange, suspect that he died an unnatural death somewhere in South America. Only one definite thing is known about his movements after fleeing Cuba in 1941: when he arrived in

Spain, he fell into disgrace and was made a prisoner in Valencia.

Sergio Cifuentes, propaganda chief of the Falange, was arrested in his sumptuous home in Vedado in May 1941. His confidential files were taken by the government and, after a trial, he managed to flee to Spain where he was received with honors by Franco and hailed as a conquering hero by the Falange.

Serrano Villarino, founder of the first Falange in Cuba, was also arrested by the police; and, although he managed to worm out of the charges, he lost one of his most treasured possessions in the process. This was a glowing letter from Fritz Kuhn, Führer of the German-American Bund, a letter which ended with the twin cry: "*Arriba España! Heil Hitler!*"

The expulsion of the Nazi consuls made things more difficult for the Falange. The Falange in Matanzas, for instance, was deprived of the educational benefits of its meetings with the Nazi group led by Clemens Ladmann. While Ladmann was still German Consul in Matanzas and Administrator of the Jarcia cord factory, he would meet with selected Nazi and Falange leaders in the Casino Español. After Ladmann was expelled from the country, Oskar Harves, German vice-consul and office manager of the Jarcia plant, remained in Cuba to carry on. But the meetings at the Casino Español had come to an end. Although Harves succeeded Ladmann as Number One Nazi, he had to transmit his orders to the Falange through intermediaries.

In Havana, in Matanzas, in Camaguey, and other cities Cubans began to petition their government to break off relations with Franco Spain and to jail all the Falangistas. This growing sentiment frightened the Falange and shook its supporters.

Pepin Rivero and Raoul Maestri began to think seriously in terms of newsprint. Roosevelt was backing the accursed Russians in their war with the Nazis—and newsprint was still controlled by Canada and the United States. So Pepin, hiding the medals he received from Hitler, Mussolini, and Franco, and Maestri, forgetting his own published works, started a flirtation with the American Ambassador, George Messersmith.

Through the good offices of the American Embassy, Maestri was invited to lecture in the United States, at the expense of our government, on Latin-American problems. And when an American magazine took a healthy swipe at the Falange, Pepin, and Maestri, the first man to rush to Maestri's defense was Ambassador Messersmith. As if to make this defense stick, Messersmith posed for a picture with Pepin, Maestri, and other *Diario de la Marina* executives—a picture the paper displayed prominently in its rotogravure section.

Then, for reasons which will some day make interesting reading, Pepin Rivero was awarded the 1941 Maria Moors Cabot Prize for outstanding journalism in the cause of North and South American mutual understanding. He traveled to New York in triumph, picked up the medal and the cash award from Nicholas Murray Butler at Columbia University, turned on all of his charm at a New York banquet, and proclaimed himself a life-long admirer of democracy.

Shortly after Pepin got his medal, Messersmith was transferred from Cuba to Mexico. Cubans express great gratitude to the American Government for having appointed Spruille Braden to Messersmith's old post.

On September 24, 1941, Francisco Alvarez Garcia, chief of the Falange in Cuba, received a coded cable at the Spanish Consulate. They were his orders to return to Spain at once. Francisco de la Vega, an important official of the Spanish Consulate in Havana, also received a cable. He had been appointed the new chief of the Falange. Señor de la Vega was taking over the jobs of both Inspector General Villanueva and the Cuban Territorial Chief.

But getting out of Cuba was not to prove an easy task for Alvarez Garcia. Lieutenant Francisco Padrone, of the

Cuban Secret Police, tipped off that the Falange chief planned to leave on the Spanish steamer *Magallanes* early in October, felt that the Axis agent owed the Cuban Government a long series of explanations.

Waiting only until Alvarez Garcia had boarded the ship, Padrone and his men seized the Fascist's baggage. Alvarez Garcia, aided by the ship's officers, escaped from the boat and took refuge in the Spanish Consulate. Here, despite the fact that the Urgency Court of Cuba was demanding his appearance, Alvarez Garcia hid for a full month under the diplomatic protection of a "friendly" nation. The police surrounded the Consulate for the length of Alvarez Garcia's stay there.

The people of Havana, although angered, were not blind to the humor of the situation. The siege of Alvarez Garcia became the butt of hundreds of jokes, and even the subject of improvised ditties sung by the wandering street singers of the Cuban capital.

While the legal authorities maneuvered to force the Spanish Consulate to disgorge Alvarez Garcia, Padrone and the Cuban Police made a detailed study of the Falange leader's baggage. Like Genaro Riestra, Garcia had taken a complete file of pictures and documents along to prove to von Faupel that he had done his job well. The pockets of the expensive suits in his trunks were filled with letters, military orders, and other official records. In one of the trunks there was a complete collection of *Arriba España*, the official organ of the Falange in Cuba.

But the prize item in the baggage of Francisco Alvarez Garcia was four thousand feet of 16 mm. motion-picture film, much of it in color. A Cuban who was present at one of the many screenings of this film at Police Headquarters describes it as a complete documentary movie on the four years of Falange activities in Cuba. It showed everything from meetings of the Falange to the Auxilio Social of the Falange, military drills, parades, and intimate views of activities in Falange headquarters. The actor who "stole" the entire picture was, in the opinion of all who saw it,

Pepin Rivero. He dominated every sequence he was in, and, say the eyewitnesses, he was in most of them.

Francisco Alvarez Garcia was finally permitted to return to Spain via Spanish steamer in November. While he was on the high seas, the Japanese bombed Pearl Harbor. Two days after Pearl Harbor, Cuba declared war on the Axis powers.

As in Manila, the Spanish legation in Havana took over the diplomatic representation of German, Italian, and Japanese interests when the war brought on the complete break. While scores of Nazis, Italians, and Japanese were rounded up and sent to the Cuban internment camp for enemy aliens on the Isle of Pines, the less prominent Axis agents went into hiding.

Somewhere in the interior of Cuba, shortly before Pearl Harbor, a Japanese secret agent met with certain Falangistas and turned over to them a large sum of money, earmarked for the common cause of all the Axis nations.

The funds of the German organizations, from the Nazi Party to the Winter Hilfe, seemed to have vanished into thin air. But in the files of the Cuban Secret Police there is a complete record of the number of visits Walter Lademann, treasurer of the Nazi organizations, paid to the Spanish legation before Pearl Harbor. Lademann is now imprisoned on the Isle of Pines.

Many of the other Nazi agents who regularly visited the Spanish Consulate before Pearl Harbor became prisoners on the Isle of Pines with Cuba's declaration of war. The Spanish Consulate became their legal adviser. For a long time the Spanish Consulate was able to arrange for the Nazis to receive visitors in the internment camp. Manuel Alvarez Reymunde, commercial attaché in the consulate, made frequent arrangements for former Cuban Minister of State Cortina to visit Nazis on the Isle of Pines. This precipitated so great a scandal that, in August 1942, the government clamped down on all visitors' permits to the camp.

The temper of the government and the people has put the

Falange and the Spanish diplomatic corps on its guard. But the 30,000 Falange members, after seven years of training, are far from inactive. Nor are they carrying on with empty hands.

The present leadership of the Falange is held by Francisco de la Vega, who operates out of the Spanish Consulate in Havana. High in the ranks of the current Falange leadership are:

Lopez Santo, Santa Clara 164, Havana
Aureliana y Faustino Tarnos, Campostela 707, Havana
José Martinez Gorriaru, Muralla 209, Havana
Esteban Uriarte, Merced y Picota, Havana
Jesús Humara, Havana.

Instructions and propaganda still reach the Falange via Spanish ships, which ply the seas with complete freedom. The Spanish diplomatic pouches are kept fairly free of incriminating correspondence, since trusted and secret Nazi couriers on board Spanish ships can carry messages and funds in total obscurity.

The most recent line of Falange propaganda as sent to Cuba from Madrid has an eerie ring. Booklets printed in Madrid and Santander preach Hispanidad as usual, attack President Batista for his "liberal" policies and his "inferior racial origins," hail Charles A. Lindbergh as the "great caballero of the continent," and—hopefully—assert that this war will finally prove the inherent inferiority of the democracies and the strength of the Axis. Many Cuban citizens who receive these booklets in the mails promptly turn them over to the police.

Currently, the Falange is trying to organize a Latin-American Youth Congress in Madrid in 1943. Literature of the Falange says that the delegates from Latin America will be taken on a tour of the New Spain, and that the first step on this tour will be the tomb of *El Apóstol*—José Antonio Primo de Rivera.

The powerful Spanish set which openly and covertly

supported the Falange since 1936 is, today, far from quiescent.

The Spanish crowd in the Lonja del Comercio, under the inspiration of the Falange, is engaged in open warfare against the war policies of the Batista government. Early in the course of the war, Batista pushed through a set of price-fixing laws and created an official agency, the ORPA (Office of Price Regulation) to enforce these laws. They were designed to prevent inflation.

Many of the Lonja members who backed the Falange have persistently broken the ORPA laws, particularly those relating to food prices. As a result, prices in Cuba are in some cases nearly 50 per cent higher than they were at the start of the war.

Certain known Falangist businessmen in Havana are hoarding alcohol for greater profits. This not only creates great fire hazards, but it also keeps much-needed alcohol from reaching the war industries of the United States.

In politics, the wealthy Falangistas and their friends pour vast sums into the political campaign funds of enemies of the Batista coalition.

The *Diario de la Marina*, still the spokesman for the Spanish set, plays a careful but dangerous game. On the surface, the paper is all for the democracies. But the *Diario de la Marina* is still violently pro-Franco. It raises issues like the hazards of a Russian victory in this war, and attacks win-the-war Cuban policies like price control, fair labor legislation, and the diversified agricultural program designed to grow less sugar and more food.

Attacks on price-control legislation are far more serious in Cuba than in most other countries. For the great majority of Cubans are employed in the sugar fields—where there is work for only two months of the year. The slightest rise in prices spells catastrophe to almost the entire population; a catastrophe which benefits only the Axis powers. Like the price-control measures, Batista's labor and agricultural diversification programs are designed to keep Cuba from falling down in her war tasks. Should these programs be wrecked, Cuba will become, not an asset, but a liability to the United Nations.

Early in 1942, the Cuban Government put an unofficial but nevertheless effective embargo on the trans-shipment via Cuba of war supplies from South America to Spain in the ships of the Compañía Transatlantica Española, the shipping line owned by the Spanish State. The Nazis had been receiving Chilean nitrates and other vital war materials over this route. The *Diario de la Marina* fought vigorously and successfully for the lifting of this embargo.

With the outbreak of the war, the Cuban Government issued restrictions against publishing certain types of shipping information, on the logical grounds that such information would be valuable to the commanders of the Nazi submarines in the Caribbean and the South Atlantic. The *Diario de la Marina* violated these restrictions so flagrantly in April 1942 that the government was forced to seize one issue of the paper and take legal steps to prevent further violations.

Of the 500,000 Spaniards in Cuba, only 30,000 joined the Falange. The overwhelming majority of the Spaniards in Latin America, like their brothers in Spain, are sworn enemies of the Falange and the Fascist Axis of which it is a satellite. Cuban Spaniards, those of long residence and those who fled to Cuba as refugees from Nazi Spain, are the firmest allies the Cuban Government has in its unrelenting war against the Falange. The Casa de la Cultura, largest of the refugee Republican organizations, has over 30,000 active members. Many of them have risked their lives to get evidence against the Axis Fifth Column in Cuba. More than one cell of the Falange in Cuba and Latin America has within its ranks Spanish Republicans who joined the Falange only to act as unpaid, unsung, and unknown agents of the governments which shelter them.

The average Cuban, far from having any inner desires once again to be part of the Spanish Empire, is aggressively anti-Axis, fervently pro-United Nations. An indication of how the Cubans feel about the Spanish Empire and the war can be found at any Cuban baseball stadium. Baseball is as popular in Cuba as it is in Brooklyn; and the Cuban fans, like the Dodger rooters, look upon all umpires as their natural enemies. For forty years, when Cuban fans really wanted to tell an umpire what they thought of his larceny, they flung but one choice epithet at his head: *"Guerrillero!"* The *Guerrilleros* were the storm troopers of the Spanish monarchy in Cuba. Today the Cuban fans have another epithet. The call the umpire a *quinta columnista*, a Fifth Columnist.

Although the *Diario de la Marina* is considered by some Americans to be Cuba's leading paper, it falls behind anti-Axis papers like *El Pais* and *El Mundo* in circulation.

The Cuban labor movement, an important factor in the nation's political life, is all-out in its support of the war and the Batista government. The daily newspaper of the Cuban Confederation of Workers, *Hoy*, started from scratch four years ago and now has a larger circulation than the *Diario de la Marina*. For four years its pages have sailed into the Falange tooth and nail, and its ace reporters like Diego Gonzalez Martin and Fernando Carr have put more than one Falangista on the road back to Madrid—or in jail.

Fulgencio Batista, more perhaps than any other statesman of the Western Hemisphere, understands the role of the Falange in this war. Cubans in and close to the government make no secret of the fact that Batista wants to break off diplomatic relations with Hitler's Spain. The only thing, they say, that keeps him back is fear of treading on Washington's toes.

Many democratic Cubans, encouraged by the language and the actions of Spruille Braden, our present Ambassador, feel that Cuba will have the full support of Washington if the Antillean republic breaks with Spain.

Perhaps they are not being overoptimistic. But as long as Axis Spain retains its legations in the New World, the Falange will remain an undercover Fifth Column that does not lack for direction, leadership, and funds.

CHAPTER FOUR

Meet the Gray Shirts

THE AFTERNOON OF FRIDAY, October 6, 1937, began normally enough in Havana. Then, like locusts, cards began to descend upon the city. They were four inches long and five inches wide, and they were in many colors. But whatever their color, they all bore the same printed message, a message that made many Cubans pinch themselves to see if they were really in Havana. The full text read:

CUBAN:
Attend the first meeting of the LEGION OF NATIONAL REVOLUTIONARY SYNDICALISTS at the Central Park, Saturday, October 7, at 8 P.M.
EXALTED NATIONALISM
    ABSOLUTE CUBANIDAD
From the legionaire platform all the defects will be explained to you, who are involved. And all the evils caused by Communism, Judaism, politicians' chatter, and the false revolutionaries; and how the LEGION OF NATIONAL REVOLUTIONARY SYNDICALISTS through its CREDO will finish off such perfidy.
Speakers: F. Fernandez, Blas Hernandez, Elicio Garcia, Arturo E. de Carricarte, Abelardo Gonzalez Vila and Jesús M. Marinas.
No more politicians' talk. No more hunger. No more betrayal. No more Jews. No more Racism between Cubans.
Bread and shelter for all Cubans . . .
For a free Cuba, independent and sovereign.
CUBA ARISE!
        Commission of Press and Propaganda.

The next evening, in Havana's pretty Central Park, against the background of the classic Capitolio designed along the lines of the Capitol in Washington, Jesús Marinas made his debut as the leader of a Fascist movement.

He wore a gray shirt, as did his small corps of Legionaires, and an armband bearing the insignia of a dagger and an open book. His small mustache was a cross between the brush under Adolf Hitler's nose and the classic Spanish *moustachio*. He affected at one and the same time the stern serenity of the official portrait of young Primo de Rivera and the frenetic hysteria of the Nazi Führer.

It was a truly amazing performance. To a curious audience of Cubans—probably the least anti-Semitic people in the Western Hemisphere—Marinas ranted and shrieked about the Jewish menace in Cuba. From the Jews, Marinas shifted his attention to "Imperialism." This monster was responsible for Cuba's hunger. But as he went on, Marinas made clear that he was not speaking about German, or Japanese, or Spanish imperialism. What he meant was "Yankee Imperialism," and he meant it in no uncertain terms. With the Jews and Imperialism, Marinas linked Communism as the third of the great problems weighing on the Cuban people.

There was something only too familiar about this credo. Jesús Marinas had but recently changed his Falange Blue Shirt for the Legion gray shirt, and had changed it on orders from his chief, Francisco Alvarez Garcia. The Legion of National Revolutionary Syndicalists was merely a subsidiary of the Falange.

It was the Cuban prototype of Adolf Hitler's Latin-American trump card. Although it never became known outside of Cuba, the Gray-Shirt movement represented the menace of the Falange in its most acute form—the Falange disguised as a native organization without foreign ties of any sort.

This type of false-front Falange organization epitomizes the careful planning of men like Wilhelm von Faupel. Organized while the Falange was still legal, it was created for the primary purpose of providing a base of operations for the Nazis if and when Axis Spain was finally forced to openly go to war against the democracies.

An intimate knowledge of the machinations and the secrets of the Gray Shirts in Cuba provides the key to the operation of Falange-front organizations all over Latin America—including the Sinarquistas of Mexico, whose 500,-000 members form a dangerous anti-American bloc on our borders. When and if Axis Spain makes its belligerency official and the Spanish diplomatic network which nourishes and guides the Falange is dissolved, scores of organizations like the Gray Shirts—many of them already in existence—will arise to carry on the tasks of the Falange Exterior in the Americas.

Just as the Falange inherited the Latin-American funds of the Germans, Italians, and Japanese after war was declared, so, too, will fronts like the Gray Shirts inherit the resources of their parent organization if Spain goes to war. The story of the Gray Shirts which follows, then, should be viewed in the light of a pattern for much of the Fascist activities that will develop in Latin America as the war progresses.

In political parlance, the Gray Shirts were originally established as a "stink-bomb" movement. By beclouding as many issues as they possibly could, by stirring up all sorts of national troubles, the Gray Shirts would theoretically keep many anti-Fascist Cubans from worrying too much about the Falange. In time, as the Gray Shirts grew in numbers, their whole membership would make excellent whipping boys to absorb blows aimed at the Falange.

The Japanese had a slight hand in the Gray-Shirt movement, too. Having studied the Cuban domestic situation for over a decade, they were aware that the island's large Negro population suffered from many instances of racial discrimination. (They also knew that the men responsible for this discrimination were the men behind the Falange.) Tokio has for years spread propaganda among Negroes to the effect that the Japanese Army is fighting the battle of all the dark races. While the Gray Shirts were being formed, the Japanese sent in a Cuban who became one of its leaders. This

Japanese agent—his name is known to the Cuban police—inserted the plank about "no racism between Cubans" in the Legion platform.

Marinas started to draw his membership largely from the ranks of the petty middle class. Unlike the Falange, which in Cuba at least attracted the cream of high society, the Legion was largely a *sans culottes* outfit. Marinas organized a feminine section and a Student Legion, wore himself hoarse speaking to small crowds in half-filled auditoriums, and waited patiently for orders.

In the beginning, the Legion's magazine, *Acción Legionaria*, was expensively printed. One of its early issues ran a tear-jerking tribute to young Primo de Rivera; all of them found something worthy of praise in Italy, Germany, Japan, and Franco Spain.

But propaganda was not the primary mission of the Gray Shirts. The Legion was created to stir dissension in Cuba, and when its membership reached the three thousand mark Marinas, on orders, launched the National Workers Committee, an affiliate of the Legion. This committee was designed to raid the existing labor unions for membership.

Legion officials launched the National Workers Committee in a unique manner. They offered the strong-arm squad of the Gray Shirts to certain firms on the Havana wharves as union busters. The offer was accepted—but only once. It led to something Marinas had not bargained for. The union he chose to break remained unbroken, which was more than could be said for the heads of some of Marinas's Legionaires.

The Legion of National Revolutionary Syndicalists remained a stepchild of the Falange until the war in Spain came to an end. They did not really figure in the von Faupel plans for Cuba until the second phase of the Falange in the Americas was under way. But as the invasion of Poland neared, the Falange began to pay closer attention to the Gray Shirts.

Francisco Alvarez Garcia, Chief of the Cuban Falange,

had a trusted Falange official make a private survey of the Gray Shirts. By July 1939 they still stood at the three-thousand mark, with possibly another thousand in their Student Legion. Their strongholds were Havana, Camaguey, Cienfuegos, Caibarien, and Matanzas. Under Marinas's leadership, the Gray Shirts had developed into the proper nucleus of a Fascist terror corps. Many of the students, like the adult Gray Shirts, were in the habit of carrying guns and knives. At their public meetings, the Gray Shirts mauled opponents who showed the slightest disrespect for the speakers.

The Gray Shirts had also established close relations with the Nazis. There was quite a quarrel between the Falange chief and his Gray Shirt underling when a Falange inspector, snooping in Marinas's files, found a letter sent by Luis Miries Diaz to the Legion chief on July 18, 1939. Diaz, the Legion's chief of press and propaganda, wrote a long letter to Marinas about Legion affairs. Toward the end of the letter were these sentences:

Antonio Rodriguez has just told me that the sportsman, Bubi Rugchi, is in Havana, and I have agreed to go with him to visit the Legion on Sunday. So you, or the Chief of the Militia, receive him so that he is introduced. He belongs to the Nazi Youth of Germany.

Alvarez Garcia, who suspected that Marinas was trying to get at Nazi funds without his knowledge, threatened to remove him as the Legion leader. Marinas, who felt that he had not been treated properly by the Falange, defended himself vigorously. The quarrel ended with the Falange leader promising Marinas more funds and more jobs for Legion members. Marinas, in turn, had to promise to create more discipline in his ranks.

Discipline came to the Gray Shirts in the person of A. P. Golowchenko, a round, short, rasp-voiced martinet who claimed to have been a captain in the Czarist Russian Navy.

Golowchenko, who spoke Spanish with a heavy accent, arrived in Havana in 1940 to assume the leadership of Cuba's Ukrainian Nazis. There were only two hundred Ukrainian Nazis in Havana but, as Michael Sayers and Albert Kahn revealed in their book, *Sabotage*, the Ukrainian Fascist movement has for many years been used by the Germans and the Japanese as a reservoir of terrorists all over the world. Havana's two hundred Ukrainian Nazis were all hard-bitten, veteran terrorists—ready to commit any act, including murder, at the command of their leaders.

All of the Axis groups in Cuba grew to know Golowchenko well. He had close relations with the Japanese and the Italians, but his particular job seems to have been as drill-master for the Gray Shirts and the Falange. He was a hard taskmaster on the drill fields, training his men in the methods approved by the Czar's army in 1914 as well as in tricks he had learned from the Japanese.

Not only Golowchenko, but also some of his Ukrainian Nazi followers, devoted most of their waking hours to the Legion. They participated in public and private meetings of the Gray Shirts, adding a weird international flavor to the fiercely nationalistic Legion.

The Nationalism of the Legion became as tainted as the nationalism of Franco's "nationalists." In their files was Nazi propaganda, printed in Germany, in the strangest languages. One of the choice exhibits was the assortment of propaganda printed in Hungarian, by German Nazis, for distribution abroad. It became one of the odd jobs of the Gray Shirts to hunt up stray Hungarians in Cuba and press this German propaganda upon them. Other pieces were printed in English and German.

The Russian-Finnish War also served to dilute the nationalism of the Gray Shirts. No sooner had it started than the Legion organized, within its ranks, a Committee for Aid to Finland. The Finnish Consul, Guillermo Evert, was much touched by this action, and on March 6, 1940, he wrote a formal letter of thanks to Marinas on the stationary of the consulate. It had an interesting salutation: "I join you in the cry of Long Live Finland and Independent Cuba!" The Gray-Shirt slogan the Finnish Consul quoted, *"Cuba Independientes!"*, had a particular meaning. It referred to a Cuba independent of "Yankee Imperialism," as everyone in Havana knew.

By this time, the Falange had started to treat the Gray Shirts as a useful factor. In preparation for their coming role, the Gray Shirts were ordered to gain a modicum of respectability and to seek some sound advice.

In February 1940 Jesús Marinas started to see Pepin Rivero. Between visits, they exchanged a most cordial—and revealing—correspondence. There was, for instance, the letter Pepin sent Marinas on March 18, 1940. This letter said, among other things:

I have received yours of the fifth, in which you remind me of your pleasant visit in company of the members of the Supreme Council of the brave League of National Revolutionary Syndicalists.

The enormous accumulation of responsibilities that weigh over me in these times has forced me to cancel the interviews for one month. That is why I send you this letter begging you to have an interview with the secretary of my editorial staff, Dr. Oscar Cicero, who has my orders already to take care of you as you deserve and to place the pages of the *Diario* at the service of the good Cuban legionnaires.

I hope to notify you soon, granting you an interview which will be for me a sincere pleasure.

Affectionate greeting, *brazo en alto,*

Your affectionate friend, etc.,

JOSÉ I. RIVERO

This letter makes clear the fact that Rivero's meeting with Marinas and the Supreme Council of the Gray Shirts was one of a series of interviews. The *brazo en alto* salute—the Hitler salute—is not a typographical error.

The date of this letter makes it particularly interesting to American readers. When Pepin arrived in New York to accept the presentation of the Maria Moors Cabot Prize for

Journalism on November 10, 1941, there was something of a public scandal. Newspapers like PM called Dr. Butler's attention to the fact that the man due to receive the medal at Columbia University was a Fascist of long standing. They cited the fact that Pepin had received the Order of the German Eagle from Hitler, an order awarded to persons who had performed services valued most highly by the Nazis State, and they called attention to his record as a Falangista.

Pepin was forced to make a statement. He denied all. Of course, he said, he had aided the Franco's forces in Spain, but that was only to save Spain from communism. The Spanish war ended in April 1939. By March 1940, Spain had already been saved from what Pepin chose to call communism. And it was in March 1940 that Pepin was offering Marinas advice, publicity, and the *brazo en alto* salute.

Marinas received many letters from the *Diario de la Marina*. One that must be mentioned was on the *Diario* letterhead of the "Private Secretary of the Director." This letter, dated October 5, 1940, notified Marinas that an appointment had been made for the Gray-Shirt Caudillo and his aides to meet with Raoul Maestri. The letter was signed by Miguel Baguer. Miguel Baguer's name also was on the masthead of *Arriba España*, official organ of the Falange Exterior. Baguer was the Director of this Falange organ.

The Gray Shirts also sought spiritual advice in 1940. This letter, written March 13, 1940, on the letterhead of the Archbishop of Havana, was signed by the Vice-Chancellor.

Sr. Jesús Marinas
Chief National Legionaire
Distinguished and esteemed sir:—

By order of the Most Illustrious Capitulary Vicar, S.V. [Servant of the Virgin], I have the pleasure to acknowledge the receipt of your courteous letter of the 11th, and at the same time to inform you that His Illustrious Serenity will have great pleasure in receiving you next Friday at 10.00 A.M. to determine who is to be named Counselor of the Legion of National Revolutionary Syndicalists . . .

Marinas had already had one interview at the Archbishop's palace on February 27, when he first asked for a spiritual adviser. It was never revealed who finally was appointed when Marinas returned to the Palace in March, but shortly after this a whole detachment of uniformed Gray Shirts, carrying their banners, marched to the Cathedral of Havana, where they were blessed after praying for the victory of their cause.

This new respectability gave Marinas a feeling of added power. When he was ordered to hold drill sessions more frequently, he made it known that Gray Shirts who missed a single military drill would be subjected to severe punishment.

Acción Legionaria, the now mimeographed publication of the Gray Shirts, grew bolder, too. In 1940 it was coming out with issues so patently Nazi that even the Falangist high command began to wonder if perhaps Marinas was not going too far.

The issue of December 15, 1940, is a case in point. The cover featured a *Der Sturmer* caricature of a Jew and the slogan: "FUERA JUDIOS" [Out with the Jews]. Inside, illustrated with more Nuremburg art, was a long article on the subject. There was also a page by "Comrade Armando Valdes Zorrilla," which contained these choice nuggets:

SUGAR TO SWEETEN THE ENGLISH

There is a movement to get Cuba to remit tons of sugar for 'poor and unfortunate' England. The authors of this project must have souls of honey, must be melting with tenderness, to conceive that Cuba sweeten English life with Sugar. . . .

After all, it is logical that if the English are the owners of sugar in conspiracy with the Americans, that the intended shipment does not arouse notice. This is a proof that hunger only visits England and not Germany. And that for the English babies it comes in handy to get a little bit of sugar water. The Legionaires will send the needed bottles and nipples to wean the English babies.

THE AMERICAN PRESIDENT AND THE CUBANS

Recently a message was sent to the President-Dictator of the United States in the name of the Cuban people. This message called him the champion of America and the idol of the peoples of America.

It is sad that we have to clarify the fact that Cubans are not in accord with the message in question, since we feel deeply the . . . oppression of the Philippines, the slavery of the small peoples of the Continent, and all the other provocations of the President-Dictator to the peoples who are friends of Europe. When one speaks of the people one has to be very careful, señors parrots of the fostered American democracy and of the hypocritical manifestations of the INHABITANT OF THE WHITE HOUSE.

The Gray Shirts were greatly concerned about who the inhabitant of the White House should be. They had their own candidate for this job. On the public platforms, in their publications, and in handbills they shouted his name for all to hear. The name was Charles Augustus Lindbergh.

As they grew more outspokenly fascist, the Gray Shirts became strong-arm men for the Falange at many meetings— precisely the role the Falange itself had played for the CEDA and the Monarchists in the prewar Spain. Marinas tried desperately to gain a greater following by strutting and screaming on platforms everywhere. He made little headway among the average Cubans, running particularly afoul of their magnificent sense of humor. The quip that hurt most was the commonly repeated one, "poor Marinas— he tries so hard to be like Primo Rivera and Adolf Hitler, and all the time, the harder he tries, he succeeds in becoming daily more like Jesús Marinas."

Yet the Gray Shirts presented a real problem, since they had attracted to their ranks just those elements of Cuban life which form the storm-trooper armies of fascism everywhere. And just as the Brown Shirts in pre-Hitler Germany gave the early storm troopers jobs and uniforms to keep them going, so, too, did the Falange take care of enough Gray Shirts to keep them happy.

One of the places where Gray Shirts found employment was in the chain of dining rooms maintained by the Auxilio Social of the Falange. But even here Marinas found the going difficult, since the average Falangista looked down upon the Gray Shirts as the scum of the earth. More than once, Marinas was forced to take time off from more important duties to intercede for a Gray Shirt who wanted a job as a waiter in an Auxilio Social dining room.

It was one of these attempts to gain employment for his followers that gave the Cuban police one of their most important documentary proofs of the connection between the Falange Española Tradicionalista and the Legion of National Revolutionary Syndicalists. On September 23, 1940, Marinas wrote a long letter to Falange Chief Francisco Alvarez Garcia about a Gray Shirt who had been fired from an Auxilio Social job.

The other things the letter revealed are worth quoting. Marinas, addressing his letter to Alvarez Garcia as "Distinguished Comrade," went on to say:

Ties of real and sincere comradeship link me to you, and you know perfectly my demotion and affection for the glorious FALANGE.

I, as Chief of the LEGION, am honored in coming from the Blue ranks (FALANGE) and preserve very deeply in my soul the days of sadness and joy alike that the Movement of Liberation made us all feel. . . .

Could there be people who would like to intrigue between the Falange and the Legion? . . .

Brazo en alto, I am yours for a Syndicalist Spain and Cuba.

Marinas showed his terroristic hand even against his own membership. The Cuban Secret Police twice had to step in to protect Gray Shirts who tried to resign peacefully from the organization.

Fernando Sanchez Gómez joined the Student's Legion in November 1938. Before long he found himself a full-fledged member of the Gray Shirts. At first he went along and kept his mouth shut. But when he realized that he had tied up with a Fascist group, he tried to resign. His leaders, brandishing pistols, told him that resignation from a military organization was out of the question. If he resigned, they said, a "council of war" would be called to execute him as a traitor.

While the police were investigating Gómez's story, Abelardo Gonzalez Villa charged breathlessly into Havana's Secret Police headquarters. Numb with fear, Villa had to rest quietly for some time before he could even speak.

He was the secretary of the Legion of National Revolutionary Syndicalists. Like Gómez, he had grown disgusted with the Gray Shirts. He decided to resign. His resignation was not accepted. Instead, as he left the Legion Offices at Manzana de Gómez 241, he was followed by a group of Gray Shirts who warned him that he would deeply regret resigning. "The Legion is a military body," one of them warned, "and if the Legion considers you a traitor . . ."

Gómez and Villa were luckier than other ex-Gray Shirts. Placing themselves under police protection saved them from the beatings which were inflicted upon other unfortunate youths who tried to quit the terror organization.

The Cubans who swallowed the Gray-Shirt line had plenty of reasons for wanting to quit unless they were confirmed Fascists. One who did resign was beaten to within an inch of his life. To friends who asked him why he had taken a chance, he mumbled something about a letter from the German consul. Possibly he had seen the letter the Counselor of the German Legation had written to Marinas on June 25, 1940.

This German Legation [the letter ran], is pleased to acknowledge receipt of your kind letter of the 24th, of whose contents it has taken good notice.

Please accept through this means of expression the most sincere appreciation of your cordiality as to congratulations and wishes for Germany, which will be transmitted in their correct form.

Francisco Alvarez Garcia also reacted violently to this letter. He threatened to put a bullet through the Gray Shirt's head if he so much as sent a postcard to any of the Axis legations again. Marinas, it seems, just could not remember that the Legion was not the equal, but the creature, of the Falange.

As the day of Pearl Harbor approached, the Gray Shirts grew even more violent in their attack on America and all things American. Even as the Japanese admirals were planning the operations of December 7, *Acción Legionaria* was shouting:

American philosophy and that of her hired defenders in Cuba is utterly charming. These cry out that the American worker earns ten dollars daily. . . . But these gentlemen remain silent about the fact that these salaries are possible because here in their colonies and sugar plantations they pay miserly quarter-dollars in vouchers to Cuban workers.

Thirty years of friendship between governments of Cuba and the United States have only served to enhance hunger in Cuba, to increase her debt, and, far sadder, to make peoples who suffer the same misfortunes look at each other with hatred.

The same article went on to complain:

But if a Spanish writer speaks of reawakening the dormant love between Mother Spain and her American daughters, that is [considered] an aggression against liberty and a menace to the free peoples.

This was the language of the Gray Shirts as the bombs rained on Manila.

To the immense surprise of Falange officials in Havana and Madrid, however, Jesús Marinas and some of his most trusted henchmen were arrested by the Cuban police, tried, and sentenced to long terms on the Isle of Pines within a week of the attack on Pearl Harbor.

For the moment, the history of the Gray-Shirt movement has reached a dark, blank page. But the complete membership lists of the Gray Shirts are in the Spanish Consulate in Havana; and if this copy should be lost, there are other copies in the files of General von Faupel in Madrid and in the Ibero-American Institute in Berlin.

Cubans who have had much to do with combating Fifth Column activities in their country are still very much concerned about the apparently dissolved Legion of National Revolutionary Syndicalists. They know that the underground Gray-Shirt movement will not be leaderless as long as the Falange remains an entity in Cuba. They feel that the Falange is holding the Gray Shirts in reserve until Cuba begins to feel the inevitable pinch of a long war. And that then the Gray Shirts, backed with plenty of funds, will return to add blood to the Axis-muddied waters.

CHAPTER FIVE

Cliveden in the Caribbean

IN THE LATE SPRING of 1941, Cuba's Secret Police, commanded by General Manuel Benitez, received some secret information through the good offices of the Spanish Republican leaders in Havana. It was the tip that the Falange in Madrid was sending a young assassin to Cuba to commit certain unspecified acts.

Benitez ordered a vigilant watch on every incoming Spanish liner, since this was the most possible means of entry for any Falange agent. The airports in Havana and other Cuban cities were placed under a special detail. Still other police agents began to patrol the Cuban shores in small fishing boats. Sometimes small boats were lowered over the side of a ship and agents landed in them.

Early in June, a young Spaniard, arriving in Havana on board a Spanish ship, attracted the notice of two of Benitez's operatives. They searched him and his baggage carefully. Hidden in a secret compartment of his small trunk were two documents. The first, which bore a photo of the suspicious passenger, was membership book number 244921 of the Falange Española Tradicionalista. It had been issued to José del Rio Cumbreras in Cadiz on the fourteenth of February, 1939, when its owner was a student of eighteen. The second document was a tattered letter, signed by Diego Dominguez Diaz, chief of the Cadiz Falange, testifying to his complete reliability as a tried and tested Falangista.

While the Secret Police agents studied these documents, young Cumbreras tried to bolt. One of the agents brought the nervous young Fascist to his knees.

"Why did you come to Cuba?" he was asked.

Cumbreras answered by attempting to fight his way out of the arms that now held him securely. Again the question was put to him, and when he still refused to answer, he was taken to Secret Police headquarters. Here the authorities decided quietly to place Cumbreras in solitary and, for the time being, to hold him incommunicado until further developments.

Utmost secrecy was preserved. Only a handful of Cuban officials ever knew that Cumbreras had been arrested, and where he was being held. Daily the Cuban authorities tried to make the young Falangista talk. Daily he grew more stubborn. Clearly Falange Chief Diaz had not been mistaken when he put his signature to the document which attested to the fact that Cumbreras had shown "perfect and total discipline during the entire length of his service in our struggle and conducted himself to the complete satisfaction of his chiefs."

The Cuban police studied Cumbreras's luggage carefully. There were no clues to his real function. His letter of recommendation from Diaz had been written on January 26, 1940—over a year before his arrest in Havana—and had been used so much that it had all but disintegrated from wear. The young agent had evidently used it often, but whether he had carried it in Latin America or Spain was a question he refused to answer. The picture on the inside of Cumbreras's Falange membership *carnet* was the photo of a dewy-eyed young schoolboy in a uniform and a beret who bore only a faint resemblance to the sullen, pouting, wiry young Fascist in the Havana jail.

Under ordinary circumstances, Cumbreras would have been put on board the next Spanish ship to leave Havana and warned to stay away from Cuba for the next hundred years. But Cumbreras had arrived in Cuba after the police received their information about a young assassin, and until they could be sure that he was not the man they were looking for, they were determined to hold him. They felt that were Cumbreras actually an important, if unpleasant, cog in the Falange machine, the Spanish legation would in time make some move for the young *militante's* release.

So, pending this type of a break in the case, they held Cumbreras secretly in solitary confinement, questioning him with due regularity every day. And learning nothing. But the Cuban police know how to be patient.

The break in the Cumbreras case came sooner than it had been expected, and from an unexpected quarter.

On June 19, 1941, the Cuban authorities released José del Rio Cumbreras, at the request of the Panamanian Government. Young Cumbreras had ostensibly, on the 18th, signed a labor contract of the Panamanian Government, drawn up and countersigned by Dr. Antonio Iraizoz, Consul General of Panama in Havana. The contract, which bore a more recent photo of Cumbreras than the one on his Spanish credentials, was legal in every sense.

This contract called for Cumbreras to sail for Panama City within ten days after being validated. The Panamanian Government was to provide his transportation and to guarantee his food and lodging for a period of a full year. Nothing was said in the contract about the type of services Cumbreras was to perform for the Panamanian Government, but *after* the contract was presented to the Cuban authorities and Cumbreras was released, someone penned the legend "#40: MASON BRICKLAYER" on the top of the original document.

It was a neat *fait accompli*. The Cuban authorities could not risk any international complications by refusing to hand Cumbreras over to the Panamanian Government. In order to refuse to release Cumbreras they would have been forced to state why the young Fascist was being held—and "suspicion" might not have been accepted as a sufficient reason by the violently and flagrantly pro-Axis Panamanian Government of Arnulfo Arias.

Consul General Iraizoz won out and, much as they wanted to, the Cuban police for diplomatic reasons now had to refrain from asking Iraizoz a series of pointed questions.

These questions, although never put to Iraizoz, made Cuban governmental circles hum for weeks. How had Iraizoz learned that Cumbreras was in Cuba? How had the

Panamanian Consul General learned where Cumbreras was being held? Why had the Panamanian Government drawn up a contract with Cumbreras? Was the young Falangista really a mason bricklayer, or did Arias of Panama have other duties in mind for him in the Canal Zone?

The most puzzling, and the most obstinate, of the questions remained unanswered. How had the Panamanian Consul General learned that Cumbreras was being held incommunicado in solitary confinement by the Cuban police?

Some authorities felt that somewhere there was a leak in the Cuban Secret Police organization itself. Others asserted that the Spanish Consulate, informed of Cumbreras's arrest by members of the ship's crew, had deduced his whereabouts. But the most persistent explanation was voiced in but two words: "Cliveden Set."

Before the year ended, a series of events in the Caribbean countries was to bring the role of Cuba's Cliveden Set to the fore and make the Cumbreras mystery one of the secret scandals of Latin America.

The background for the most important of these events went back to 1931, when a young Harvard-educated Panamanian doctor led a successful *coup d'état* in Panama. His name was Arnulfo Arias.

Arias played a bewildering brand of politics in Latin America. Instead of assuming the presidency, he gave the post to his brother Harmodio. He himself concentrated on building a political machine and strengthening the regime he had created.

In 1934 Arias had himself appointed Ambassador to Italy. Here, lavishly supplied with funds, he became a dashing figure in the Rome diplomatic set. He spoke the language of fascism openly and fervently, became friendly with Benito Mussolini, and met Adolf Hitler.

Progressives in Panama, never friendly toward Arnulfo Arias, began to accuse him of being in the pay of the Fascist powers of Europe. They pointed to the role of the Panama

Canal in the defenses of America and wondered, aloud, how Washington felt about having the political power of Panama in the hands of a man like Arias.

The Arias canvas was further confused in 1936, when he took on a new diplomatic job. This time he became Ambassador to France, Britain, and the Scandinavian countries. The new post gave him new fields to conquer—but for whom he was conquering them became even more of a puzzle to sober Panamanians who loved their country. They knew Arias too well to believe that he was simply burying himself in Europe as a diplomat, but they could only speculate as to his real reasons for preferring a diplomatic cloak to the white horse of a native dictator.

Then, on December 23, 1939, Arnulfo Arias returned to Panama. The war had started in Europe, and Arias evidently was about to show his hand. He started by openly praising the "progress" of the Nazi armies throughout Europe. Then he resigned his diplomatic portfolios and settled down to Panamanian politics.

There was no mistaking the type of politics that was in the mind of Arnulfo Arias as the year 1940 began. He formed a small, openly Fascist *junta* composed almost exclusively of non-Panamanians. One of the most important members of this *junta* was the Count de Bailen, Spain's minister to the Republic of Panama.

Arnulfo Arias and his Fascist advisers went to work on a plan for a Fascist Panama which would be a thorn in the side of the United States. The Axis had its eyes on the Panama Canal, and in Arias they had just the sort of adventurer who would make the most useful ruler of Panama in the event that the United States went to war against the Fascist powers.

The Falange had a formidable organization in Panama, headed by Count de Bailen. Under his leadership, the Panamanian Falange became the storm troops of the coup Arias was preparing. At meeting after meeting, Count de Bailen called upon the Falangistas in the Canal Zone to hold themselves in readiness for any eventualities. While waiting for these "eventualities," the Falangistas were ordered to make propaganda for Arnulfo Arias.

At first, this propaganda was merely built about the personality of Arias as the man who had returned to his homeland to save all Spaniards from incarceration at the hands of the "Protestant-Jew-Imperialist" bandits of Washington. Falangistas, working closely with Japanese and Nazi agents, warned all Spanish-speaking persons that only the rise of Arnulfo Arias stood between them and pending doom. Rumors designed to prevent Panamanians from keeping United Nations ships sailing were also spread over the country by the Falange.

From propaganda, the Falange expanded its activities to include espionage. This espionage was political, at first. Every week fervent Falangistas had to turn in to their cell leaders new lists of Panamanians opposed to the person and the policies of Arnulfo Arias. These lists found their way to Count de Bailen, who turned them over to Arias. The ambitions doctor filed them away for future use.

Then, in June 1940, Arnulfo Arias felt ready to move. He moved straight into the *Presidencia*. The day after he assumed this office, he appeared on the balcony—like his idols Hitler and Mussolini—and greeted a cheering mob with the straight-arm salute of fascism. The Falange, mobilized in full for this demonstration, dominated the crowd which was photographed cheering and giving the new President the *brazo en alto* salute.

Once in office, Arias whipped out the long lists the Falangistas had helped prepare—the lists of his political enemies. Overnight, the jails of the militarily strategic little country became packed with anti-Fascist Panamanians who had made the mistake of voicing their political sentiments in the presence of Falange Exterior members.

The old Constitution of Panama, modeled roughly on the Constitution of the United States, was replaced by a newer, more modern, completely Fascist constitution written by

Arnulfo Arias. One of the provisions in this new constitution increased the President's four-year term to six years.

The completeness of the Fascist pattern of the new Arias government was further revealed in October 1940, when the new President held a plebescite to vote on his new order. He announced that the standard Fascist choice of simple "Yes" and "No" ballots would be made available to all qualified Panamanian voters.

But Arias, on the day of the plebescite, went a bit further than Adolf Hitler. Voters who demanded "No" ballots on plebescite day were promptly clapped into jail. Other voters, who heard about this, boldly wrote "No" across the face of the "Yes" ballots handed them at the polls. For their "treason," they were not only jailed but also, in most cases, given severe beatings.

After the plebescite was over, Arias started to flood the Canal Zone with "refugees from war-torn Europe." They were the most amazing set of refugees ever seen in the Western Hemisphere. Whatever the ostensible nationalities listed on their passports, these refugees all spoke flawless Spanish.

They were also the most fortunate body of "refugees" the world had ever known. Most of them, before leaving Europe, had signed labor contracts with Panamanian consuls—contracts exactly like the printed contract Consul General Iraizoz had awarded to José del Rio Cumbreras in Havana.

In Panama the privileged refugees were given work as laborers near the canal locks, on the new defense works, as waiters in hotels and bars patronized heavily by United States military personnel, as engineers and technicians in key public works, and as office employees of Panamanian government bureaus.

The role of Arnulfo Arias in the war plans of the Axis was becoming very plain. It became so plain that, in October 1941, his regime was brought to an abrupt end by a coup supported by all anti-Fascist elements in Panamanian life. The United States Government did not look with disfavor on the new government established by R. A. de la Guardia, a former member of the Arias Cabinet.

The immediate cause of the coup which finished Arias was the crisis which followed in the wake of his vetoing a bill permitting ships under Panamanian registry to arm themselves against Axis raiders, which were sinking them regularly. After this flagrant pro-Axis action, Arias's hours as President of Panama were numbered.

On the tenth of October, 1941, carrying a passport bearing his mother's name, Arnulfo Arias fled to Havana—to see his "oculist," he said. He had often made this trip before; the "oculist" in question was a charming lady whose name is of little bearing at this writing.

The Cuban Government pulled the welcome mat from under the ex-President's feet and, torn from the arms of his mistress, he left in a few days to seek refuge in Nicaragua.

In Cuba the end of the Arias regime had one immediate result. Dr. Antonio Iraizoz, whom Arias had appointed Consul General in Havana, found himself without a job. Iraizoz was a veteran Cuban newspaperman who had long worked for the *Diario de la Marina*. The collapse of the Machado dictatorship in Cuba had some years before sent Iraizoz fleeing into exile for a grim period. Now, with the collapse of the Arias dictatorship and his diplomatic portfolio, Iraizoz decided to return to his old profession of journalism. Few Cubans were therefore surprised when Iraizoz became a writer for Pepin Rivero's *Diario*.

Iraizoz's was not the only life in Havana to be affected by the end of the Fascist regime in Panama. There was also the Count de Bailen. In October, when Arias fled Panama, the Count de Bailen remained in the country in his twin posts of Spanish Minister and Regional Chief of the Falange Exterior of Panama. For some reason, he retained his *persona grata* status with the de la Guardia regime.

Panama observed its Independence Day on November 11, 1941, with many celebrations. But during the day one sour note was heard above all the others. The Falange held a meeting, too, and at this meeting the indiscreet Count de Bailen chose to deliver a heavily sarcastic address weighed down to the breaking point with attacks on democracy, the

United Nations, and the government of the United States.

The effect of the speech was more than mildly electric. To save the Count's life as well as to protect its own dignity, the government of Panama was forced to expel him from the country.

While the Count was packing his bags, he received a coded message from Madrid ordering him to go to Havana. The Count de Bailen obeyed his orders.

He arrived in Cuba a week later, flat broke, and carrying in his trunk the dress uniform of the former German Consul General to Panama. He leased Apartment 85, on the eighth floor of the Lopez Serano Building in exclusive Vedado, Havana's finest suburb. Gonzalez Gordon, the Havana business leader, gave him some substantial funds, and within a few hours the Count de Bailen was ready to assume his duties as one of the guiding spirits of Cuba's Cliveden Set.

The Cuban police arrested the Count de Bailen during his first week in Havana, but the combined pressure of the Spanish Consulate and the Cuban Cliveden Set was sufficient to win the Falange leader's release.

Cuba's Cliveden Set existed for many years before it received its name from a Fascist-hating Havana newspaperman. Like the British Cliveden Set, it is presided over by a number of titled ladies. (The titles, incidentally, are of the old Spanish monarchy.)

Prominent in the affairs of Cuba's Cliveden Set are the Marquesa de Tiedra (*née* Leticia de Arriba,) sister-in-law of a powerful Cuban official and immensely wealthy in her own right. The Marquesa was head of the Family Commission of the Comite Nacionalista Española, which raised funds for Franco during the Spanish War.

Nena Velasco de Gonzalez Gordon, wife of the financier who loaned Count de Bailen money, and treasurer of the Comite Nacionalista Española, is another prominent leader of Cuba's Cliveden Set. The Falangist Countess de Revilla Camargo, Gonzalez Gordon himself, Senator J. M. Casanova, a powerful Cuban industrialist and plantation owner, and some members of the Cuban Senate and lower house attend most of the Cliveden Set's fabulous functions.

The Cuban Cliveden Set, which holds endless series of dinners, banquets, and luxurious social events, is far from lacking in foreign members. At all of its functions, there is a strong representation from many foreign legations—particularly the Spanish legation. The diplomats of Vichy France were among the earliest members of the Cliveden Set.

The most interesting foreign member of the Cuban Cliveden Set is not a Spaniard, however. This person is a woman, the wife of a diplomat accredited to Cuba. Despite the name she bears, she is an Austrian, mother of two sons in the German Army, and believed to be one of the most important back-stage plotters against the unity of the Americas in the entire hemisphere. Even the Cuban Secret Police, who know both of her names well, avoid mentioning her original name. "Frau K.," they call her, and Frau K. she will remain for the present.

When Count de Bailen was released from the custody of the Cuban police, the Cliveden Set held a big private dinner for him. It was attended by the cream of "Spanish" society in Havana. The Count sat next to the Marquesa de Tiedra, with whom he maintained very close relations. At this dinner the foreign diplomats of the Cliveden Set rubbed shoulders with Cuban politicians, army and navy officers.

The Cuban Cliveden Set is unalterably opposed to all of the war policies of the Batista government. They use their weight and their influence to back all anti-Batista moves, and more than once attempts to save Falangist agents from the rewards of Cuban justice have been traced right back to members of the Set acting either singly or in pressure groups of their own.

Actually, the Cuban Cliveden Set is the social front of the old "Spanish crowd" in Cuban economic and political life. It is but another facet of expression for this crowd, as real and as effective as the Falange and the "Spanish bloc" in the Lonja del Comercio.

One of the intellectual favorites at the Cuban Cliveden Set's functions is Dr. Raoul Maestri, sub-editor of the *Diario de la Marina*. Unlike many of its members, Maestri today professes to be a great friend and admirer of the United States.

The Cuban Cliveden Set were among the first to know, on January 28, 1942, that Arnulfo Arias had flown to Havana from Yucatan on that day.

Arias, who was accompanied by a Mexican priest named Martin, escaped from both the newspapermen and the police at the airport. He went to an unknown address. None of the people who looked for him could locate his Cuban retreat.

Had they gone to the house at the corner of 19th and 8th, Vedado, they would have flushed their elusive quarry. They would have found him to be busily at work, too.

What Arias was working on in Havana at this time was hard to say. On February 3, late in the afternoon, Arnulfo Arias sent two cables. The first was to Ernesto Bellini, in Mexico City. The second was to Deputy Sabayera of the Panama Republic.

One of the few Cubans who saw Arnulfo Arias at this time was Ava de la Vega Martinez. This Martinez was far from a stranger to the Cuban police. In their drive against the Falange Exterior and other Axis satellite groups in Cuba, the police had four months previously arrested Martinez.

In the Martinez home on 24th Street, Miramar, the Cuban police had run across many pictures of great interest to their investigations. In many of these pictures they found Arnulfo Arias embracing Senator Elicio Arguelles, President of the Comite Nacionalista Española. The Martinez files also yielded scores of documents and cables of particular value to the Cuban Secret Police.

What Arias and Martinez talked about in Havana early in 1942 is something at least three government Intelligence Services would like to know. After one of his meetings with Martinez, Arias and Count de Bailen held a long, private conversation in Vedado.

On February 6, 1942, Arnulfo Arias was driven to number 420 Oficos Street, Havana, the address of the Spanish Consulate. He remained inside the Consulate for over four hours.

After leaving the Spanish Consulate, Arnulfo Arias returned to Vedado, where he dashed off a cable addressed to Ricardo Welhead, Palmito Moron, Venezuela. The text of the cable read:

I am coming by plane. Will be there on the 8th. Wait for me.

He left Havana at dawn the following day, but he did not go straight to Venezuela. He stopped at Santo Domingo and Puerto Rico before joining Welhead in Venezuela.

A study of the itinerary Arnulfo Arias followed on his trip from Yucatan to Venezuela and back, as well as of his cables, raises some interesting questions.

Perhaps it was merely a coincidence that Arias's odyssey covered the main bastions of the Caribbean just at the time that the Nazi U-boat activities broke out furiously in these waters.

Perhaps, too, the name and nationality of the man who received the Arias cable in Venezuela is a story in itself.

These are little points that the Cuban Cliveden Set, which showed such an interest in Arias during his visit, might be able to explain. But wait—the Cuban Clivedeners, like their British cousins, deny that they ever existed as a set. In fact, they deny all.

Some of them, after August 1942, even denied ever having wined and dined the dashing and slightly bankrupt diplomat and Falange Exterior leader, the Count de Bailen. For in August the Cuban Government, its patience at an end, finally expelled the Count de Bailen for being an active leader of the underground and illegal Falange in Cuba.

CHAPTER SIX

Compañía Transatlántica Española: Hitler's Bridge of Spies

LATE IN AN AFTERNOON of September, 1941, the Spanish liner N——, bound from Spain to the United States via Havana, approached the Florida shores. On the bridge the captain ordered the engineer to reduce the speed. Her engines all but idling, the liner crawled parallel to the American coastline while the setting sun bathed the red and gold flag of Axis Spain.

As the sun started to sink into the sea on this September afternoon, a small boat was lowered over the side of the N——. It was an ordinary little fishing boat, powered with a good marine engine, and not at all different than any of the fishing boats that dot the southern Florida waters.

In the boat were two men, dressed like American vacationers. They spoke perfect vernacular American English, and they carried fishing tackle made and sold in America. Their clothes came from American stores, and the small fortune they carried was in American currency.

Nevertheless, the two men who were in the small boat lowered from the Spanish N—— off the Florida coast in September, 1941, were not Americans. They were Germans. Nazi Germans. Officers of the Gestapo.

When the small boat rested on the water, one of the Gestapo agents undid the lines that bound it to the N——. His companion started the engine, pointed the bow toward Florida, and waved a cheery adiós to the Spanish officers lined up on the deck of the steamship.

On board the N—— the captain watched the small motorboat disappear across the darkening horizon. Then he nodded to the radio operator. "All right," he said. "You may send it now."

The radio operator entered his shack. He turned to a

small auxiliary short-wave radio and started to send a code signal. When he reached the station he was seeking, he sent the coded message: "All goes well."

Some 150 miles east of Havana, in the small, secret short-wave radio station to which the N—— radio man addressed his message, a Falangista sat with earphones clamped to his head. He tapped out the reply: "Message received, thank you," and then broke the contact.

A few minutes later, ranking Axis officials in Havana knew that the two Nazi agents on board the N—— had been transferred to the fishing boat. In less than an hour, the intelligence was flashed to Berlin via Venezuela.

Two more Axis agents had been landed in the United States via the Spanish network.

The ships of the Compañía Transatlantica Española, owned by the Falangist Spanish State, had after September 1939 become Hitler's chief avenue for spies and saboteurs bound for the Western Hemisphere.

On September 30, 1941, the C. T. E. liner *Ciudad de Madrid* arrived in Havana from Spain. That afternoon, two of the passengers from the *Ciudad de Madrid* were taken to the Hotel Lincoln, on the corner of Galleano and Virtudes streets in Havana.

Brought to the hotel by a friend who had met them at the pier, the two visitors signed the hotel register casually and went up to their rooms. The first of the two to sign the register was Dr. Hoguet Hornung. Although he gave his address simply as "Switzerland," he bore a Peruvian passport. The number on his passport was 178, 1938.

The second man signed the register as Enrique August Luni. He carried Passport Number 38 issued by the Republic of Honduras, declared that he came from Barcelona. He was a slight, dark, gentle traveler, thirty-one years old, and spoke excellent Cuban Spanish.

Luni was given room 408. His friend Doctor Hornung took room 410.

For four days Luni and Hornung lived the lives of average tourists. A good friend of theirs, no stranger to Havana, plied them with food, drink, and excursions to the city's varied pleasure places. Then, after four days, the two passengers from the *Ciudad de Madrid* checked out of the Hotel Lincoln and moved to the Hotel Siboney, on the Prado.

There was nothing strange about this move. The rates at the Siboney were somewhat lower than the prices charged at the more modern Lincoln. Jewish refugees from Hitler-occupied Europe had been flooding into the Siboney since 1933. No one thought it odd that Luni and Hornung should join the refugees at the Siboney.

The friend who had met them at the boat, and who had done so much to keep them amused during their first four days in Havana, remained on as a guest at the Lincoln. He had been living at the Lincoln since March 20, 1941. His name was Ricardo Dotres.

Ricardo Dotres, like his friends Luni and Hornung, had also reached Havana via a C. T. E. steamer. A typical Catalan, he registered as a native of Barcelona. He had a Spanish passport, number 10-E.

Short, thin, in his late thirties, Dotres carried himself with military erectness, moved and spoke with much poise—when dealing with men. In the presence of women—practically any women—Dotres would change. His black eyes, under their heavy eyebrows, would flash. His white teeth would gleam. The very cleft in his chin would seem to quiver as Dotres prepared to give chase.

In a city which had seen skirt-chasers from all over the world, Dotres soon became part of its immortal comic legend. His zeal knew no bounds. He courted women in five languages, being equally at home in Spanish, French, German, and English, as well as in his native Catalan. He pursued them with flowers, bonbons, night-club invitations, and an endless stream of chatter. When rebuffed, as he generally was, by the female guests and the employees of the hotel,

Dotres remained undaunted. He would hail one of the dozen cabs usually parked outside of the hotel and drive to any one of the hundred brothels where his sallies were greeted with laughter and his pesos accepted with gracious thanks.

He was a garrulous, social fellow with a lust for life and many friends on both sides of the ocean. Hardly a week went by but Ricardo Dotres received a cable from Barcelona or Basle or Madrid announcing the marriage of a friend, or the birth of a comrade's child, or the wedding anniversary of a boon companion. During the course of a month, Dotres would always send a handful of cables to friends in these cities. They were ebullient, joyous cables of congratulations and good wishes.

Dotres also sent many business cables, in code, to Basle and Barcelona. They were addressed to the Om Laboratories, a Swiss chemical concern with branches in many countries. Om Laboratories had a branch in Havana, too. It was on Cuba Street, opposite the Police Headquarters. Dotres, who had worked for the Om firm abroad, drove to the Cuban offices of Om every morning in one of the cabs parked near the Lincoln.

The Om Laboratories, evidently, were a legitimate concern. They were not then and are not now on the American black list of Axis firms in Latin America.

This was a bit puzzling to the Spanish Republicans in Havana. For Dotres was not a stranger to some of them. They knew that he had been in Barcelona during the three years of the Spanish War, and that the Spanish Red Cross uniform resting in the trunk in Dotres's room on the fourth floor of the Hotel Lincoln was not the only uniform he rated. Señor Dotres had, during the entire course of the Spanish War, been an officer of the Fascist Army. He was, in fact, one of the key men of the Fifth Column in Catalonia.

Of course, there was no proof that Dotres was still an officer of the Franco Army. Perhaps all that was behind him. Perhaps he was merely a simple chemist, working hard for an honest living at the Om Laboratories and indulging in a little relaxation from his labors seven nights a week. The only way to find out was to keep a careful eye on him, and keep an eye on him they did.

This study of Dotres's moves soon revealed a set pattern of existence. Ordinarily, Dotres divided his time between his office and his continuing chase after women. Only when a Spanish steamer arrived in Havana would the routine of the life of Ricardo Dotres change.

With the docking of a C. T. E. ship, Dotres would become a new man. His poise, his easy-going ways, his careful husbanding of his energies for the myriad women in his ken all went by the board. Instead, he would become very busy with various arriving passengers.

Like an excited mother hen, Dotres would descend upon his charges as they walked down the gangplank, whisk them into a waiting cab, and take them to one of Havana's better hotels. For days he would hover at their sides, attending to their every whim, showing them the sights, and guaranteeing their comforts. During these periods he would leave his own hotel early in the morning and return very late at night, so tired that he had hardly enough energy even to ogle any woman he might encounter in the lobby or, heaven help her, in the elevators.

But always, much to the relief of the madames of Havana's bordellos, these periods ended as abruptly as they began. Within a week of the arrival of a Spanish steamer, Dotres would slide effortlessly back into his accustomed ways—and the fathers and husbands of attractive women at the Hotel Lincoln would resume their practice of carrying weighted canes and little pearl-handled revolvers.

When summer came Dotres began to spend his Sundays at one of Havana's better beach clubs. Here, clad in crimson shorts, Dotres exposed to the sun and to the women one of the hairiest bodies that ever bared itself to the Caribbean. Covered with black, curly hair that clung in veritable mats to his chest, his back, his arms, his legs, and even his hands, he chased up and down the beach, begging females of all ages to give him the honor of teaching them to swim by a method he had developed at Biarritz.

On these excursions to the beach, as well as on week ends spent in the country, Dotres shot scores of pictures with his excellent German camera. These pictures were generally of Dotres and his new-found friends, often posed against exotic backgrounds like wharves, electric turbines, airports, reservoir sluices, and Cuban army field artillery.

Dotres led a charmed, if often hectic, life. He made friends in all circles, including Cuban army circles, and his conquests mounted like Hitler's. Nothing ever occurred to upset this routine. Not even the Japanese bombing of Pearl Harbor.

But a few days after Pearl Harbor was bombed, Dotres suddenly showed up in the lobby of the Lincoln one Wednesday morning with a slightly long face. It was just a mite longer than the face left by the hangover of a night's debauchery. "I am worried," Dotres announced, "about my poor old father."

Until that tense morning—for by then Cuba was in the war—no one had ever heard of Dotres the Elder.

"And what," asked the desk clerk, "is the matter with your father, Señor Dotres?"

The fabulous chemist heaved a mighty sigh. "My old father," he said, "is in Manila. The cablegram pad, please."

And Ricardo Dotres sent the first of his many cables to Manila. Not until *after* José del Castano and the Falange handed Manila over to the Sons of Nippon did Ricardo Dotres receive a cable from Manila. Between that day and the morning Dotres left Havana, he received other reassuring cables from Japanese-held Manila.

On April 11, 1942, Ricardo Dotres approached an employee of the Hotel Lincoln. This employee was known to him as an ardent Spanish Republican.

Dotres smiled his most ingratiating smile. *"Amigo,"* he said, "tomorrow I go back to Spain. If you have any Republican friends or relatives in Spain, I'd be glad to bring them some gifts or a confidential message. I always sympathized with the Republicans myself, you know."

This employee smiled politely, "Señor Dotres," he answered, "I have a more reliable way of reaching my Republican relatives and friends in Spain. And please do not call me *amigo*."

With the crack of dawn the next morning, Ricardo Dotres sped to the Rancho Boyeros Airport. Here he boarded a Pan-American Airlines ship for the first leg of a flight to Caracas, Venezuela. He traveled light, carrying only a small valise. His trunk was left behind in the store-room of the hotel.

Three days later, thirty postcards, mailed by Dotres from Caracas, were delivered to the Hotel Lincoln. Evaristo Fernandez, the owner, received one. The waiters, the elevator operators, the bartenders, the kitchen help, the prettier female guests—everyone but the one Spanish Republican employee received cards.

On the heels of these postcards came a cable from Dotres to Fernandez. Like the cards, the cable had also been sent from Caracas. Dotres asked the hotel manager to please open his trunk, take out the five chemical books he would find there, wrap them well, and airmail them to: "R. Dotres, c/o Pan American Airways, Port-of-Spain, Trinidad, B.W.I."

Fernandez, who had contributed money to the Franco forces during the Spanish War, sent the five chemical books to Port-of-Spain at a personal expense of twelve dollars. Two months later, the five chemical books were returned to Havana, marked "Unclaimed." Fernandez shelled out another twelve dollars and put the books back in the trunk, where they rested next to a picture of Dotres and some Cuban officers.

They remained in the trunk until October 1942, when a visiting American investigator learned of their existence and realized that the volumes contained more than chemical formulae.

Dotres simply disappeared. He never sent for his trunk, and he never sent another postcard to the Hotel Lincoln. Whether he went the way of Villanueva, or whether he became the contact man for Axis spies in another Latin-

American capital is still not known. Some Spanish Republicans at one time had reason to believe that Dotres had quietly returned to Cuba. But to date, Dotres has still not been found.

Like Dotres, Dr. Hoguet Hornung, one of the two *Ciudad de Madrid* passengers whom the contact man had brought to the Hotel Lincoln, simply vanished from Havana.

Enrique August Luni, the handsome younger passenger, remained in Havana for exactly thirteen months.

The beginning of his stay was marked by days of idle loafing. He frequented many bars, took many sight-seeing tours, and saw the insides of most Havana night clubs. Waiters grew to like him for his liberal tips and for his unassuming friendliness.

One waiter, let us call him Pancho Vivaldi, which is not his real name, became a great friend of Luni's. This waiter, a man of Luni's own years, grew to look forward to the idler's daily visits to the *cantineria* at Virtudes and the Prado. Before long, Luni was confiding to Pancho that he had but recently inherited a tidy fortune in Honduras. A day later Luni told Pancho that he was tired of doing nothing, and was looking for a business in which he could invest some of his money.

"But I can't work too hard," Luni explained. "You see, Pancho, I have a bad touch of rheumatism."

Pancho had a wife, Maria, who worked at home as a dressmaker. Maria was as skilled with a needle as are few women on this earth, thought Pancho. With a little capital, Maria could no doubt become one of the great fashionable dressmakers for the "high-life" set of the city. Besides, if Maria did all of the work, Señor Luni would not have to strain his rheumatism too much.

Young Señor Luni listened gravely to Pancho's musings. Modestly, he admitted to always having had a secret yearning to own as gentle a business as a fashionable custom dress salon. After glancing at some samples of Maria's labors,

Enrique August Luni knew that his dreams had come true. He dipped into his apparently ample coffers to open a factory on busy Industria Street.

Maria, Pancho, and Luni became equal partners in the new firm. While the happy seamstress and her simple husband fixed up the workrooms, Luni moved a large diathermy machine into a corner of the atelier. "It's for my rheumatism," he explained. "They object to my using it at the hotel."

But once the factory started production, Luni felt self-conscious about taking diathermy treatments in the plant. He took a room next to Maria and Pancho on Teniente Rey Street, and moved the machine there.

To his room Luni also brought a cage with four canaries. All his life, he explained, he had wanted canaries. He spent little time in the business establishment he was financing, but he was far from aloof toward his new friends. When he went on a shopping spree for tubes, coils, condensers, and other radio parts, he took Pancho along with him.

On one of these trips, he bought a pair of "Junior G-Man" telegraph keys for a quarter each in Woolworth's. "For my nephews in Barcelona," he said.

Then, after buying all the parts "to build a radio myself," Luni passed a shop window in the gleaming, streamlined America Building on Galleano Street. There, at a bargain price, stood a powerful American console radio. Luni bought it for cash, and had it delivered to his new room.

In the house at Teniente Rey Street, the American radio began to boom until all the windows shook. Some of Luni's new neighbors protested. They suggested that, when Luni felt like listening to his super-radio, he should at the very least close the transom over his door if he could not play it with less power. This Luni refused to do, until one day, while he was listening to the radio, he decided to let his canaries have the freedom of his room. Before he could say "Don Quixote de la Mancha," two of the four canaries were through the transom and out of the house.

After that, whenever Luni liberated his canaries, he always did so with the transom tightly closed and the door locked. Since he always had the radio on while the canaries were out of their cage, his neighbors began to be increasingly thankful that canaries were made with wings.

Luni spent very little time in Maria's dressmaking shop. Instead, he chose to while away many hours at places like the Porto Chico bar, on the water front, a stone's-throw from the Spanish Consulate.

These, however, were not hours idly spent. For here Enrique August Luni really went to work. Here he met with officers of Spanish ships and plied them with endless questions. Here, too, he used to set up drinks for Cuban customs officers and pier officials.

The sidewalk tables of the Porto Chico, like the front windows of the Spanish Consulate, commanded a panoramic view of the Havana wharves. Nothing could miss the scrutiny of a trained pair of eyes at a Porto Chico table —all ships entering and leaving the harbor, all loading operations, everything.

When Luni wanted a closer view of a ship in the harbor, he merely borrowed a small boat and rowed out to look the ship over.

Between visits to the water front, Luni would repair to his room on Teniente Rey Street, close the transom, lock the door, and turn on his radio to the maximum of its power.

Then, while boleros and congas rattled the plaster of the room, Enrique August Luni would open the locked steel door of his diathermy machine. From one of the drawers of his dresser he would take out a coil of wire and a set of earphones. From another drawer he would get one of the Woolworth toy telegraph tickers. A few deft maneuvers with pliers and screw driver were then enough to convert the diathermy machine into an ultra high-frequency short-wave radio station.

The radio drowning out the clicking of his nursery-room telegraph key, Enrique August Luni would tap out brief, but vital, messages to the commanders of Nazi submarines lurking in the South Atlantic and the Caribbean. Sometimes the messages went to other Lunis, seated at similar clandestine two-way radios, in Santo Domingo, Argentina, Venezuela, Guatemala, and Chile. The Chilean Luni was a man named Robinson. Often, they themselves reached Enrique August Luni in Havana through their radios.

On the high seas, Axis submarine commanders, guided constantly by these radios, started to sink United Nations ships in great numbers. Guided by such excellent intelligence, they had things all their own way.

In addition to his radio messages, Luni also sent daily letters to certain business firms in Barcelona and Lisbon. Each letter was signed by a different name. Answers to these letters, also sent to different names each time, were rerouted to Luni by their recipients in Havana.

When Luni moved from the Siboney to the room on Teniente Rey Street, he neglected to notify his correspondents abroad of this change of address. Within two days, he had an angry letter from Barcelona, rebuking him for this oversight.

The Barcelona letter was signed, "Manuel Alonso." Luni broke into a cold sweat when he saw the signature. For at that address in Barcelona there was no Manuel Alonso. This was the name used on all letters addressed to Heinrich Himmler, chief of the Gestapo. And Luni knew a thing or two about the Gestapo.

Señor Enrique August Luni, resident of Barcelona and Havana, citizen of Honduras, was a fiction; a figment of Manuel Alonso's imagination.

In 1910, in the city of Hamburg, Germany, the Italian wife of a German importer named Luning bore him a son. The boy was christened Heinz August Luning. Thirty-one years later, this boy stepped off the gangplank of the *Ciudad de Madrid* in Havana as Enrique August Luni.

Young Heinz Luning had grown up looking like the

image of his Latin mother. While in his early 20's, he had been gripped by the wanderlust. It had led him to far away places he had read about in his schoolbooks. Puerto Rico, Santo Domingo, Venezuela—the Caribbean had early colored his fancies. When he was twenty-five, Heinz August Luning returned to Hamburg, where his father and his uncle still ran an importing business. Hitler now ruled Germany, and Luning joined the Nazi Party.

As the war clouds began to grow darker over Hamburg, Luning started to look for something safer than a spot in the front-line trenches. His search led him inevitably to the Gestapo, where he figured that his newly acquired knowledge of Spanish and his most Latin appearance would stand him in good stead.

The Gestapo enrolled Luning early in 1940, and sent him off to a special school for foreign agents in Bremen. Here, under expert instructors, Heinz August Luning was trained in the manufacture and use of secret inks, radio, telegraphy, and kindred skills.

From the Bremen school Luning was sent to Madrid, where he was given special courses in Central and South Atlantic geography and vernacular Cuban Spanish. Once this training was completed, Luning proceeded on to Barcelona. Here he was trained to memorize codes and key addresses, given his Honduran passport, and put on board the *Ciudad de Madrid*.

Heinz August Luning did not lack for company on board the C.T.E. ship. Among his fellow passengers were many fellow graduates of the Gestapo school in Bremen. They were bound for points as divergent as Santiago de Chile, Buenos Aires, Baltimore, Los Angeles, and Port-of-Spain.

The Gestapo agents had the run of the ship during the entire voyage. They ate with the captain, lolled in the sun, and practiced taking and developing pictures with their new miniature cameras. Luning was later to say that this voyage was one of the most pleasant in his whole life—but this was much later.

Luning's letters to Barcelona and Lisbon from Havana were all sent via air mail. All of them had to clear through the offices of British censorship in Bermuda. Some time after he started sending them, the letters began to attract the attention of alert British agents in the Bermuda station. The British made photostatic copies of each letter, put the originals back in the envelopes, and allowed them to proceed.

But when the British had collected enough photostats of Luning's letters, they realized that, although each was signed by another name, they were all the product of one individual. Similarly, they were able to spot the answers to the Luning letters, as well as the additional directives which were mailed to the Gestapo agent from Spain.

When they were sufficiently certain of these basic facts, the British communicated with the American Federal Bureau of Investigation, which maintains an office in Havana. The F.B.I. immediately checked with the Cuban Secret Police.

For months the Cuban censorship watched for letters to and from Barcelona and Lisbon. Each letter was carefully studied by American and Cuban secret agents, photostated, and then filed away. The different Havana recipients of the letters from Barcelona and Lisbon which the United Nations intelligence officers suspected were for the unknown spy they sought, were watched like hawks.

Finally, on August 15, 1942—after operating his radio station for nearly eleven costly months—Luning was revealed to the Cuban and American investigators as the man they were after. Captain Faget, of the Cuban Secret Police, and F.B.I. Agent Sweet, acting together, nabbed Luning just as he was getting ready to send the information which would lead to the sinking of another American ship.

Only the German High Command actually knows how much United Nations shipping, how many men perished in the deep seas because of Heinz August Luning alone. All estimates are frankly a guess, but persons close to the

Luning case feel that the actual figures are staggeringly large.

So complete was the intelligence job done on Luning that the spy had no choice but to confess to his true role almost immediately. He was quickly sentenced to death by the Cuban military court which tried him. But as the door of his death cell clanged shut, Heinz August Luning was not without powerful friends in Cuban life.

Tremendous pressure was brought to bear on President Batista and other members of the government to commute Luning's sentence to a "reasonable" term of imprisonment. (This despite the fact that a Cuban ship had been sunk by a Nazi raider shortly before Luning was caught.) Pro-Falange newspapers in Havana began to run long sob stories about the gentle and patriotically misguided character of the young Nazi spy. One paper even went as far as printing a ballot asking its readers to select their own punishment for Luning.

A group of powerful men in Cuba forced the Luning case to the Supreme Court, in a legal test of the military tribunal's right to try a civilian spy.

Throughout the nation, simple people began to curse the slowness of their government. They were afraid that the "high-life" Spaniards would succeed in saving Luning's neck.

The case dragged on. The Supreme Court was still considering the case on October 10, 1942—Cuba's National Independence Day. And on this day Luning's doom was sealed. It was not the Supreme Court that acted on October 10; it was the Cuban people.

All the anti-Axis organizations of the nation united with the government that day to stage the official celebration of National Independence at the National Theater. The square outside of the theater was blocked off and filled with seats. Loud-speakers carried the speeches of the day to the square, to the crowds in Central Park. Every radio station in the country had a microphone on the platform inside.

On the platform, Prime Minister Zaydin stepped up to the microphone to deliver the main oration of the day. He talked about Cuba's long struggle for independence, about the United Nations, about the meaning of the war to every Cuban. Then, bringing the speech closer to home, he mentioned the Luning case as an example of United Nations vigilance.

The audiences—those in the theater, in the square outside, before thousands of radios all over the island—stirred restlessly.

Suddenly Zaydin shouted: "Luning must, Luning will die before a firing squad!"

The crowd inside sprang to its feet even as every man and woman in it started to shout. The cheer that welled up from their lungs would have given Wilhelm von Faupel an apoplectic stroke could he have heard it. It contained the anger, the honest hatred, the determination of a simple people enraged to the breaking point. Not since the shouts of relief which rang through Havana on the day Cuba declared war on the Axis had such a roar been heard in the land. Long after silence was restored within the hall, the cheers continued rolling in from the square outside.

The people had passed sentence on Heinz August Luning, and the Supreme Court was quick to ratify their decision.

Luning faced the well-oiled rifles of a Cuban firing squad in the courtyard of the Havana fortress on the morning of November 8, 1942. He faced them with an angry sneer on his lips. The soft charm he had so carefully cultivated—the charm which had so captivated Pancho, and Maria, and the feature writers of so many Havana papers—was no longer useful. It was discarded. Bareheaded, his chest strangely shrunken, Heinz August Luning chose to stand revealed as a Gestapo agent, a Nazi spy contemptuous to the very end of the democracies which had trapped him.

The Nazi died secure in the knowledge that, even as the Cuban bullets whipped through his eyes, other Spanish ships carrying scores of other Lunings were on the high seas—bound for North, Central, and South American ports.

The C.T.E. ships are still delivering Axis agents to our side of the ocean.

It was the day after Zaydin proclaimed that "Luning must, Luning will die," that I heard the first-hand account of the voyage of the *Magallanes*, sister ship of the *Ciudad de Madrid*.

Tomás told it to me. He is a Spanish Republican who has never stopped fighting Hitler.

"The *Magallanes*," he said, "left Spain on the seventh of September, 1941. Passengers were shocked at the great number of Germans on board, Germans bound for the Americas.

"The ship reached Port of Spain, Trinidad, on the 17th. There was a United Nations convoy of over 100 ships in the harbor at the time. The British authorities checked on all the passengers when the ship cast anchor.

"Two of the passengers assumed new identities. One became a sailor. The other a ship's machinist. The British, who separated the crew from the passengers, examined the papers of the passengers only.

"The man who posed as a sailor was Leopoldo Sanchez Carbojal. He is a Spaniard trained by the Gestapo in Germany. He was not the only Gestapo-trained Spaniard on board ship. He and the fake machinist took pictures of the convoy and the defenses of Trinidad with telefoto-lens German cameras.

"There was a third person on board; a third key person the British passed over. He was the chief radio operator, and the Falange chief of the ship. He had two radios. One was for regular wireless uses. The other transmitted details of the convoy. This man was the famous Camarada Martinez who twice escaped from the Cuban police. His full name is Miguel Barcelo Martinez.

"When the ship arrived in Cuba on September 26, many Cuban officers were waiting on the dock. They boarded ship as the social guests of the Company. They had dinner on board, and after dinner were shown Fascist films in the ship's theater.

"The officers of the ship were Falangistas. They brought over instructions and propaganda materials for the Cuban Falange."

Tomás is a man of few words. He neglected to say that his life was in danger during the entire crossing.

CHAPTER SEVEN

Puerto Rico: Gibraltar or Pearl Harbor?

TINY, TRAGIC, OVERCROWDED PUERTO RICO—the island's population of nearly two million makes it the fourth most densely peopled country in the world—is very much in the news. The island, less than two-thirds the size of Connecticut, means many things to many people. To Puerto Rico's nationalists, it is America's India. To Puerto Rico's Spaniards, it is the Lost Colony of the Holy Motherland. To serious-minded Latin-American thinkers, it is the touchstone of our relations with all of Latin America. To the naval and military High Commands in Washington, Puerto Rico is today primarily the Gibraltar of the Caribbean.

A glance at the map is enough to tell why Puerto Rico bulks so large in our defenses. American-owned anchor in the Antilles chain of islands, it guards the approaches to the Panama Canal and sits squarely in the path of Axis sea raiders of the South Atlantic.

Puerto Rico is today a bristling garrison. An important American garrison.

The civilian defense organizations of Puerto Rico—like the civilian defense organizations of Manila on Pearl Harbor Day—are packed with Falangistas.

Perhaps it is because of the Falangistas and their friends in the Puerto Rican civilian defense bodies that many worried Puerto Ricans talk the way they do. Freedom-loving, decent Puerto Ricans who look to a United Nations victory as the key to the ultimate solution of Puerto Rico's gravest problems always include one idea in their discussions of the Falange menace on the island. "Puerto Rico," they say, "is called the Gibraltar of the Caribbean. Pray God it does not become the Pearl Harbor or the Manila instead."

For it was in Puerto Rico, during the Spanish phase of World War II, that the Falange Exterior built one of the most effective of its branches in the Americas. And today, although the Falange of Puerto Rico has been officially dissolved since January 10, 1941, the leaders and *militantes* of the Puerto Rican Falange are still very much among the present on the island.

Puerto Rico became a colony of the United States after the Spanish-American War of 1898. Under the Spanish rule of the old Bourbon Empire, life had always been harsh for the people who tilled the soil and cooked the meals, and who made up all but a minor percentage of the population. Under the administration of the United States, the island's population nearly doubled, but the conditions of life for the average Puerto Rican were far from improved.

The small set of Spanish colonial planters and businessmen who dominated the economic life of the island under the Empire grew somewhat smaller with the American occupation, but they survived as a body. Most of them retained their Spanish citizenship. They sold most of their good soil to large American sugar corporations and retained for themselves the control of the mercantile commerce of the colony.

Sugar became the one industry of Puerto Rico. The island, which never grew enough food for its own needs, grew less than ever after the land was given over almost entirely to sugar. During its entire history as a Spanish colony, the island's people had never been permitted to develop native manufacturing industries. Under American domination, this taboo was maintained—if only in an economic form. (A bitter example of how this works and one which came home to roost after Pearl Harbor, is the experience of a group of Puerto Rican capitalists who attempted to establish a native pineapple canning industry. While the cannery was being established, a large Hawaiian grower dumped enough canned pineapple in the island to ruin the native industry.)

The wealthy Spaniards on the island took control of the shipping industry, the importing business—now greater than ever, and most wholesale and retail trade. Like their fellow Spanish businessmen in Latin America, they invested sizable portions of their Puerto Rican profits in various enterprises of the mother country across the seas. The advent of the Spanish Republic grated on their sensitive pocket-book nerves as violently as it grated on those of their brothers in Spain.

Socially, the wealthy Spaniards of Puerto Rico were a set apart from the Puerto Ricans and the Americans on the island. They looked down upon the Puerto Ricans as an inferior, mongrel assortment of peasants and servants. The Americans, whom they also considered their inferiors, were accepted by the powerful Spaniards as a necessary evil. The aspirations of the various native movements for national independence were never shared by the Spaniards—who were content to pay lip service to the new American masters while they dreamed of the island's ultimate return to the Spanish Empire.

The cleavage between the Spanish set and the other cultures of Puerto Rico is physically evident in the three great cultural centers of the island. In San Juan, the Spaniards flocked to the Casa de España, while the Puerto Ricans centered their cultural and social life around the Ateneo Puertriqueño. The buildings stand within a stone's throw of each other. In Rio Piedras the University of Puerto Rico stands as a bastion of the third culture in the colony—the American culture.

A year after the Spanish Republic was established, the Spanish business crowd in Puerto Rico found itself faced with a new potential menace. This was the New Deal of Franklin Delano Roosevelt.

The outbreak of the Spanish War found the Spanish colony of Puerto Rico torn between the real menace of the Spanish Republic and the social legislation of Washington. When Hitler and Mussolini openly sent their troops against the Spanish Republic, many of the wealthier Spaniards in Puerto Rico correctly interpreted the war as being the first stage of the war against the United States as well as against Spain. Whether they saw the Spanish War as purely a Spanish affair or not, the wealthy Spaniards of Puerto Rico united as one behind the banners of Francisco Franco in the war for the etxermination of democracy in Spain.

The Franco-Hitler-Mussolini partisans of Puerto Rico lost little time in organizing for action when the fighting began in Spain. In San Juan's largest daily paper, *El Mundo*, they had a spokesman made to order for their cause. The weekly *Puerto Rico Illustrado*, published by the *El Mundo* owners, was similarly impartial—on the Fascist side. Not until January 1937, with the appearance of the first issue of *Avance*, did the Falange bring out their official organ.

Dionisio Trigo, the president of the Spanish Chamber of Commerce of Puerto Rico, assumed the leadership of the Franco forces. Burgos—then the seat of the Axis power in Spain—appointed Trigo the official representative of the Franco government in Puerto Rico.

Trigo was the brother-in-law of the insular Chief of Police, Colonel Enrique de Orbeta, and an individual of much power in the Spanish community. Always a spokesman for the most reactionary elements in insular life, he was a natural leader for the Axis cause. His close associates in the Franco movement were millionaire Spaniards like Gonzalez Padin, Leopoldo Ochoa, Secundino Lozana, and José Maria del Valle.

Trigo and his intimates were men to whom money talked louder than all creeds. Their primary idea of how to best aid the armies protecting their interests in Spain was simple: money. Like Elicio Arguelles in Havana, Trigo concentrated on the raising of funds for the Fascist forces in Spain.

This campaign was phenomenally successful. No less an authority than Elicio Arguelles, who was not exactly raising a pittance for the Fascists himself, recognized Trigo's efforts as a major contribution to the Falangist war effort. In a letter sent from Havana on October 26, 1937, Arguelles told Trigo:

Here we fight with great firmness but not with the success

you have had. . . . Without any argument, Puerto Rico and you have shown the best and most positive examples that we owe to the new Spanish Crusaders. For the high spirit of adherence to the cause, the patriotism which prevails and the successes obtained in your subscriptions, it is necessary to place Puerto Rico in the place of distinction and honor. We, less fortunate, fight with faith and will continue to prosecute our task until we are able to see the ONLY SPAIN, Great and Free. . . .

Acting informally, without an official organization, the Puerto Rican supporters of the Fascist armies in Spain raised close to a million dollars in less than a year. This the men of Burgos appreciated, but money was not the prime need of von Faupel. What was needed was a functioning section of the Falange Exterior. For Puerto Rico figured very much in the plans of the architect of the invasion of Spain.

The initial edition of *Avance,* dated January 1937, was the first formal move of the Falange in Puerto Rico. The cover of this issue, which featured young Primo de Rivera's portrait, bore two emblems on its masthead—those of Puerto Rico and of the Falange Española. The inside masthead listed Alfonso Miranda Esteve, a lawyer, as director, and two sons of Dionisio Trigo as members of the staff.

Three interesting features appeared in the third issue of the then biweekly Falange organ. The first was the official program of the Falange Española Tradicionalista de la J.O.N.S.—the famous twenty-seven (now twenty-eight) points quoted in full in Chapter I. The second was a little notice headed: "Falange Española." It announced that the Puerto Rican Falange would soon be formed. The third was a long, lyrical pro-Franco article signed J. Fidalgo Diaz—a name which will come up later in this chapter.

The young Fascist organ was crammed with large advertisements from the very first issue on. Firms like Bull Insular Lines, headed by Honorary Japanese Consul Miguel Such, Mendez & Company, large shipping agents, the Fajardo Sugar Company, bought space immediately. Other firms, a bit more discreet, paid for full-page complimentary but anonymous advertisements.

In February 1937, *Avance* published an interesting schedule of short-wave broadcasts in Spanish. Heading the list was station DJQ of Berlin. Although the list included two American stations as a matter of form, it included one other Berlin station, two in Rome, and five in the then Fascist-conquered parts of Spain, the Canaries, and Spanish Morocco.

Notices appeared in both March issues about the impending formation of the Puerto Rican Falange. In April the Franco slogan—*"Una Patria, Un Estado, Un Caudillo"*—appeared in *Avance* for the first time. This slogan, which appeared constantly in the magazine after that, was handed to the Falange by the Nazi experts called in by General von Faupel to mold the Falange as an Axis instrument. It is a translation of the Nazi war cry, first heard in Austria and Czechoslovakia—*"Ein Volk, Ein Reich, Ein Führer."* One People—Spaniards; One State—Fascist Spain; One Leader—Franco.

Despite its publication of the anti-American Twenty-Seven Points and of this slogan, *Avance* was never stopped by the United States postal authorities.

The July 1, 1937, issue featured the face of one Leo Ribilzki on its cover. A long caption explained that the Señor was the radio speaker on short-wave stations DJA and DJN, of Berlin, whose speeches about the cause of the Fascists in Spain meant so much to Puerto Rican listeners. The same issue also carried an article by Alfonso L. Garcia, an instructor at the University of Puerto Rico. This article praised not only Franco, but also Italy and Germany.

In issue after issue *Avance* continued to lay the groundwork for the organization of the Falange under the American flag. By September, when Franco dispatched a traveling "ambassador" to Latin America, the Falange banner was flying from the radiators of half of the cars parked outside of the University of Puerto Rico every day.

Luciano Lopez Ferrer, the first of Franco's official "ambassadors at large," reached San Juan in September 1937. His party included Dr. Francisco J. Almodovar and a Captain Julio de la Torre, of the Spanish Fascist Army.

Dignified, venerable, very much on the stuffed-shirt side, Lopez Ferrer had a simple mission to perform. While glad-handing and flattering the wealthy Spaniards of the countries he visited, he acted as a perfect front for serious Falange agents like de la Torre.

The Captain had a mission of his own in Puerto Rico. He was charged with getting the Falange Exterior branch formally organized.

Hard on the Captain's dashing heels came another Falangista from Burgos, charged with the task of making the organization stick. This individual was no stranger to Latin America, or to the Falange—where he rated as an "Old Shirt," the Spanish equivalent of a Munich Beer-Hall Putsch veteran in the Nazi Party. His name was José Gonzalez Marin.

The New World escapades of Gonzalez Marin have made him almost as fabulous a creature as Ricardo Dotres, the woman-crazy Falangist who acted as Axis liaison agent in Havana. Gonzalez Marin, however, never bothered with women. He had been to Puerto Rico and other Latin-American countries long before the Spanish War. He had for years been one of the leading *recitadors* (poetry readers) in Spain. With the coming of General von Faupel, Gonzalez Marin became one of the first of the many noted Spanish actors, musicians, and dancers to make international tours as Axis agents disguised in the robes of artists.

It was as an artist that Gonzalez Marin arrived in Puerto Rico in the fall of 1937. He gave some public performances, including a benefit show for the Fascist side in Spain, handed out pictures of himself giving the Fascist salute while wearing the Falange uniform, and then went to work in earnest.

The results of Gonzalez Marin's labors were soon made plain. The December 1 issue of *Avance*, on page 17, ran a half-page photo of the speaker's table at a dinner given by the Spanish Societies of San Juan at the Casa de España. Present are seven men, each of them giving the *brazo en alto* salute. Gonzalez Marin is the man in the center of the group. At his side stands Alfonso Miranda Esteve, identified in the caption as: "The Chief of the Falange Española and Director of *Avance*."

The Franco forces of Puerto Rico thrilled Gonzalez Marin. While he was in San Juan, he was taken to see the building occupied by *El Imparcial*, a daily newspaper whose press was bombed in 1937 when the editor had the temerity to print a story giving the Republican viewpoint of certain events in Spain. He was shown the hold the pro-Falange groups had on the Casa de España, and heard for himself the difficulties the anti-Fascists of Puerto Rico encountered at every turn in their battle against the Falange.

The Falange of Puerto Rico had finally been launched. Satisfied with his handiwork, Gonzalez Marin boarded the plane for Venezuela. His "artistic tour" ultimately included a visit to the Falange of New York—but that is a story for a later chapter.

International law became a mockery in Puerto Rico where Spain was concerned. Dionisio Trigo, whose position as official representative of the Franco government had no legal standing in the United States, attended official functions at the Governor's Palace—La Fortaleaza—regularly. More regularly than Jacinto Ventosa, the consul of the Spanish Republic, the only Spanish government recognized by the State Department.

Enemies of the Fascists in Spain found it next to impossible to broadcast simple truths over the radio. Dr. Antonio J. Colorado, spokesman for the Asociación Pro-Democracia Española de Puerto Rico, was forced to evade the unique censorship in a spectacular manner. Since the censors forced him to delete all references to the fact that Hitler and Mussolini were even interested in the Spanish War, Colorado wrote his scripts around the magic word *censura*. In time, radio listeners knew what Colorado meant when he declared, "Franco is fighting with the *censura* armies of the *censura* of *censura* and the *censura* of *censura*, who has a little mustache."

The Fascists in Puerto Rico were never forced to resort to such devices by the censors, nor were their presses ever bombed.

Even before Gonzalez Marin arrived in Puerto Rico, *Avance* was publishing the standard Hitler attacks on democracy. He was particularly impressed by the unsigned editorial which had appeared on June 1, 1937, a piece called "National Socialism and Democracy."

This editorial made the interesting point that only in Germany did the truest democracy exist since

. . . the repeated plebiscites held in Germany indicate that its government is a faithful expression of the conscience of the people. And if no credit is given to that institution, it is enough to travel through Germany and talk to all classes of people to see that an intimate bond exists between the government and the people.

After demolishing the idea that democracy existed in England and France, the editorial went on to declare:

As to North America, President Roosevelt has just said in his second inaugural speech that one-third of the population has no food or sufficient clothing. That cannot be said of Germany or Italy. And there you see where democracy is effective, and where it is merely an illusion; where the government is for the people and by the people.

Editorials like this one made it clear to everyone but Americans like Governor Winship, Colonel John W. Wright, head of our garrison on the island, and Federal Judge Robert A. Cooper, that the Falange of Puerto Rico was involved in something more serious than preventing "communism" in Spain. These three gentlemen were the most important American officials on the island, and their cordial relations with the Falange crowd became the subject of a most enthusiastic report Gonzalez Marin delivered to his Axis masters in Madrid.

Early in February 1938, after Gonzalez Marin had left, the German warship *Meteor* steamed into San Juan's harbor. Flying two enormous swastika flags, the Nazi vessel tied up at the docks and held open house for the "high-life" Spanish set of the city.

The Spanish Fascist societies of San Juan welcomed the Nazis as heroes. They hung a great picture of Adolf Hitler in the Casa de España and invited Henry Fiese, Honorary German Consul in San Juan, and the officers of the *Meteor* to a banquet.

When called upon to speak at this banquet, the commander of the Nazi warship said: "Today we find ourselves in the Casa de España as guests of a nation whose sons, far away from their land, follow the events of their motherland with ardent hearts. They support the same struggle against Bolshevism that held Germany on the border of ruin. . . . I give my most expressive thanks and I greet their motherland, the noble Nationalist Spain. *Viva Franco! Arriba España!*"

The Nazis and the Spaniards then posed for two interesting pictures which appeared in the Puerto Rico *Illustrado* of February 12. The first picture showed thirteen Spaniards, including five members of the Falange, under Hitler's picture. The second showed Fiese and the officers of the *Meteor* standing before Franco's portrait.

Publication of these pictures had no seeming effect on the good relations the Falangistas seemed to enjoy with the Insular and American authorities. On February 19, the Spanish Republic's Consul Ventosa was forced to issue a pained statement to the press:

For quite a while now there has existed little cordiality between this Consulate and the Executive of Puerto Rico [Ventosa revealed]. There are concrete cases that indicate that the Governor, to our mind, has not proceeded with absolute impartiality in accordance with international law. We have been able to see in certain of these official acts this manifest tendency. . . . This [*Meteor*] incident is considered by the Executive as of no value and as a purely social and private affair. On the other hand, this Consulate, as much as for the ideas shown as well as for the people who have participated, considers it public because of the facts involved.

Puerto Ricans who recognized the implications of this statement were, at that time, starting to encounter the repeated spectacle of uniformed Falangistas marching behind Franco's banners through the cities of the island. To many of them, the continued official indifference to the anti-American, openly Fascist tenets of the Falangistas became the yardstick by which they measured the democracy of the United States.

Consul Ventosa himself became a symbol to thousands of Puerto Ricans. Secrets are very hard to keep, scandals impossible to hide on the island. Thus, when Ventosa was insulted and threatened by gun-waving Falangistas in the Pardo Restaurant of San Juan, the whole island knew that the authorities had ignored the incident.

Some time after this gun-waving incident, Ventosa delivered a lecture at the Ateneo Puertoriqueño. While he was on the platform, Francisco Cerdeira, a pugnacious Franco partisan, rushed up and jammed a pistol into the Republican Consul's abdomen. In plain sight of the entire audience, Cerdeira pulled the trigger.

The gun jammed. Ventosa pushed his assailant to the floor. A group of men present at the scene grabbed the gun and hid it in the piano. Cerdeira was subdued, and a call was sent for the police.

Six of Puerto Rico's most distinguished professional men signed the complaint against the gunman. The magistrate before whom the charge was brought complained that there were too many witnesses.

D. A. Frankel appeared as attorney for Cerdeira. Frankel was the son-in-law of Miguel Such, the wealthy Spanish shipping man who served as honorary Japanese consul in San Juan. Cerdeira himself was the author of a laudatory biography of Señor Such.

The trial was postponed. It remained postponed until after Ventosa had departed forever from Puerto Rico; then the case was heard. The judge chose to accept the testimony of a waiter who claimed that the gun had belonged to Ventosa. Cerdeira was acquitted, and the stock of democracy sank still lower in Puerto Rico.

Voices raised against the Falange in Puerto Rico were generally heard with great difficulty by the people. Even the voice of Father Martin Bernstein, a Dutch friar at Catanzas, was drowned out by the thunderous barrage of Falangist propaganda in the press, the cathedral, and over the radio.

Father Martin's little weekly paper, *El Piloto*, was one of the first publications in Puerto Rico to denounce the Falange. Like the average Catholic in Spain, Father Martin looked upon the Falange as being anything but a holy crusade for Christianity.

In January 1937 Father Martin wrote the most classic of his denunciations of the Falange. More than any one single piece of writing, this denunciation sums up the attitude of the vast majority of Catholics in Spain and in Latin America toward the Falange and explains why they fought the Falange in Spain and abroad. Father Martin wrote:

In Spain there is fascism. There it is called Falangism or National-Syndicalism. We have already said . . . that Spanish Falangism is also to be condemned from a Catholic point of view. Falangism is incompatible with the Christian ideology.

Falangism as a system tends to what is called totalitarianism, absolute State Power. As such, it is an enormous danger for personal liberty and for Peace. As such, it preaches exaggerated national pride, imperialism, militarism, violence, hatred, and vengeance; violence against all those who do not submit to what a Falangist leader deems to be the "dignity of the State" or "national integrity."

We do not exaggerate. Here are the words from the official manifesto of the Falange:

> To the realization of this task [to strengthen, elevate, and enlarge the supreme reality of Spain], it will be necessary to *subordinate inexorably* the interests of individuals, groups, classes. Our will is Empire. . . . Our state shall be a totalitarian instrument. We will make a militaristic conception of life to permeate all Spanish life. . . .

That [charged Father Martin] is a purely fascist program. It is the totalitarian monster with all its pride, intransigeance, coercion, violence. It is a system in which there is no room for virtues of humility, indulgence, respect, and love. Fomenting violence, it foments hatred: unhealthy hatred, against Jews, Masons, etc. . . . The very essence of Christianity is precisely love, universal love, a love which will exclude no one, a love which will presuppose a deep respect for human liberty and dignity. Falangism, therefore, is as such incompatible with the genuine Christian ideology.

Father Martin's blunt words earned him the wrath of those sections of the Hierarchy which had a stake in Spanish fascism. Many Spanish priests canceled their subscriptions to Father Martin's paper when he continued his attacks on the Falange. The Falangistas of Puerto Rico denounced the white-haired friar. But his words struck home.

In many instances, Father Martin's words were a long time in taking their effect. There was, for instance, the case of Father Victor Jesús Herrero Padilla.

Father Padilla is a Spaniard, a citizen of Spain. He was the priest of the Monserrate Church in Santurce, and originally a Franco partisan. In fact, on April 1, 1939, Father Padilla took the Falangist oath and received membership book number 305 in the Puerto Rican branch of the Falange Tradicionalista Española de la J.O.N.S. He held his book until October 1, 1940. Then, without a word of explanation, he formally resigned from the Falange. Puerto Ricans close to the Padre of Monserrate broadly hinted that Father Martin's writings on Falangismo had caused this resignation.

The uniformed Falangistas preferred the writings of *Avance* to the columns of Father Martin's *Piloto*. In the issue of January 1, 1938, *Avance* hailed the Japanese recognition of Franco as the legal head of the Spanish State—more than a year before the Republic fell—in words the German origin of which was unmistakable.

Japan could not be missing among those powers who offer us their company and their friendship [*Avance* announced]. Japan is a hierarchical believing nation, fundamentally honest with the ethical principles of society, noble in her aspirations, and an intelligent nation. She has to be with us hand in hand, heart to heart, with conscience and with unshakable will to fight Communism . . . who will not yield until the definite defeat of the Red credo is inflicted—defeat to Judaism, Masonry, the Soviet . . . Spaniards! For this victory of today . . . cry out with me: Long Live the Japanese Empire, as of today the intimate friend of our Spain!

The same issue of *Avance* also denounced the "russo-yankee press" and the Jews for the "calumnies" against Falangismo many Spaniards had noticed on the Island of Puerto Rico.

Two weeks later, *Avance* printed a speech by Oliveira Salazar, the Caudillo of clerico-Fascist Portugal—a speech praising Franco for his role on the Iberian Peninsula. On April 15, 1938, *Avance* carried the latest regulations of the Falange Exterior as promulgated in Burgos.

Alejandro Villanueva, General von Faupel's Inspector General of the Falange in the Americas, visited the Falange of Puerto Rico in June 1938. According to *Avance*, Villanueva's visit was merely an inspection trip, since the Inspector General was due to sail for Spain in August. Perhaps it was as a result of Villanueva's visit that the Falange organization of Puerto Rico was shaken up. Leopoldo Martinez Ochoa, a wealthy businessman of San Juan, replaced fiery young Alfonso Miranda Esteve as regional chief, and the pace of all Falange activities was stepped up.

Dionisio Trigo, the elder statesman of the Puerto Rican

Falange, went to Spain shortly after Villanueva. He never returned to Puerto Rico. His visit to Franco Spain had inevitably led him to Nazi Germany. In Frankfurt, Trigo underwent an operation and died.

The Falange turned out in full uniform to attend a Mass for Trigo in San Juan on October 20, 1938. It was the most spectacular Falangist mass until the one they celebrated in April 1939 upon the victory of the Franco forces in Spain. At both Masses the Falangistas and the feminine section of the Falange donned the Fascist uniforms and carried the Falangist flags into the Cathedral.

The Falange kept growing in Puerto Rico until the advent of the British and French declarations of war on Nazi Germany. Many Falangistas who thought of the American Government in terms of Governor Winship were rudely shocked by the obvious feelings of Franklin Roosevelt. Word had already filtered through to the New World that the Germans were gobbling up all of Spain's resources. Many Puerto Rican Falangistas who had looked to Franco to guard their investments in Spain were shocked to discover that the Nazis were keeping all funds from leaving Spain—even dividends due Spaniards in Latin America.

The Presidential Executive Order freezing Axis funds early in 1940, while it chose to overlook Spain's being part of the Nazi Empire, sent many of Puerto Rico's wealthier Falangistas scurrying to their bank vaults. They had no illusions about the fact that Spain was an Axis nation, and most of them felt that Spanish funds would inevitably be frozen under the terms of this order. In their panic, they began to sink vast sums into real estate—causing an astonishing land boom on the poverty-stricken island.

Many of the more timorous rich Falangistas resigned from the organization and tried to cover up their pro-Axis records. They began to talk in terms of seeking United States citizenship, much to the disgust of the Franco consul in San Juan. From the Spanish Consulate the Axis consul sent angry reports to Madrid and to the Spanish Embassy in Washington. He complained of the cowardice of the frightened Falangistas on the island, and followed up these complaints with a number of scathing personal denunciations.

But the economic forces which had originally drawn the wealthy Spaniards of Puerto Rico into the Falange were now operating to force them into at least a tactical retreat. The New Spain might be glorious and real democracy might exist only in Italy and Germany, just as *Avance* wrote. Nevertheless, the prosperous Falangistas were confronted with the reality of a German *Gauleiter* who had already frozen all Latin-American investments in Spain and the spectacle of an American President who had frozen the funds of Italy, Germany, and Japan in the New World. The logical next step of freezing the funds of Axis Spanish firms would place them economically between the German anvil and the Yankee hammer. Economic common sense, therefore, dictated that the Falangistas in Puerto Rico should take all possible measures designed to protect their funds in the Western Hemisphere.

The wealthier Falangistas began dropping out of the organization. Those who were Spanish citizens immediately began to apply for American citizenship. What remained in the Falange was, by and large, exactly that element which the Nazis wanted most—the young, fanatical, emotional Fascists who had nothing to lose and everything to gain by an Axis victory in World War II.

Not even the voluntary dissolution of the Falange of Puerto Rico in January 1941 bothered Spain's Nazi masters. The pocketbook panic which had given the older Falangistas such hysterics was a perfect cover for changing the form of the Falange in Puerto Rico. By 1941 it suited von Faupel's plans to have the United States Government accept at face value the fact that the Falange no longer existed in Puerto Rico. The seeds which had been planted in 1936, and nursed along by such master Fascist gardeners as Gonzalez Marin, Julio de la Torre, and Alejandro Villanueva, had produced a plant which could not be killed by a formal act of a small group of frightened men.

As war approached, the United States started to increase the Puerto Rican garrison. Blanton Winship and Colonel Wright disappeared from the scene. Winship was succeeded for a time by Admiral Leahy, who in turn was succeeded by Guy Swope and then by Rexford Guy Tugwell.

When the former New Deal Brain Truster became Governor of Puerto Rico in September 1941, he inherited one of the greatest headaches in our government. The forty years of American bungling which had succeeded four centuries of Spanish misrule had brought Puerto Rico to the brink of the war in a condition conducive neither to good government nor to sound military defense. The island could produce practically no food for the suddenly increased garrison, let alone its own people. An inadequately fed people lived in inadequate houses in shocking sanitary conditions. Only the temporary emergency jobs provided by the defense projects stood between thousands of Puerto Rican families and ruin.

Governor Tugwell had plans for Puerto Rico, plans which would have made it both a better place to live in and a sounder base of operations for the defense of the Caribbean and the Panama Canal. These plans included projects for a safe water system, cheap sanitary housing, and the enforcement of the 500-Acre Law begun in 1941 after four decades. This act, written into the original Puerto Rican charter when the island first became a colony of the United States, was designed to keep the small Puerto Rican farmers from being made landless. It limited the size of all farms to five hundred acres. Had it been enforced, Puerto Rico's history as a stepchild of the American Government might have been a brighter one. Instead, the fertile bottom land of one-third of the island was absorbed by forty-two sugar plantations owned by absentee American and Spanish corporations.

The wealthy Spaniards who had flocked to the Franco banner were quick to join hands with the American sugar corporations who declared war on Tugwell. Supporters of Tugwell were more numerous on the island than his enemies. Their voices, however, found fewer effective forums and newspapers at their disposal.

The bombing of Pearl Harbor ended the reconstruction programs of Governor Tugwell. Nazi submarines in the Caribbean, guided by scores of Heinz Lunings, sank supply ship after supply ship. The island's food shortages, always serious, became catastrophic. The completion of the naval and military defense projects added to the island's unemployment.

In Madrid, General von Faupel had the satisfaction of learning that the war had brought Puerto Rico to the state of acute crisis. He had the additional satisfaction of learning that in Puerto Rico, as in the Philippines, the Falange and its friends had swarmed into the civilian defense organizations.

The civilian defense organization of Puerto Rico, established in 1941, has sixty thousand workers. Prospective air-raid wardens and other civil defense volunteers were accepted into the ranks and given their credentials without investigation.

Puerto Rico's scrambled political lines had their reflection in Governor Tugwell's appointee as the Executive Secretary of the civilian defense organization. Against his better judgment, Tugwell was maneuvered into appointing to this important post Enrique de Orbeta, former Insular Chief of Police, brother-in-law of Dionisio Trigo and uncle of two outstanding Falangistas.

Orbeta's nephews, Juan Trigo de Orbeta and Dionisio Trigo de Orbeta, are today in the civilian defense organization of Puerto Rico. Both held membership cards in the Falange; Juan was a member of the *Avance* staff. Bonifacio Fernandez, who was also a Falange member, is a lieutenant in the civilian defense organization. His brother, Telesforo

Fernandez, who carried a Falange card, is in the State
Guard.

José Fidalgo Diaz, who was both a member of the Falange and a contributor to *Avance*, is not only in the civilian
defense organization but also the personal secretary to
Sergio Cuevas, the Insular Government's Secretary of the
Interior. Eliado Rodriguez Otero, contributor to *Avance*,
is in the civilian defense organization of Rio Piedras.

The list of proved former members of the Falange in
Puerto Rico's civilian defense organization is huge. In certain communities, the people who suddenly awoke to discover that the Falangistas had taken over the local civilian
posts raised such a scandal that the offending wardens had
to resign.

Former Falangistas and Franco partisans have also
swarmed into the U.S.O. Wives and daughters of Falangistas who marched through the streets in the uniforms of
the feminine section of the Falange yesterday are now
serving coffee and cakes to American soldiers in U.S.O.
clubhouses.

Among the outspoken Franco partisans now engaged in
U.S.O. work is a society woman of Arecibo. Her case is
typical of the new conditions in Puerto Rico.

On Pearl Harbor Day, as the news of the Japanese bombing attack came over the radio, she was in a store in Arecibo.
The news excited her. "Viva Hitler!" She cried. "*Este es el
hombre que necesitamos!* (He is a man we need here!)"

She is now active in the U.S.O. of Arecibo. In this sea-
coast town there are also a group of Spanish priests who
were and are violently pro-Franco. On Labor Day 1942 a
dozen American fliers got reeling drunk at the parish house.
The fliers were from the emergency air base the Army built
near Arecibo.

This air base was built in great secrecy. As soon as it
was finished, the Vichy-controlled Martinique radio put
on a special Spanish broadcast beamed at Puerto Rico. In
mocking tones two announcers congratulated the Americans upon the swift completion of the base and then

launched into a solicitous critique of its various shortcomings.

The effect of this broadcast on the Puerto Ricans was about as shocking as the well known fact that the Nazi submarine commanders in waters around Puerto Rico have never made the mistake of sending a torpedo into a ship carrying dynamite. Submarines which torpedo dynamite ships are in danger of being sunk by the resulting concussion—a dynamite ship, in exploding, acts like a depth bomb. But the Nazi submarine commanders who prey on Puerto Rican shipping seem to have an uncanny idea of what is in the cargo hold of every ship that crosses their periscopes.

Pearl Harbor sent many once-proud Falangistas scurrying to the Federal Court with petitions for American citizenship. Early in 1942, twenty-one Spanish residents of Puerto Rico, all of them admitted members of the Falange during its official existence on the island, applied for American citizenship before Judge Robert A. Cooper.

It was the most spectacular court hearing in Puerto Rico since Judge Cooper had found the leaders of the Nationalist Party guilty of treason in 1937. At that time, Cooper had ruled that the Nationalist program of independence for Puerto Rico constituted treason.

In the case of the twenty-one Falangistas, the official program of the Falange Española Tradicionalista, like the program of the Nationalist Party, was on trial. Puerto Ricans, well-acquainted with those points of the Falange program which called for the restoration of the Spanish Empire, looked for fireworks from the bench.

They had good reason to expect drama. In an earlier citizenship hearing, on September 15, 1941, Judge Cooper had made a strong pronouncement. "Any person who belongs to organizations opposed to the United States," he declared, "cannot be considered a good citizen, cannot fulfill his oath to defend and support the Constitution of the United States."

When the hearings began, however, it was not the Judge

who provided the fireworks. First blood was drawn by Alfonso Miranda Esteve, Director of *Avance* and first chief of the Falange of Puerto Rico.

Esteve was not an applicant for citizenship. He was one of the chief attorneys for the petitioners. He beamed when the Judge decided to hold court on Washington's Birthday, since, "In these days of emergency, one cannot lose time in festivities." * He sat unruffled through the early skirmishes, smiling softly to himself as he laid his trap.

Before Esteve could spring his surprise, the Falange Oath used in Puerto Rico was introduced into the evidence. On the face of it, it seemed enough to disqualify the petitioners who had signed it. In a faithful translation, it reads:

I SWEAR to give myself always to the service of SPAIN.

I SWEAR not to have any other pride than that of the Motherland and of the Falange with obedience and joy, impetus and patience, gallantry and silence.

I SWEAR loyalty and submission to our Chiefs, honor to the memory of the dead, unswerving perseverance in all vicissitudes.

I SWEAR that wherever I may be or be ordered to obey, to respect our Command from first to last rank.

I SWEAR to reject and consider unheard any voice of friend or enemy that may weaken the spirit of FALANGE.

I SWEAR to maintain above all the ideas of unity: UNITY between the lands of SPAIN, UNITY in man and among the men of SPAIN.

I SWEAR to live in the holy brotherhood with all those of FALANGE and to lend all aid and oppose all differences whenever this holy brotherhood is invoked.

After the Falange oath was introduced, Esteve maintained his amused calm. He sat quietly at the counsel table while·Benecio Sanchez Castano, associated with him in the case, agreed with Judge Cooper on the importance of

---

* This and other speeches made at the hearings are translated from the accounts appearing in *El Imparcial, El Mundo,* and other Puerto Rican newspapers at the time.

denying citizenship to members of subversive organizations. Nevertheless, Castano asserted, the fact that a person had been a member of the Falange was not grounds for the denial of citizenship.

When Castano was done with this argument, Esteve himself started to answer the Judge's questions. He began by explaining that, after the war began in Spain, a group of Puerto Ricans organized an association to aid the cause of the Fascists. Then, Esteve said, the Comite de las Damas —the Women's Committee—was organized in 1937 to collect funds for Franco. "The organizers were all rich people," he said, "and contributed money of their own."

The Falange in Puerto Rico, Esteve said, was organized in 1938. (This would have made the announcement in the December 1937 issue of *Avance* of which Esteve was the Director a lie.)

At this point Judge Cooper asked Alfonso Miranda Esteve whether the Falange Española Tradicionalista was the same as the Nazi Party of Germany.

Esteve was ready with a very glib answer. The Falange, he said, was quite different. The Falange was for a corporate state like that of Portugal, and supported Franco because he promised to support its Twenty-Seven Points. "The Falange of Puerto Rico," Esteve said, "stood for the same program as the Falange of Spain."

The first leader of the Puerto Rican Falange and director of its official magazine belittled his own efforts. Never, he told the court, had the Falange on the island reached a membership of more than 250—a figure which startled all Puerto Ricans who had seen the streets darkened on more than one occasion by processions of uniformed Falangistas.

Then, mopping his lips with a limp handkerchief, Esteve launched into an apparently pointless story of the celebration held at the Casa de España to celebrate the Franco victory in April 1939. Innocently, he started to describe the celebration in detail. He blandly mentioned the names of many notables who attended the fiesta.

Courtroom spectators gasped as some of the names slid from Esteve's lips. At the Franco victory celebration there had been many high officers of the American Government and the Army. Esteve named them all, pausing between names for effect. He cited then-Governor Blanton Winship, Colonel Wright, Judge Martin Trabieso, of the Puerto Rican Supreme Court.

Esteve paused again, exchanged a queer look with some of the petitioners. He revealed that the band of the regular United States Army garrison performed in the Casa de España at that celebration. And then he named another prominent person who he saw in the Casa de España that day. The name was—Judge Robert A. Cooper!

Had he hurdled the bench, tied a string of giant Chinese firecrackers to the Judge's robe and ignited the fuse, Esteve could not have created a greater sensation in the San Juan Federal Court on that memorable Washington's Birthday.

When order was restored, the Judge spluttered an indignant denial. He hotly denied that he had attended the celebration, or even that he had been invited to attend. But he felt that he owed some sort of explanation, for he asserted that if he was in the Casa de España on that day, it was merely to play a game of billiards. Judge Cooper also felt constrained to remind his listeners that billiards was his favorite game.

Puerto Rico has been a land without laughter for four centuries. Judge Cooper's hasty explanation, however, made many suffering Puerto Ricans laugh. For reasons best known to themselves, they thought it was very funny.

Miranda Esteve continued to dominate the hearing. He went on to tell the court that the Puerto Rican Falange was disbanded after the Spanish War, since it no longer had any reason to exist. But he did not explain why the Falange waited for nearly two years after the Franco victory before disbanding for this stated reason. Answering another question, he said that the Falange still existed in Spain.

"Is it true," the Judge asked Esteve, "that the relations of Franco and the Falange are similar to the relations between the National Socialist German Workers Party and Adolf Hitler?"

"In essence, yes," Miranda Esteve replied. "They are similar. But the Government of Francisco Franco," Esteve added, "is not opposed to political parties." (There is only one legal political party in Spain.)

"Is the government that now exists in Spain a representative government?" the Judge asked.

"Not exactly," Esteve answered.

The Judge glanced at the petitioners before he put the next important question to Miranda Esteve. "How do you think some persons can advocate one form of government for one country and swear loyalty to another system of government under which they live?"

The answer was quite frank. "I don't know."

Puerto Rican democrats took heart from the Judge's reaction to this answer. Cooper said that he did not "understand how a person wishes to swear loyalty to a system of government different from one he aided in organizing in another country."

Not even the parade of high-placed character witnesses who appeared for the petitioners shook the faith of some spectators in Cooper's determination to refuse comfort to Axis partisans. The imposing array of character witnesses was headed by Dr. Muñoz MacCormick, director of the Puerto Rico Defense Council. He was followed to the stand by Filipe de Ostos, head of the Puerto Rican Chamber of Commerce and leader of the anti-Tugwell forces. Both MacCormick and de Ostos testified for Petitioner Emeliano Mendez. Alfonso Valencia, of the Bull Insular Lines, testified for a group of the petitioners.

So imposing was the weight of the testimony about the Axis character of the Falange, that, at one point, the Judge was forced to postpone the hearings in order to study the record. At this point, Judge Cooper sounded what seemed to many listeners like the closing of the door to all citizenship petitions by Axis partisans.

"My attention has been called to the possibility that the activities of the Falange Española in Puerto Rico might be anti-American. I do not know if the assertion is correct, nor if it includes the petitioners. I want it to be understood," the Judge said, "that in postponing their cases I am not prejudging their admissibility. I believe I must proceed with a detailed examination of these petitions. . . .

"Lately, we have discovered that (some) political organizations are much more powerful than we believed. Of course, citizens may be in disagreement, but there should be no discrepancies at least as to certain fundamental principles.

"For example," Judge Cooper, the former Governor of South Carolina, pointed out, "it has been resolved that the principles of the Ku Klux Klan were anti-American. If proof were offered that a candidate for citizenship belonged to the Ku Klux Klan, it seems to me it would be my duty to clarify the situation before making a decision as to his admissibility."

Again, in these words, the foes of the Falange found much promise. For the Ku Klux Klan, while as Fascist as the Falange in its principles, never demanded that any state or colony of the United States of America be restored to a foreign empire. On these grounds alone, the Puerto Ricans who backed the United Nations in the war against the Axis felt that at Judge Cooper's hands the Falange of Puerto Rico was finally to receive a setback.

These hopes were all blasted on March 10, 1942, when Federal Judge Robert A. Cooper, having studied the evidence, prepared to hand down his decision. "If I had any doubts regarding the good faith of the petitioners," Judge Cooper declared, "I would plainly refuse their request. . . . No matter what may be said for or against the Falange," Cooper said, he was "satisfied that the petitioners would take the oath of loyalty in good faith."

The twenty-one Spanish Falangistas, four months after Spain's Axis partners and masters declared war on the

United States, were admitted to American citizenship by the judge who played billiards at the Casa de España.

Few judicial actions have ever given Fascists in American territories the encouragement Judge Cooper's decision gave the enemies of democracy in Puerto Rico. It came at a time that Nazi submarine raiders in the Caribbean were reaching the peak of their destructive efficiency, when democracy meant only increased starvation on the island.

Before Judge Cooper handed down his decision, the American authorities in Puerto Rico had appeased Franco in a manner that had made Puerto Ricans writhe. When the garrison was increased, the authorities had to find a suitable headquarters for the U.S.O. Two buildings proved physically and geographically suitable—the Ateneo Puertorriqueño and the Casa de España. Both had ballrooms, meeting halls, social rooms, and quarters for libraries and buffets. The Casa de España, which flew the Franco flag, was bigger and more modern than the Ateneo. It stood as a symbol of Axis power on the island, while the Ateneo was the only meeting place for pro-United Nations citizens of the island.

Perhaps the authorities did not know all this when they decided to take over the Ateneo Puertorriqueño for the U.S.O. Nevertheless, they could not have aimed a heavier blow at the pro-United Nations forces of Puerto Rico than when they took the Ateneo. The U.S.O. banner now flies from the Ateneo's standards, and the dispossessed Puerto Rican intellectuals gag every time they pass the near-by Casa de España and see the Franco flag waving insolently in the lazy breezes of the troubled colony.

The Franco flag waves in Puerto Rico, which has very few secrets. Disheartened Puerto Rican democrats, who see the Falange in its true colors, can see only danger ahead in the continued tolerance American officialdom seems to show for the most outspoken of the Axis partisans of the island.

In the meanwhile, Franco supporters and former Falangistas move about the island in perfect freedom. They dominate the civilian defense organizations and the U.S.O., they hold positions of importance in the government, and they rub shoulders with American soldiers.

A case in point is one Obregon, headwaiter at La Mallorquina, one of San Juan's smartest restaurants. American army and navy officers often eat and drink at this expensive café, and many of them talk shop. Obregon is a recent arrival from Santander, Spain. He boasts of having been an important Falange leader in Santander, where, he claims, he personally liquidated many enemies of Spanish fascism. Today he pours rum and whisky for the officers of America's Gibraltar.

Dr. Juan Homedes Cortiella is another Spaniard who moves about in San Juan in perfect freedom. Cortiella was living in Barcelona with his family when the Spanish War started. He went to France, where he wrote to Dr. Roldan, head of the Puerto Rican Auxilio Muto and asked for a job. He reached Puerto Rico early in the course of the Spanish War and went to work as an intern in the Auxilio Muto clinic.

When Dr. Cortiella reached San Juan, he visited the Spanish Republicans. He was, he told them, an old anarchist and a foe of the Falange. He started to attend pro-Loyalist meetings and make anti-Franco declarations. During all of this time, however, he was attending various Falange functions. On February 24, 1939, Dr. Cortiella joined the Puerto Rican Falange and was given card number 100. He resigned from the Falange on July 1, 1940, the date the President's order freezing Axis funds took effect.

Many outspoken supporters of Franco and the Falange own large estates which touch on the coastlines of the island. These estates are all capable of sheltering and shielding Axis agents with radio equipment more powerful than the clandestine sender Heinz August Luning operated in Havana.

Wherever one turns in Puerto Rico, the Falange and its most open supporters appear in high places. Only after Pearl Harbor was the daughter of a leader of the feminine section of the Falange removed from her confidential post in the postal censorship office. A high-ranking military officer who exchanged a glowing correspondence with Franco during the Spanish War today holds an important command on the island.

Between the Falangistas, sworn enemies of the democracies, and the American authorities, who evidently choose to ignore them, stand the vast body of Puerto Ricans. The lot of these Puerto Ricans is an increasingly unhappy one. Starvation and unemployment are increasing in their ranks. America has failed them. The most articulate of their numbers welcomed America's entry into the war as the catalyst which would stimulate the factors which can bring democracy and its benefits to Puerto Rico. Today, they are losing hope. In the continued official tolerance of the Falange and its leaders on the island, Puerto Ricans can see only the negation of all the democratic war aims.

CHAPTER EIGHT

Mexico: Falange Concentration Point

IF GENERAL WILHELM VON FAUPEL ever writes an autobiography, he can well rate his successes in Mexico on a level with the Fifth Column he created for the Axis in Manila. Through the Falange and its chief Mexican subsidiaries—the Acción National and the Sinarquistas—he has established on the borders of the United States of America one of the most dangerous Axis centers in the entire world. He has created a co-ordinated movement embracing well over a half-million followers engaged in espionage, arms smuggling, propaganda, and sorties of violence often reaching the scale of actual warfare. And von Faupel has forged this Axis army in the space of less than a decade.

Perhaps, if Carlton J. H. Hayes, the American Ambassador to Spain, who in February 1943 chose to make a statement praising the "wise" peace policies of Francisco Franco, had taken time to study the end results of this policy in Mexico—perhaps the Ambassador would have tempered his words. For in Mexico the mistakes the Western democracies made during the Spanish War between 1936 and 1939 have given birth to one of the grisliest of Appeasement's Frankensteins.

Falangismo reached Mexico three years after the Germans had set up a widespread and expensive Nazi network. In addition to their legations, the Nazis had sixteen organizations for Germans in Mexico—organizations ranging from the Mexican branch of the Nazi Party to the Ibero-American Institute and German sports clubs. The Gestapo had a smoothly-running center in Mexico City headed by Georg Nicolaus. Nazi cells functioned from Guatemala to Texas. Something like twenty thousand Germans all over Mexico paid their dues to the Nazi collectors and carried out the orders of their local leaders.

In the early part of 1935, the Nazi leaders of Mexico received orders to cultivate the wealthier members of the Spanish colonies of Mexico. The Spaniards in Mexico owned about 60 per cent of the agricultural acreage, most of the real estate in Mexico City, and many mining interests. More than two-thirds of the textile mills in Mexico belonged to Spaniards. The Spanish Colony had a virtual monopoly of the domestic mercantile commerce of the nation, the printing and publishing business, and the processed-food industries.

The men who owned these enterprises looked down upon Mexicans as inferiors and viewed the Mexican Republic as something alien to their best interests. They had important investments in Spain and, generally, considered the Spanish Republic to be an instrument of government as menacing to themselves as the Mexican Republic.

When Hitler invaded the Spanish Republic in 1936, the upper crust of Mexico's Spanish Colony required little prodding to jump on the Axis steamroller. The Falange program was one that appealed to their hearts and their purses, not only as the program that could do them the most good in Spain, but also as an eminently desirable blueprint of the ideal Mexican State. The Nazis in Mexico were able to sell the Spaniards on the idea that the triumph of the Axis in Spain would be the preliminary to the establishment of a Falangist state in Mexico.

Under Nazi supervision, the Falange was created in Mexico within weeks of the start of the Spanish War. By the time the German, Italian, and Japanese legations were expelled by the Mexican Government in 1941, the Axis had, in the Mexican Falange, an instrument capable of continuing its anti-American activities from the strategic and valuable Mexican base. Since Pearl Harbor, the Falange network in Mexico has, if anything, grown stronger and more menacing. It is not only the Axis Fifth Column nearest the United States borders; it is also the most powerful anti-American force in the hemisphere.

Nominal chief of all Falange activities in Mexico is

Augusto Ibañez Serrano, a Spaniard who had lived in Mexico for many years before the Nazis gave him their· blessing in 1936. He sometimes signs his letters as "Personal Representative of Generalissimo Francisco Franco in Mexico." Although he receives his mail at 123 Calle Articulo, Mexico City, visitors to this building would have great difficulty finding Ibañez Serrano. The best place to find him is in the office he maintains in the Portuguese Legation in Mexico City.

Mexico, the only country in the Western Hemisphere which had aided the Spanish Republic, has never had diplomatic relations with Axis Spain. Portugal looks after Spanish diplomatic interests in Mexico. All Spaniards who visit the Portuguese Legation for any reason must first be cleared by Ibañez Serrano before they will be received by the Legation's officials.

From his offices in the Portuguese Legation, Ibañez Serrano today directs all Falange activities in Mexico. He is the direct link between the Nazis in Europe and the secret Fascist armies on the American border. Through special couriers, Ibañez Serrano keeps in constant touch with Colonel Sanz Agero, the current chief of all Falange activities in Central America, and with the Spanish Embassy in Washington. Colonel Agero is the Spanish Minister to Guatemala.

Ibañez Serrano operates primarily through three close lieutenants, all of them lawyers. They are Alejandro Quijano, Gómez Morin, and Carlos Prieto. Quijano is Ibañez Serrano's legal adviser. Morin supervises the activities of Mexican groups organized and run by the Falange. Prieto, among other things, keeps contact with Nuñez Iglesias in the Spanish Embassy in Washington.

These four men have the intimate and varied activities of Falangismo in Mexico at their fingertips. They see to it that the various organizations under their control contribute on an average of three hundred thousand pesos each month to defray part of the expenses of running the network. Under the watchful eye of Gestapo-trained members of the Spanish Secret Service in Mexico, the four top leaders disburse these funds where they will do the United Nations the most harm.

The official Falange Española Tradicionalista de la J.O.N.S. en Méjico has about 50,000 uniformed, dues-paying members. Although the majority of its members are Mexicans of Spanish descent, Mexican citizens are not permitted to hold important posts in the organization. The chief strongholds of the formal Falange in Mexico are centered in Puebla, Vera Cruz, Mérida, Comitán, Guadalajara, Morelia, Mazatlán, Guanajuato, Tampico, Monterrey, Torreón, and Guaymas. Here corps of blue-shirted Falangistas, trained by a succession of German and Spanish military officers, are at the service of General von Faupel and his subordinates in the Americas.

As the hour for Pearl Harbor approached, von Faupel considerably tightened the organizational controls of the Falange in Mexico. The most important move made for this purpose was the assignment given to Eulogio Celorio Sordo, who was sent from Spain to take charge of the uniformed Falange of Mexico in July, 1941. Celorio Sordo's title is Provincial Chief of the Falange in Mexico. He receives his orders directly from Madrid, and is equal in rank with Ibañez Serrano, the nominal chief of Falange activities.

Celorio Sordo works out of Messones 127, Mexico City. He heads the delegation of Falange leaders chosen in Spain, rather than in the office run by Ibañez Serrano at the Portuguese Legation. These Madrid-chosen Falange officers include personalities like María Luisa Gavito, chief of the feminine section and the Auxilio Social of the Falange, and Felipe Yubrita, chief of the Falange in Mexico City.

As Provincial Chief of the Falange, Celorio Sordo supervises all the activities that the Falangistas themselves classify as "illegal." This, however, is not a moral classification. The term is used merely to designate those Falangist actions which happen to run counter to the laws of Mexico—a judicial code the Falange recognizes only as an unavoidable nuisance.

These activities vary greatly, but a mere glance at a few representative Falange tasks in this category is enough to explain why they cannot be performed legally in Mexico. Three examples picked at random tell their own stories.

A member of the Falange ran a leather-goods shop in Mexico City. Tourists visited the shop for handbags and tooled-leather belts. Falange shock troops visited the shop regularly—but never as customers. They went to the shop for sealed orders, and for packages containing rifles, bullets, and machine-gun ammunition.

A certain business firm whose offices overlooked the blue waters of the Gulf of Mexico at Vera Cruz received regular shipments from Spain that never were entered in the books of the corporation. These special shipments arrived on Spanish ships of the C.T.E. line—and consisted of trained agents of the Axis assigned to work in Mexico or one of the Central American republics.

A well-known garage in Mexico City is also the center of the transportation system used by agents of the Falange and the Spanish Secret Service.

Centers such as these are supervised by Celorio Sordo and his aides all over Mexico. To keep them working at top efficiency, the Falange in Spain has been sending about five hundred *militantes* to the Americas each month since 1939. These Spanish Falangistas cross the ocean in C.T.E. ships as tourists, business men, educators, and artists. Upon arrival in Mexico, they are given new papers and new identities by the Falange chiefs and then go to work as Falange agents.

The important Falangistas are attached to Falange cells all over the country. In Mexico they are concentrated mainly in Puebla and in provinces of northern Mexico—the regions nearer the United States. Chief of these centers are Morelia, Guanajuato, and Mazatlán.

All of the visiting *militantes* are trained in the basic principles of sabotage, espionage, and secret warfare. Many won their spurs originally as officers in the Franco forces during the Spanish War, and in Mexico most of them train Falangist shock troops and other military organizations. Acting on orders received even before they left Spain, they keep out of the limelight entirely in Mexico. They hold no offices in the local Falange cells and remain under cover whenever the Falange groups they instruct hold any type of public demonstration.

These *militantes* were originally under the direct supervision of Hans Hellerman, a veteran Nazi agent who was sent to Spain by General von Faupel as early as 1934. Hellerman remained in Spain until 1937, when he returned to Berlin for a short term as chief of the Spanish division of the Nazi Party. He reached Mexico late in 1938, and took charge of the military training of the Falange. Pearl Harbor, which precipitated Mexico's entrance into war, ended Hellerman's career as generalissimo of the Falange shock troops in Mexico; but nearly a year before Pearl Harbor, von Faupel sent a new military chief to the Mexican Falange.

The man chosen to supplant Hellerman was Major José Enrique Carril Ontano, one of the most ruthless commanders of the Fascist armies during the Spanish War. Major Carril Ontano had a specialty: he had developed to a fine art the technique of razing and looting undefended Republican villages. He sailed from Spain for Havana in January 1941. After his arrival in Havana, the Spanish Republican émigrés learned that he was in Cuba—and the Major went into hiding. In May of that year he sneaked out of Havana and went to Mexico City.

The apartment maintained by the Major at 2 Oriente Street in Puebla is seldom used, since he travels over Mexico constantly. Major Carril Ontano goes nowhere without his picked guard; Mexico has many Republican refugees, and the Major is in constant terror of his life. When he is in Mexico City, he stays in the vicinity of the Hotel Colisco.

Two Spanish army officers who also arrived in Mexico shortly before Pearl Harbor are Carril Ontano's chiefs of staff. They are Major Francisco Garay Unzuenta and Captain Carlos Aravilla. Like their chief, they are constantly on the move, checking on the work of the *militantes* in the Falange cells all over the country.

Carril Ontano's military delegation, while nominally under the direction of Celorio Sordo, receives its orders and directives from General Mora Figueroa, chief of the Spanish Falange and Minister in the Spanish Cabinet. Figueroa, in turn, sends the Falange military delegation in Mexico directives drawn up by General von Faupel and his staff. For the main part, these instructions deal with creating anti-American forces in areas close to the American border.

The Falange militia in Mexico is not an army without arms. Spanish ships cross the oceans with great regularity, and many of them are little more than munitions ships at the service of the Falange Exterior. Just before Pearl Harbor, three Spanish ships reached Guatemala within a period of two weeks and unloaded cargoes of munitions which were then trans-shipped to Chiapas, Mexico. The arms these and other Spanish ships succeeded in smuggling into Mexico have not been wasted for mere training purposes; they have gone and continue to go into the vast secret arsenals the Falange maintains in scores of Mexican strongholds.

There have been times in the past three years, however, when bullets from these arsenals have been put to real use. Among their other duties, the imported *militantes* from the Falange Fatherland act as executioners when the Falange· passes judgment on local Falangistas who are tried and convicted by the organization's own courts-martial: Death sentences are handed out to Falangistas who try to desert the blue-shirt ranks or sell the secrets of the Fifth Column. Other infractions can send errant Falangistas into one of the private jails maintained by the Falange Exterior—sometimes for sentences of five years.

The undercover militia represents only one aspect of Falangismo in Mexico. Dangerous as it is, this organized army represents only a token force. Von Faupel entertains no pipe dreams about using it to invade Texas, and, under any circumstances, it would prove no match for even the Mexican Army. Were the Axis to make any serious moves in the Western Hemisphere, however, this Falange secret army in Mexico could and would be used to immobilize a sizable United Nations force and weaken our defenses.

The Falange campaign in Mexico goes much further than the maintenance of a secret Axis army. Its objectives are very clear. Vicente Lombardo Toledano, head of the anti-Axis Latin-American Confederation of Labor, summed up the Axis aims in Mexico in a speech delivered a month before Pearl Harbor. He declared that the Axis wants:

1. To use Mexico as the nearest base for Nazi espionage in the United States.

2. To use our country [Mexico] as a source of raw materials for its war.

3. To make Mexico a center for organized acts of sabotage against the United States, as well as against our own export trade, so that we may be prevented from sending help to the countries fighting the Axis.

4. To establish a center of Fascist provocation against the United States, thus distracting that country's attention from the European and other theaters of war.

5. To secure a center from which Fascist propaganda can be directed to all of Latin America.

6. To instigate provocations against the government of Mexico from within our country itself, so that the government will be obliged to retaliate with restrictive measures. Afterward, these measures will be used to discredit the present regime in Mexico, and turned against democracy within and without our country.

Here, in a nutshell, is the master-plan of the Falange in Mexico.

The first point of the program, that of establishing Mexico as the nearest base for Nazi espionage against the United States, has become one of the cardinal tasks of the Falange.

Nazi espionage in Mexico was a going concern when

Francisco Franco was still waiting for the Nazis to invade Spain. With the establishment of the Falangist state in Spain in April 1939, the *Reichswehr* accepted von Faupel's recommendation that Spanish Fascists be trained by the Gestapo to work for the Axis in Latin America.

Special schools for Spaniards were established in Hamburg, Bremen, Hanover, and Vienna; institutions with German experts as instructors in sabotage, espionage, radio, secret codes, map-making, microphotography and allied subjects. Candidates for scholarships in these spy colleges were drawn from the ranks of the Spanish Falange. Preference went to those Falangistas who had joined the Franco movement before 1936 and had been wounded in action during the three-year war against the Republic. The most acceptable candidates, however, were those Spanish Fascists who had remained behind Republican lines as Falange agents during the war; men like the band of Fascists in Madrid whose co-operation with the four Axis columns converging on the city gave the world a new war term to remember—the Fifth Column.

Graduates of these special schools were commissioned as officers in the Spanish Army's Intelligence Service, the SIM. A small number of them were detailed to duties under the supervision of Gestapo officers in Spain. The rest were sent to Latin America to work under the direction of Gestapo and Japanese officers abroad.

The work of the SIM in Latin America was intensified after the German legations in most of the hemisphere were closed in the summer of 1941. While the diplomatic break did not eliminate more than 5 per cent of the Axis espionage personnel in Latin America, it did add greatly to the importance of the SIM. The numerous Spanish legations now became the diplomatic fronts for all Axis espionage, and SIM agents became liaison men between the Gestapo and the Spanish diplomatic network.

In line with his master-plan, General von Faupel took steps to strengthen and prepare the SIM to carry the major burdens of Axis espionage in Mexico. In December 1940, von Faupel had Alberto Mercado Flores, a veteran Spanish Falangist official, sent to Mexico. Flores was placed in command of the SIM operations for Mexico.

Flores has made his headquarters in a small town near the United States border. He owns at least three false passports, which he uses when traveling to San Francisco, Los Angeles, and Washington—where, of course, he is known by other names. He is responsible for SIM operations in the United States and Central America as well as in Mexico.

The SIM chief has two principal aides: Colonel Sanz Agero, the Spanish Minister to Guatemala, and Major Eugenio Alvarez Cano. The latter works out of an apartment at the corner of Lopez and Independencia streets, Mexico City. His movements are guarded and very hard to trace. Twice, since April 1941, he has made trips to New York, where he conferred with Spanish officials and shipping men. In Mexico City Cano works very closely with Ibáñez Serrano, co-ordinator of all Franco activities in Mexico.

The SIM organization that Flores directs in Mexico is an espionage machine built along the lines of the Gestapo, which created it. The work of its agents falls into two definite categories: military and economic espionage, and "control" of the Spanish colonies of the country and of those non-Falangist Spaniards known to have relatives in Spain.

The military espionage arm of the SIM operates in co-operation with the hordes of German and Japanese spies still actively at work in Mexico. Since Pearl Harbor, the ranking military officer of the Axis espionage network in this section of the world has been Colonel Sanz Agero. His is Flores's chief adviser in military matters.

Part of the SIM network's fantastic efficiency can be traced directly to its utilization of thousands of unpaid Falangistas and members of Falange-controlled Mexican organizations as part-time assistants. Much of the routine "donkey work" which takes up the energies of a professional spy is performed for the SIM by these fanatical followers of Falangismo. Every paid SIM agent has at his disposal at least one functioning cell of the Falange Exterior: a cell which in most cases includes a Spanish *militante* sent from Madrid to keep it functioning at maximum efficiency.

For this reason, the field headquarters of the SIM are located in cities where the Falange concentrations are strongest. The SIM maintains its chief field branches in the following Mexican centers: Monterrey, Torreón, Mazatlán, Tampico, Vera Cruz, Guadalajara, Puebla, Jalapa, Mérida, Tapachula, and Comitán.

There is scarcely a hamlet in Mexico without at least one SIM agent in its fold. Often the SIM operative in a tiny Mexican village will also turn out to be the Spanish *militante* of the local Falange, or the home-town leader of one of the Mexican subsidiaries of the Falange. Mexico City, on the other hand, has over a thousand Gestapo-trained SIM agents working out of no less than eleven offices in the capital alone.

The SIM has a complete list of Falangistas and Franco partisans in Mexican government bureaus, business houses, shipping companies, and other offices. Using these lists as their levers, the SIM has established pipe lines of information in all of these places.

The Nazis have been flooding all of Latin America with SIM operatives since 1939. Sources close to Madrid ruling circles estimate the SIM delegation in Mexico and Guatemala at close to ten thousand paid agents. Their routine reports reach Europe via Spanish boats, but scores of secret radio stations in Mexico often flash important intelligence to relay stations in Venezuela. The SIM in Venezuela sifts and transmits these reports to Madrid within minutes of their reception. Often, SIM agents visit Spanish ships arriving in Mexican ports and arrange to use the ship's radio for their transmissions. The radio operators on Spanish boats are hand-picked Falangistas—like the notorious Axis agent "Camarada Martinez," who is marked for immediate arrest if the Cuban authorities ever catch up with him.

The propaganda of the Falange in Mexico is as energetically anti-United States as are the activities of the SIM and the *militantes*. The Falange controls a number of publications and radio stations, openly or covertly as suits the plans of its leaders.

José Castedo, a veteran of the blue-shirt ranks, edits *Hispanidad*, the official magazine of the Mexican Falange. Here, assisted by Falangistas Adolfo Caso, Julio Luna, Delfin Sanchez Juarez, Francisco Ramirez, Marco Almazan, and A. Perez, Castedo produces a standard Falange Exterior organ along the lines of magazines like *Avance* of Puerto Rico, *Arriba España* of Buenos Aires, *Yugo* of Manila, and the other official publications in the Americas. This magazine is sold openly, unlike the *Boletin del Partido*, a weekly distributed only to Falange members.

Ibañez Serrano has a personal organ in *El Diario Español*. *La Semana* and *Mexico Nueva* carry the Falange line, and, like *Omega* and *El Hombre Libre*, are controlled by the Falange. The weekly *El Sinarquista*, published by the Falange-operated Sinarquist movement, is one of the most potent propaganda enemies of the United Nations in Mexico. *La Nación*, a weekly edited by Gómez Morin (one of Ibañez Serrano's three principal aides) and Alfonso Junco, Mexico's foremost apostle of Hispanidad, outdoes nearly every other Falangist publication in its campaign for the Axis.

The venom of the Falangist press is reserved almost exclusively for the United States. Thus on November 14, 1942, Luis G. Orozco blandly anounced in *Omega* that "Roosevelt is pushing his people into the pit of Bolshevism." This was in an article called "The Catholic Church and the World Revolution," which also said:

Whether they know it or not, those members of the clergy who have declared themselves in favor of the "democracies" are working in favor of Bolshevism. . . . How is it possible that members of the clergy have made speeches from the same platform with members of the Masonic order?

This article appeared after *Omega* described the American landings in North Africa as a "treacherous attack."

Omega also runs large advertisements for books like *Jews over America,* by "Dr. Atl, whose competence as an expert on international affairs is universally recognized." The chapters of the book include: "El Kabal, Roosevelt Is a Jew on All Sides"; "Jews in the New Deal"; "A Jewish leader to be feared: Felix Frankfurter."

From *El Hombre Libre,* a year after Pearl Harbor, come such choice nuggets of Axis propaganda as this:

The people of the United States are still under the influence of a government that tries to make them believe in a final victory, so that they may accept all the sacrifices imposed upon them by this war—a war that in the final balance will not take a very great toll of their lives anyway, for individuals of these races never fight, and the armies that march beneath the banners of John Bull and Uncle Sam are made up of colored peoples—black and brown—considered as inferiors by the Anglo-Saxons, who have always looked down upon them.

This was more than a mere parroting of the stock Nazi lies; it was part of the campaign being waged against compulsory military service and the sending of Mexican troops to fight the Axis armies abroad. The article then went on to carry the old Hispanidad line:

The world can well understand why nations with large populations like England, France, Belgium, Holland, Germany, and Italy have sought to build up colonial empires. The United States, however, has a great amount of territory and only her ambitions, her thirst for dominating other people, have driven her to try to form a colonial empire with the Philippines, Puerto Rico, Panama, the Pacific Islands, and the British possessions that have fallen into her hands. Still unsatisfied, she now wants control of all the countries of Latin America, rightful sons of Spain.

The quotation which sums up the complete line of the

Falangist press in Mexico is the following, taken from *Omega.*

A democratic government is a thousand times more danger-ous than a dictatorship like Hitler's or Mussolini's. Democracy exploits and deceives the people in the name of liberty, equal-ity, and fraternity. The democracies are protecting us from Hitler by throwing us into the arms of Roosevelt, who is the greatest danger of all those that menace Latin America today.

This theme, embroidered with anti-Semitism and gilded with Hispanidad, is reiterated day after day in the Falange publications south of the Rio Grande. In radio broadcasts over Station XEZ and other outlets, the Falange both scat-ters this line and issues coded instructions to its *militantes.* In books, meetings, pamphlets, and forums the Falange spreads this Nazi version of world affairs to millions of Mexicans. It has had a distinct and unpleasant effect on Mexico's war effort, and has been responsible for the spread of anti-American feeling in many sections of the country.

The Falange in Mexico has developed more "front" or-ganizations than in any other country in the world. These fronts range from dignified cultural bodies like the Acade-mia Española de la Lengua to the Fascist legions like the National Union of Sinarquistas. They all play specific roles in the Axis campaign to disrupt life in Mexico and make things difficult for the United Nations in the Western Hemisphere.

The Academia Española de la Lengua is the leading cul-tural organization in Spain. It is the source of all Spanish intellectual briefs for fascism, and has branches in many Latin-American lands. Only the élite are invited to the Academia sessions—the élite which can most effectively influence public opinion. The Academia works on news-paper publishers, college professors, statesmen, and dis-tinguished clerics.

In Mexico Ibañez Serrano is the official representative

of the Academia Española. He has delegated the actual work of running the affairs of this cultural front to his aide, Alejandro Quijano, and to Alfonso Junco, editor of *La Nación*. These fanatical enemies of the democracies run very exclusive forums at which the invited guests hear arguments for fascism, for Hispanidad, and for anti-Semitism couched in intellectual terms by the leading pundits of Falangismo. The Academia Española influences a small group of Mexicans, but their importance far exceeds their numbers.

Somewhat lower on the intellectual scale is the Escuadra de Acción Tradicionalista. These "Action Squadrons" are just what their name implies: shock troops. They are organized along highly secret lines; so much so that only a handful of members know the identity of their supreme commander. He is Major San Julian of the Spanish Army, a Fascist killer who joined the Falange some time before the Spanish War. Of Major Julian, it was said during this war that ice water would have frozen in his heart. Like Major Carril Ontano, San Julian was a past master in the art of liquidating whole Republican villages.

San Julian's talents as a shock-troop leader won him the post of chief of the Escuadra de Acción Tradicionalista of Mexico. Here, aided by Leon Osorio—a member of the Mexican branch of the German Nazi Party—San Julian commands a terror army of hand-picked Falangistas and Mexican Fascists. There are probably no more than 5,000 men in these "action squads," but they are the most violent of all the Falange fighters in the Americas.

In action, the Escuadra de Acción Tradicionalista assumes a role very similar to that assigned by Spanish fascism to the Falange in Spain before the Nazis entered the picture. Like the pre-1936 Spanish Falange, the Escuadra is at the service of *all* the Fascist organizations in Mexico. They do all the dirtiest jobs, for rewards which can best be imagined.

More cultural than the Escuadra de Acción, but far less exclusive than the Academia Española, is the newly formed Liga de Hispanidad Ibero-América. This League of Hispanidad was established to spread the racist doctrines of the Council of Hispanidad. Its first leader, chosen by Gómez Morin, was Octavio Elizalde, a Mexican who corresponds regularly with Andres Soriano, late of Manila. Elizalde resigned after a few months of spreading the Hispanidad creed.

The league is now led by José Castedo, editor of *Hispanidad*, the official organ of the Falange Exterior in Mexico. Two friends of Ibañez Serrano's assist Castedo in managing the affairs of the League. They are Francisco Cayon y Cos and Adolfo Caso, a Mexico City lawyer.

The P.A.M. (Partido Autonomista Mexicano) is a small storm-troop party led by a noted rabble-rouser named Pedrozo, who is financed and supervised by the Falange. It is one of a handful of groups including the Vanguardia Nacionalista, the Dorados, and the Frente Anti-Communista, financed and controlled by the Falange. These groups all have one commodity they place at the disposal of the major Fascist groups in Mexico: violence. They are scattered all over the country, and are responsible for much disunity in Mexico.

Next to the National Union of Sinarquistas—probably Wilhelm von Faupel's Mexican masterpiece—the Acción Nacional must rank as the most important of the Falange fronts in Mexico.

The Acción Nacional, formed shortly after the Falange appeared in Mexico, is a Fascist party directed by Gómez Morin, one of the three principal lieutenants of Ibañez Serrano, Franco's personal representative in Mexico. It is one of the most "respectable" of the Falange fronts in Mexico, opening its doors only to the wealthier and middle-class elements in the Spanish colonies and business circles of the country.

The program of the Acción Nacional is simple: a corporate state for Mexico and "absolute Hispanidad." It has close relations with some sections of the Spanish Catholic Church, and is heavily subsidized by the Falange Exterior. Gómez Morin is in constant touch with José Maria Peman and Carlos Peroya—two of the leading Falange propagandists in Spain. Under his leadership, the Acción Nacional has planted the Fascist doctrines of the Axis in exceedingly fertile soil. It has become the perfect vehicle for those prosperous pro-Franco Spaniards of Mexico who lacked the physical courage to join the uniformed military ranks of the Falange Española and yet wanted to join the *movimiento* of El Caudillo. Because of its composition, the Acción Nacional is in many respects the most menacing of the Falange groups in all of Mexico. It cannot, however, hold a candle to the National Union of Sinarquistas.

On May 23, 1937, in the provincial city of Leon, a group of idealistic Mexicans, "motivated by the moral, political, and economic disorder precipitated in the Republic, resolved to form one union which would fight for the Christian Social Order." These men, Salvador Abascal, José Olivares Manuel Zermeno, and a third named Urquiza, thereupon formed the National Union of Sinarquistas—which in 1943 has 500,000 devoted members in Mexico.

Thus runs the official Sinarquist version of the movement's actual origins.

The facts, however, are slightly different. While the date is accurate, the three actual organizers of the Sinarquistas were Hellmuth Oskar Schreiter and the brothers José and Alfonso Trueba Olivares. The Sinarquistas' organization papers, as filed with the government, listed these three and Melchor Ortega and Adolfo Maldonado—governor and general secretary of Guanajuato Province—and I. G. Valdivia, a Mexican lawyer, as the founding fathers of Sinarquismo.

Schreiter was anything but a Mexican idealist. A native of Germany, he carried an old, "low-number" German Nazi Party card. His dues to the Nazis were paid up to date on May 23, 1937. By profession Schreiter was a chemical engineer; but for quite some time he had been following other callings in Mexico. He had a job as professor of languages in the State College of Guanajuato, and served as president of the province's Nazi Fichte Bund. His real job in Mexico can be described quite simply: Hellmuth Oskar Schreiter was a Nazi agent.

The Trueba Olivares brothers were powerful Spanish *haciendados* whose great Mexican estates were veritable feudal domains. They were leaders of the Falange Española.

The movement these three men created in the Sinarquistas was a Nazi-Falange legion identical in structure and aims with the Fascist parties of both Germany and Spain. From the beginning, Nazi agents like Paul Klement, Alexander Holste, Otto Hilbert, and Frederico Heinn were assigned to work with the frustrated country lawyers chosen to serve as the nominal heads of the movement. These Nazi agents were ultimately replaced by whole corps of Falange *militantes* and advisers sent from Spain to Mexico.

Like the Nazi and the Falange parties, the Sinarquistas promised all things to all men. If the Sinarquist slogan, "Faith, Blood, and Victory" was more than faintly reminiscent of the beer-cellar mysticism of Nazism and Falingismo, its program was simply a Mexican carbon copy of Fascist platforms the world over.

Because the Sinarquist movement today has 500,000 members below the United States border—and quite a number of devoted followers above the Rio Grande—an examination of its program is in order. It is of importance to all Americans to know exactly why one of the last issues of Coughlin's *Social Justice* to appear before that publication was banned from the United States mails for sedition carried these revealing words:

Advocates of Christian social justice in America, Christian Americans who once dreamed of a national union to effect a 16-point reform, and who have watched the progress of the Christian States headed by Salazar, De Valera, General Franco, and Mussolini, will want to hear further from Mexico's Sinarchists with their "16 principles" of social justice.

The program of Sinarquismo calls, first of all, for a

Corporate State—which is a Portuguese, Italian, and Spanish euphemism for fascism. The official publication of the Sinarquist movement describes this state in these terms:

The members of the same craft or profession must unite, building corporate groups. Over these professional or corporate groups, a superior power must be established, in charge of their mutual relationships and directing them to the common good. Similar professional corporations must unite within themselves, submitting to a supreme authority [a dictator] embodied in the political structure of the Nation.

The "supreme authority" will be so great, according to the official program of the movement, that:

Among us one does not discuss—there is our strength. Take away discipline, take away loyalty to the leader, and Sinarquismo is nothing.

This corporate state, however, must not be an independent or free Mexican state. "Let us return to Spain" is one of the chief slogans of the Sinarquistas. In the April 1939 issue of *El Sinarquista*, an official organ, they declare:

All those who have been concerned with dignifying the life of Mexico, as well as those who have wanted to point the way to the real aggrandizement of Mexico, speak of Spain. To put it more concretely, they speak of the work done by the Mother Country during the historical colonial period. She showed us the road and gave us our bearings. So Mexico must cling to its traditions to find the meaning of its future. Thus, those who feel the desperate uncertainty that today hangs dense and heavy over the nation, want to return to Spain.

The Sinarquist propagandists picture Mexico under Spanish domination as a paradise. The May 15, 1941, issue of *El Sinarquista*, for example, described pre-Republican Mexico in these idyllic terms:

In the eighteenth century Mexico was the largest, the most

cultured, richest, most illustrious, most powerful nation of the Continent.

Spain protected the workers by means of unions and the peasants by means of Indian legislation. All this without any need to resort to strikes and fights, simply because the State knew its duties and protected the worker, considering him a son of God, worthy of the same benefits as the rich.

The government of two hundred years ago was sincere, the present ones are deceitful. In New Spain [Mexico] agriculture was entrusted to the workers and landlords. The King told the landlords that if he permitted them to till the soil and get benefits, it was only so that they would in turn dedicate themselves to improving the material and intellectual lot of the Indians they governed.

El Sinarquista, the weekly paper of the movement which constantly recalls the glories of colonial Mexico, links its lamentations for past glories with one pat explanation for the destruction of Spanish power in Mexico: the United States of America, as part of a Masonic-Protestant conspiracy, subsidized and lent military support to Hidalgo and Juarez and the other liberators of Mexico.

The National Union of Sinarquistas, which clamors constantly for a Christian Social Order, has never presented a complete blueprint of this order to the Mexican people. But among the things they have attacked as being contrary to the concepts of such an order are free non-clerical public schools, social-security legislation, and the land reforms of Cardenas and Madero.

The land problems of the nation contain the key to the power of the Sinarquistas. The varied land-reform programs attempted during the past three decades in Mexico, while distributing vast tracts to thousands of landless peons, have nevertheless left the bulk of the great *haciendas* pretty much intact. The overwhelming majority of the peons are still landless. World upheavals since 1929 have added to the normal hardships of the peons' life in Mexico. While increased misery is the lot of the peasantry, the powerful *haciendados* eat well and have plenty of money, but in the back of their minds is always the fear of further and greater land reforms which may some day affect their own estates.

The Sinarquistas, in the classic Fascist manner, managed to win both the *haciendados* and the landless peons to their banners—just as Hitler won both the landed Junkers and the simple *Bauern*.

The *haciendados* were won over by promises of eternal war on the very principles of land reform. The Sinarquistas denounce land reform as a by-product of the Mexican Revolution and declare, in their manifesto, that "Sinarquismo was born fighting the Revolution: Sinarquismo was born aggressively anti-revolutionary."

The peons were drawn to the Sinarquist ranks by the fervor with which the Nazi-Falange cabal in the movement's leadership exploited their misery. Concretely, the Sinarquistas promise the peons nothing: their appeal is, rather, along the lines of the "every-man-a-king" panaceas offered by Huey Long. Mysticism, violence, marches, military demonstrations—the cheapest sort of circus—are utilized by the Sinarquistas in their work among the landless peons. They convince the peons that the only solution for their problems lies in the destruction of the Republic—and they promise them arms and a chance to kill those Republican evildoers "responsible" for their misery.

Sophisticated Americans living in large cities like New York or Chicago might snicker at the idea of a new empire created out of Mexico and parts of the American southwest. But the Sinarquistas have presented, and successfully, the dream of a new Spanish domain—El Gran Imperio Sinarquista—with a brand new capital city, "Sinarcopolis," built in what are now the plains of Texas. Hitler's dictum about the greatest lies being the ones that gain the widest acceptance has not been lost on the architects of "Sinarcopolis."

The Sinarquist leaders, aided by Falange specialists assigned to work exclusively with the movement, have been giving their followers military training for six years. The Sinarquist peons are too poor to afford uniforms; their only "military dress" is the armbands they wear. But wearing only their everyday clothes and these armbands with the emblem of the movement, Sinarquist storm troops drill with sub-machine guns, rifles, and other arms kindly supplied by the Nazis via Spanish boats.

From time to time the leaders stage a military demonstration intended to bolster the ardor of their troops and to impress all onlookers with the futility of opposing the wave of the future. One of these maneuvers is still talked about: an exercise which, on May 18, 1941, saw some 30,000 well-drilled Sinarquistas "capture" the city of Morelia in forty minutes. Although the staff work was done by Spanish Falangistas, the tactics used in the "storming" of the city were unmistakably German.

Mexico's entry into the war against the Axis has converted these peaceful marches into smaller but violent sorties. Shortly after Mexico became a belligerent, the Sinarquistas became the sponsors of a new organization—the Liga Antibelica Mexicana—which seems to exist on paper only. In the name of this Antiwar League, the Sinarquistas distribute leaflets with calls like the following:

Mexicans! Be alert! Watch out for seducers. Stay out of the war. You have no quarrel with any other country. Mexico of Christ the King and Santa Maria de Guadalupe, you must not be enmeshed in the Jewish International.

When the Mexican lawyer and prominent Catholic layman, Mariano Alcocer, speaking in the name of the Archbishop, called upon all Mexicans in 1942 to unite behind President Comacho in the war effort, the official organ of the Sinarquistas attacked him for condemning Germany rather than Russia and "equally atheistic" England. The Sinarquistas raised the battle call, "Death to compulsory military service." Their prime objective became the hampering of the war effort.

In December 1942 the National Union of Sinarquistas issued a manifesto at their annual congress which proclaimed that the existing "Mexican government is not republican, not representative, and not democratic." It is rather, according to the manifesto, "based on fraud and violence," possessing "all the characteristics of a primitive dictatorship."

This congress set the stage for the series of raids the Sinarquistas began to stage on defenseless towns. Brandishing excellent arms, employing the tactics taught them by the Falangistas who led them on these raids, the Sinarquistas began to assault villages all over northern Mexico. In December 1942 three villages in Zacatecas were attacked by frenzied Sinarquist storm troops who, shouting "Death to compulsory military service and Cardenas," killed some thirty Mexicans, including the mayor of Miguel Auza and his small son. In Nieves, the Sinarquistas—like the old Cristeros—killed the local public-school teacher, Adolfo Lozano. (The Cristeros, a clerico-Fascist movement which reached its peak in 1927, waged unending war against non-clerical teachers.)

These attacks were synchronized with the actions of roving bands of Sinarquist troopers who disrupted railway communications and, like one armed battalion near the city of Pastora, cut and burned hundreds of telephone and telegraph lines. An organized formation of Sinarquistas battled federal troops near Temoac for eight hours before retreating in January 1943.

Since December 1942 these outbreaks have come in sudden waves all over northern Mexico. Early in 1943 the Mexican National Civil Defense Committee delivered a sharp memorandum to the government declaring that "the Axis powers are carrying on their Fifth Column work in Mexico through the leaders of Sinarquismo." The Chamber of Deputies, Mexico's lower house, voted for the dissolution of the National Union of Sinarquistas in January 1943—but the movement is still flourishing.

Early in its existence, the Sinarquist movement started to clamor for the right to settle 100,000 of its followers in the arid waste lands of Lower California. The idea, they said, was to prevent "a hostile foreign power" from annexing the sparsely settled peninsula. Everyone knew that this hostile power was the United States of America. Lazaro Cardenas, then President of Mexico, turned the offer down without a second thought.

The Sinarquistas went on campaigning for the Lower California colony. In the spring of 1941 they repeated their offer to President Avila Comacho. They claimed that they were willing to organize industries and construct certain planned roadworks at half of the amount set aside for this purpose in the Mexican budget. Comacho asked them to submit further details, and a year later granted the Sinarquistas permission to settle a great number of their members on the Peninsula.

Mexicans bitterly refer to lower California, today, as the "Republica Sinarquista." To the shores of this "republic" have come German and Japanese submarines for smuggled shipments of valuable Mexican mercury. Within its borders the Sinarquistas have established a state within a state, and a potential powder keg of far from minute dimensions. The *caudillo* of the Sinarquist settlement is Salvador Abascal, former "supreme leader" of the movement itself. He has been having some difficulties with certain of his followers who accuse him of personally grabbing funds of the colony for his own pocket. The current "supreme leader," Manuel Torres Bueno, has backed Abascal in his present conflict.

Were the Sinarquistas and their influence confined to Mexico alone, their existence would still be cause for alarm. However, Sinarquismo has long since crossed the borders to the north. It has become an American, as well as a Mexican, problem.

The Sinarquist movement has established itself like a cancer in many centers of Mexican population in the United States. Los Angeles, one of Sinarquismo's American strongholds, has a Mexican population of 300,000. Towns in Texas, New Mexico, and Arizona have suddenly discovered that local branches of the Sinarquist organization are terrorizing their Mexican quarters, producing bloodshed and disorder. The offices of an anti-Sinarquist Mexican organization in Chicago were invaded and wrecked by an armed mob of Sinarquistas late in 1942. In places as far north as the Bronx, New York, F.B.I. agents have arrested Sinarquist agents who were inciting loyal Mexican-Americans to treason.

In Los Angeles the movement is so well intrenched that it publishes a special edition of *El Sinarquista*, the official organ of the Mexican parent organization. In Los Angeles the Sinarquistas are aided by notorious figures like Jesús M. Jiminez, whom President Cardenas exiled for Gold-Shirt and Nazi activities, and by members of German and Italian organizations dissolved after Pearl Harbor. The Los Angeles Sinarquist movement has been held directly responsible for a crime wave which broke out among unemployed Mexican youths in 1942, and figured as a prime factor in at least one California murder case.

The California editon of *El Sinarquista* calls for blood. In October 1942 it wrote:

Do not expect our struggle to go smoothly and peacefully. Never gossip about your leaders. Understand that this struggle cannot fail, and that blood and suffering will bring us victory.

An idea of what the American aspects of this "struggle" are can be glimpsed in the resolution passed by the C.I.O. Union Council of Los Angeles, which has many loyal Mexican members. In November 1942, at the request of its Mexican members, the Council made a study of Sinarquist influence in the United States. The result was a resolution characterizing the Sinarquistas as an "evil influence among Mexican workers in the United States whose program coincides with that of Franco's Fascist Spanish regime." The resolution went on to reveal that:

The Sinarquistas are telling the Mexican people in the United

States not to enlist in war activities, such as Civilian Defense and the Red Cross, not to purchase war bonds, and in general not to support this country's war effort, because the "Mexican people have nothing to gain from an Allied victory."

Shortly after this resolution was made public, the Office of War Information started a drive to explain the war aims to the Spanish-speaking peoples of California and the Southwest. The campaign was made necessary by the power of Sinarquist propagandists operating in the United States.

In Mexico the Sinarquistas have been making statements designed for United States consumption only—ambiguous statements which give their defenders in America an opportunity to defend the Sinarquistas as a patriotic and Christian legion interested only in saving the Western Hemisphere from Bolshevism. This subterfuge does not fool bureaus like the F.B.I., however, which recognizes the Sinarquist movement for the Axis instrument it really is.

The Spanish canvas of Mexico grew more crowded than ever in 1939, when the Falange and anti-Falange colonies woke up to find themselves with a new antagonist. He was a handsome, middle-aged gentleman whose passport described him as Luis Gonzago del Villa, the Marqués de Castellon of Spain.

The Marqués announced himself as the official representative in Mexico of the Spanish Monarchist Union. To all who would listen, the titled visitor explained that the Spanish Monarchists had broken with Franco. He and a small group of aides set up shop in Mexico City and started to reveal secrets about Franco Spain and the Falange. Their revelations were often accurate, but never news to the Mexican Government. In brief—they were revealing facts already known.

Although the Monarchists in Spain had every reason to be pleased with Franco, the Marqués declared that they were out to overthrow Franco. Of course, this overthrow would not be followed by the restoration of the "Bolshevik"

Spanish Republic. Perish the thought! What they wanted was the restoration of the old Spanish monarchy.

Seemingly well-supplied with funds, the Marqués ran lavish parties for the Mexican and American society crowds in Mexico City, and special parties for the diplomatic social sets. He established good relations with the Archbishop of Mexico, saw only the very fashionable people, and generally cut quite a figure.

Rumors began to fly about Mexico City after Pearl Harbor that the British Government was backing the Monarchists, that the United States looked upon their cause with favor, and that a Monarchist Spanish government-in-exile was about to be formed. The exiled Spanish Republicans in Mexico became worried, and they started to check up on the Marqués's history.

The Marqués claimed to have been both a Lieutenant-Colonel in the Spanish Army and an aide-de-camp to General Mola. Neither fact showed up in any Spanish military directory of the period. To the Republicans, these omissions were challenges.

Some months later—it was in May 1942—the Republicans presented grave charges to the Mexican authorities. They presented a dossier on the Marqués which indicated that all was not as it seemed. According to this dossier, the Marqués was not Spanish, but a Mexican named Luis Sevilla, whose parents still lived on Mexico City's Calle de Insurgentes. It went on to say that in 1931 Luis Sevilla sailed for Spain while out on bail pending charges of swindling a sum of money from General Limon.

The dossier disclosed that during the Spanish War Sevilla worked in Marseilles as an agent of Franco's Secret Service —posing, during this period, as an agent of the Spanish Monarchist Party. In 1938 Sevilla, carrying letters of safe conduct, visited Premier Juan Negrin in Barcelona, told the Loyalist leader that the Monarchists were against Franco and the Falange, and tried to negotiate a deal whereby the Republic would yield in favor of a monarchy. In 1939 he went to Mexico where, according to the Republicans, he maintained relations with Ibañez Serrano, Franco's official representative.

The dossier on the Marqués caused a blast which reverberated throughout the Spanish-speaking world. The Marqués proceeded to quietly disappear, but in withdrawing he left some troubled suspicions floating over the Mexican capital. Anxious anti-Axis Mexicans and Spanish Republicans wonder if the Marqués really had some of the non-Axis backing he claimed to have.

CHAPTER NINE

Patagonia to Panama

THE PHILIPPINES, Cuba, Puerto Rico, Mexico—the Spanish-speaking countries which have the most direct bearing on the United States—tell the story of Falagismo on the march. But by no means the whole story. If the preceding chapters have dealt with the Falanges of these sectors at greater length, it is because they affect the lives and the security of all North Americans more immediately than, say, the Falanges of Argentina or Peru.

The complete story of the Falange penetration and organization on the South American continent and the Central American republics is being compiled in scores of government bureaus in the Americas. In July 1942 a report on the Falange was submitted to the Venezuelan Congress by a special sub-committee—a report which named many government officials as members of the Falange Española. In Uruguay the Consultive Committee for the Political Defense of the Continent—an official investigating body supported by the democracies of the Americas—continues to accumulate evidence proving that the Falange is growing more dangerous hourly. From all over the hemisphere documentary data continues to pile up—evidence that in the Falange Exterior the nations of the Western Hemisphere are confronted with one of their most pressing problems.

The complete dossier on the Falange in South and Central America lists names of over a million active adherents between Patagonia and Panama. It lists secret arsenals, radio stations, fueling bases, military shock troops, and espionage centers in country after country. It lists names of hundreds of known statesmen and military leaders whose ties to Falangist Spain are far more binding than the formal ties they maintain with Washington. It is, in short, a dossier that cannot be revealed in its entirety until the Axis is completely crushed.

But certain facts that make up this dossier should be known now. Facts like those contained in the report submitted to the Argentine Congress in 1941 by Deputy Raoul Damonte Taborda, chairman of the Congressional Committee investigating Axis activities—the report which the Castillo government has suppressed completely.

The Taborda Report, which covered the Nazi penetration in the Argentine, deals briefly with the Falange Exterior as an instrument of the Nazi Fifth Column in that country.

In this report, Taborda revealed the close link between General von Faupel and his Ibero-American Institute and the Spanish Falange. Speaking of the Ibero-American Institute, Taborda said:

Its real objective: while, on the one hand the Germans build their "aryan minorities" with German Nationals abroad, on the other hand they attempt to stir up the nationalistic sentiments of the masses of Spanish origin.

Taborda maintained that the greatest obstacle to this campaign was the Spanish people themselves.

The proven liberalism of the Iberian residents [in Argentina] constitutes a barrier for the Falangistas who try to group them as a minority.

The report quoted von Faupel as declaring that: "The Panamerican idea is an unsound invention, and it is necessary to oppose to it the idea of an Iberian America. The countries of South and Central America are nearer to Spain than to the United States."

After declaring that "Germany and Italy sponsor the imperialistic policy of Franco," the Taborda report reviewed the career of Germany's regent in Spain—Wilhelm von Faupel. It revealed that, while serving as military counselor to the Argentine Army, von Faupel, "in his teachings about Patagonia . . . advised that it should be abandoned in case of war, considering it defenseless." The report went on to prove that the Nazis are behind the current agitation for the independence of Patagonia—thereby underlining the fact that fully a decade before the Reichstag Fire, Wilhelm von Faupel was playing the Nazi game in Argentina.

The Taborda report declared that Von Faupel's "stay in Spain served, among other things, to found in San Sebastian in May, 1938, a Nazi college for Argentine citizens. From there would come the future directors of the Fascists of the Argentine Republic." In its way, this college is concrete evidence of the complete domination of Franco Spain by the Nazis.

The suppressed Taborda Report minced no words in its analysis of Falangismo:

With Franco, the Spanish Falange triumphed in the Motherland. With the Spanish Falange, the Ibero-American Institute triumphed in Berlin. In exact terms—Nazism. The Falange is a copy of the Nazi Party—a blueprint to such a point that it made a literal translation of all the principles that fascism uses to plant the seeds of propaganda. Nazi technicians take part in their plans, directing them politically. Their work in the Latin-American countries is oriented toward the forming in solid blocks of the great Spanish masses, an attempt to achieve what the Nazis achieved with the German "blood comrades." It is a strong Ibero-Americanism practiced from Berlin. The simplest reading of the program of the Falange tells us to beware of it.

Then the Report goes on to quote points 3, 4, and 5 of the Falange Program (*see* Chapter I) to prove the subversive nature of Falangismo; and then:

The Spanish Falange aspires to set back the clock of history by two centuries, but it will not succeed. But insofar as it is alive, it is a factor of disorder that should be annihilated.

Since Argentina has remained at peace with the Axis, the Argentine Falange is still kept in the background as part of the greater Nazi network. The Nazis not only have organized the Germans there, but also control and finance a number of native Fascist organizations. The Taborda Report, revealing that this Fifth Column operated clandestine radio stations and secret military bases, declared that it works alongside a Nazi-Falange secret service which has up-to-date maps and data on roads, bridges, waterways, and detailed plans of arsenals, bases, electric plants, and vital factories.

Do not believe that we are shouting in the dark [says the historic report, citing the Nazis' own estimate that] 22,000 perfectly disciplined men are ready, plus 8,000 Germans from the Nazi Party, 14,000 members of the German Workers Front, 3,000 Italian Fascists, 15,000 Falangistas, and many others from the Juventud Germano Argentina and many other thousands affiliated with the Alianza Nacionalista Argentina—all ready to strike.

Although Taborda's hard-hitting report was suppressed by the Castillo government, the rising anti-Axis sentiment of the Argentine people themselves has continued to grow since the war began. Despite the diplomatic stand taken by President Castillo, the Argentine Government has had to rely on Franco Spain to an increasing extent in its dealings with the Axis. After Pearl Harbor it was a foregone conclusion that Spain was going to loom larger than ever in the Argentine diplomatic picture. Argentine democrats expected Spain to make a big move early in 1942—but the Spanish Falangista chosen to make this move was a surprise even to those Argentine foes of fascism who had grown used to expect all sorts of insolence from the Nazi puppets in Madrid.

In May 1942 Spain dispatched a trade mission to Buenos Aires—a mission headed by one Eduardo Aunos. If ever a cabal gave away its intentions by a stroke of over-confidence born of arrogance, the men that chose to put Aunos at the head of this mission committed just this blunder.

Aunos was admittedly a man of many talents—but foreign commerce was not one of his specialties. A lawyer by profession, Aunos had served as Minister of Labor in the old Primo de Rivera dictatorship in Spain. After the fall of the de Rivera government, Aunos wrote *The Corporate State* and a number of other books proving that fascism was the solution to the problems of the world.

Early in the course of the von Faupel-Sanjurjo conspiracy to destroy the Spanish Republic, Aunos was admitted into the inner councils of the Spanish conspirators. He joined the Falange in 1935, and was named Counselor of its National Council.

After joining the Falange, Aunos paid the first of his many visits to "La Fragate," a modest villa overlooking the sea at Biarritz, then the main headquarters of German espionage in southern Europe. The secret radio under its tiled roofs broadcast daily instructions to Nazi and Falange agents in Spain, Spanish Morocco, and the Canary Islands between the summer of 1935 and July 19, 1936.

These visits proved both instructive and fruitful. With the German-Italian invasion of Spain in 1936, Eduardo Aunos moved to Paris, where he established himself as the chief of Falange espionage in France at 21 Rue Berri. He remained at this post for two years.

As chief of Falange espionage in France, Aunos made his reports to the Exterior Service of the Falange, then located in Salamanca, Spain. His reports to Salamanca were relayed through another high-ranking officer of Fascist espionage, Colonel Sanz Agero, then stationed near the Franco-Spanish border at Irun. Sanz Agero is today the Spanish Minister to Guatemala.

Aunos did a good job for the Axis in France; so good a job that in 1938 he was appointed Ambassador of Franco Spain to Belgium. His diplomatic duties never were allowed to interfere with his other work. In Belgium Aunos established extremely "cordial" relations with the Rexists—the Belgian Fascist party proven to have been controlled by the Nazis. Eduardo Aunos remained in Belgium until the Germans occupied that little nation in 1940. (The Rexists, who helped ease the way for the Nazis, later sent a token force to fight alongside of the Spanish Blue Legions in the Nazi armies at the Russian front.)

These facts about Eduardo Aunos were not exactly a secret in diplomatic circles when he embarked for Buenos Aires. Despite the reams of publicity put out by Axis and appeasement sources in Argentina—propaganda aimed to make Argentinians believe that the commercial pact between Spain and Argentina would bring great prosperity to the country—Argentine democrats looked to other directions for a line on what had really brought Aunos to Buenos Aires.

While speculation as to the nature of the Falangist mission raged, Argentine Foreign Minister Ruiz Guinazu—whose anti-United Nations feelings are seldom camouflaged—attended a banquet held in Aunos's honor in Buenos Aires. The foreign Minister made a long speech in which he not only praised Aunos and Franco Spain, but also predicted a trade treaty between Spain and Argentina that would be of immeasurable benefit to both countries.

Then word began to leak out that Aunos was in Argentina for the negotiation of a pact of more than merely commercial significance. While Aunos and the other Falangistas of his mission met with scores of government and political leaders, careless attachés of the Spanish Legation in Buenos Aires took to boasting in cafés and drawing rooms about a new Madrid-Buenos Aires airline, about a cultural pact with trick hidden clauses, and about a mysterious about-to-be-established Argentine free port in Spain.

A special Spanish commission prepared a complete memorandum on the planes of the war-grounded Italian Lati Air Line—especially the transports "interned" in Brazil after the Rio Conference. Papers in Madrid spoke out about using these planes in the establishment of an air line linking Spain and Argentina.

Falangist papers in Buenos Aires like the *Diario Español* and the *Correo de Galicia* began to paint vivid pictures of the great benefits—both economic and moral—Argentina would derive after the trade pact was signed. They went to great pains to point out that the wheat rotting in the warehouses, the corn being used as fuel in locomotives, and the millions of pounds of unsold beef in the packers' storage houses were being wasted because the United States was utilizing the war as a device to destroy Argentine agriculture. On the other hand, ran the Falange propaganda line, immortal Spain, the great Mother Country which had slain the twin dragons of liberalism and communism, not only needed Argentine agricultural products to sustain herself, but also had the ships and the gold to pay for them. And as for Argentina's growing shortages of manufactured goods and machinery—why, Spain would probably be able to barter manufactures for food.

This was the official line, and to make it stick, Aunos began to flood the Argentine with imported Spanish lecturers, movies, and entertainers. For the head of a commercial mission from a land ravaged by starvation to a nation with a tremendous food surplus, Eduardo Aunos exhibited a surprising lack of desire to get a pact signed as quickly as possible. The negotiations seemed to drag on for months on end.

Perhaps, if Aunos's sole mission in Buenos Aires was the trade agreement, the pact would have been drawn and signed within a month of the start of the talks. The truth about the Aunos mission was that its chief was concerned primarily with the Falanges of South America first and the commercial treaty second.

Aunos had arrived in Buenos Aires with great powers delegated to him by the Falange Exterior National Council in Madrid. During his entire stay in Argentina—and he did not return to Spain until October—he was acting as von Faupel's Extraordinary Inspector General of the Falange Exterior in the Americas. Most of his time was spent with delegates of the Falanges of Latin America and Argentina. He reviewed the reports they had to make on the Falanges in their respective countries and gave them orders both for their groups and for the Spanish diplomatic legations which worked with their groups.

The Aunos mission played its cards with a finesse that astounded all observers. In August 1942, for example, Aunos saw to it that Argentine President Ramon Castillo received the Grand Collar of the Order of Isabel—one of Spain's rarest decorations. After the decoration was received, Aunos ordered the press attaché of the Spanish Embassy in Buenos Aires, José Ignacio Ramos, to hold regular joint meetings with the envoys of Germany, Italy, and Japan—sessions at which the all-Axis propaganda drive was planned and coordinated.

Not until September 8, 1942, was the Aunos-Guinazu pact finally signed. By the time it was ready for the signatures of pro-Franco Argentine Ambassador to Madrid Escobar and Spanish Foreign Minister Gómez Jordana, it had become both a trade and a cultural pact.

The text of the agreement was never made public. But as in earlier agreements between Franco Spain and Argentina, the Iberian Axis nation promised to barter manufactured goods for Argentine grain and beef. In January 1941 Argentina had sent 350,000 tons of corn to Spain—which, in payment, was to deliver an unspecified amount of iron and steel. Argentina is still waiting for the metals. A later barter deal became a cash deal after Spain had received Argentine cattle and beef—and paid for them out of the earnings of the Compañía Argentina de Electricidad, subsidiary of Chade, the Spanish utility trust.

Spain, whose exports of food and minerals to Germany are now at an all-time high, is today receiving vast shipments of Argentine food under the terms of the new pact. The projected air line between Madrid and Buenos Aires, while covered in the treaty, has not yet been established. It has, instead, become another of the aces in the Spanish blackmail deck; an ace the Axis will not hesitate to play whenever further concessions are sought from the democracies. The cultural angles of the pact were made quite plain on October 12, 1942—Columbus Day.

The Falange celebrates Columbus Day in Latin America as El Día de la Raza—the Day of the Race. In Buenos Aires there were many celebrations, official, religious, and political. Foreign Minister Ruiz Guinazu, in a speech broadcast to Spain as well as over the Argentine networks, exchanged sentiments with Madrid short-wave speakers in a special two-way radio celebration staged by both countries.

Guinazu pledged that Spain and Argentina, "which find themselves traveling the same road and which have parallel interests," would be bound by still closer bonds—bonds, he declared, that would be created "not with words but with deeds."

President Castillo celebrated the day by attending a solemn ceremony devoted to extolling Franco Spain and the concept of Hispanidad—which calls for the return of Argentina to the Spanish Empire.

Later in the evening, two great Fascist rallies were held in Buenos Aires, and the speeches made at these rallies were broadcast over the radio to the entire country. The larger one was held by the Alianza de la Juventud Nacionalista, the Fascist party organized and backed by the Germans and the Falangistas. Its leader, anti-Semitic General Juan Bautista Molina, had been formally charged with treason by the late President Ortiz, and his trial was still pending at the time.

Flanked by Argentine and Falange flags draped around signs reading "HOMAGE TO SPAIN," Molina delivered a violently anti-Semitic, pro-Axis, and anti-United States speech that had his frenzied 18,000 followers cheering and giving the stiff-arm Fascist salute between paragraphs. Among the things assailed by Molina and other Fascists at the Columbus Day rallies were Pan-Americanism, Jewish Imperialists, the United Nations, liberalism, Roosevelt, Sumner Welles, and the Atlantic Charter.

These speeches were all broadcast. But the radio microphones were absent from one other meeting held in Buenos Aires that night—a meeting that was held only after a prolonged fight with the government for permission to stage it. Not only were its speeches not broadcast, but the papers were forbidden to report their texts the next day. This meeting was staged by labor and liberal organizations of Buenos

Aires to affirm the pro-United Nations sentiments of the Argentinian people. Its speakers included Deputy Raoul Damonte Taborda, Colonel Francisco Galan of the Spanish Republican Army, and many Argentine labor leaders.

The press did not report the keynote speech delivered by Pedro Chiaranti, the noted Argentine labor leader, who shouted:

We in Argentina can aid the Spanish people by fighting the Spanish Falange and by forcing our country to take the side of the United Nations against the Axis Powers.

Shortly after the Columbus Day celebrations, Argentine Deputy Juan Antonio Solari, who succeeded Taborda as chairman of the congressional committee investigating anti-democratic activities, made a report which explained the cultural and political results of the Aunos mission more fully.

Solari exposed the fact that the Fascist parties of Argentina were now relying more than ever before on the façade of Falangist Spain as a front for their attacks on the democracies. In his report, which was neatly squelched by the Castillo administration, Solari charged that the Spanish Ambassador, José Coll Mirambell, was supervising the activities of the Falangist Casa de España—ordered closed by President Ortiz in May 1939.

The Deputy further revealed that the Spanish ships which crossed the ocean to take on cargoes of Argentinian grain and beef brought not manufactured goods but tons of Falangist propaganda to Argentina. This propaganda was all openly pro-Axis. These, then, were the benefits Argentina received from the Aunos mission—propaganda and increased Falangist activities. (Aunos himself was rewarded handsomely by von Faupel for his mission: He is now Minister of Justice in the Spanish Cabinet.)

The complete dossier on the Falange in the Americas would not overlook Argentina's democratic neighbor to the west, the Republic of Chile. Here the strength of the Chilean labor movement and the organized democratic political parties has forced the Falange to keep its thirty-five Chilean cells well under cover.

The Falange in Chile is confined largely to the southern part of the country, which has an enormous German population. The anti-Falange sentiments of the Chilean people are so marked that after Pearl Harbor Madrid sent a confidential memorandum ordering all Spanish Falangistas in Chile to seek Chilean citizenship and to cease appearing in public in the Falange blue shirts.

The bombing of Pearl Harbor, however, made the Falange and the Spanish diplomatic network in Chile very important to the Axis. In January 1942 the Falange sent José Gonzalez Honares from Spain to Chile. Honares, the chief liaison man between the Japanese and the Falange, was ordered to Chile to take over the work of the Japanese on that west-coast South American bastion.

Today, Honares and the Spanish diplomats are the chief Axis agents in Chile, but their efforts are not made any easier by one of the most vigilantly democratic peoples in the world.

The anti-Falangist, anti-Axis feelings of the Chilean people are so pronounced that in at least one instance known to United Nations Intelligence services the Falange in Chile has been forced to distribute Spanish propaganda through the diplomatic machinery of a certain Latin-American legation in Santiago de Chile.

Brazil takes up a surprising amount of space in the complete dossier on the Falange in South America.

Late in 1940, the Falange in Madrid announced the formation of the All-Iberian Confederation of Portuguese and Spanish Falange parties. The organization was a joint committee of the Fascist parties of both Portugal and Spain, and as such had governmental backing in both Lisbon and Madrid.

With the launching of the Confederation, Spain sent a

new ambassador to Brazil. He was Raimundo Fernandez Cuesta, the former chief of the Falange in Spain and one of its earliest members. Although sadly lacking in experience as a diplomat, Cuesta needed little coaching in the theory and technique of operating a Falange Fifth Column. Before Brazil entered the war, and prior to the arrival of the Aunos mission to Argentina, Cuesta directed all South American Falange activities from his embassy in Rio de Janiero.

The Falange leader not only managed the continental Falange Exterior affairs, but he also set up an organization in Portuguese-speaking Brazil which added to his laurels in Madrid. Cuesta had five secretaries in the Embassy. They were all trained Falange officials who, protected by their diplomatic passports, aided Cuesta in his tasks of propaganda and organization.

Cuesta camouflaged the Hispanidad line in Brazil. Instead, he appealed to the Portuguese origin of Brazilians by linking Salazar, Dictator of Portugal, and Franco as the joint chiefs of a great Iberian empire-to-be. The All-Iberian Confederation became Cuesta's wedge in Brazil, and he used it with telling effect.

From Rio, Cuesta set the Falange propaganda line for the entire continent through *Nueva España*, the Falangist paper published at 70 Avenida Porto Alegre. Through this paper and through news furnished the Berlin radio by the Spanish Embassy at Rio—news the Berlin radio rebroadcast to all of Latin America—Cuesta kept Falange propaganda going along the paths determined in von Faupel's Madrid office. The great bulk of Ambassador Cuesta's large staff was composed of Falangist inspectors who maintained liaison between their chief and the Falanges of neighboring countries.

When Brazil broke with Germany, one of Cuesta's five secretaries, Manuel Montero, was entrusted with the mission of taking confidential documents of the closed German Embassy to Spain for trans-shipment to Berlin. He sailed on the *Cabo de Hornos* in May 1942, just as Aunos was arriving in Argentina.

The war forced all of the Falanges in South America to

pull in their horns. In Brazil all members of the small but influential section of the Falange Española were given copies of the confidential circular which was published in Madrid and sent to the Spanish legations in Latin America. The Brazilian edition of the circular, which bore the heading, "Extraordinary Bulletin of Instructions," said, in part:

Complying with orders received from our Superior Chiefs, because of special difficult circumstances that have arisen and affected our propaganda in America . . . all work will be interrupted until further notice. Persecuted by certain governments at the service of International Jewry, we must forbid all visits to our meeting places, even if they remain open for purely commercial ends. The following orders have been received—

1. Avoid visiting the Embassy, and only in cases of absolute necessity call for information at Department 142. Any other consultation should be made personally with the chief of the group to which each member belongs. Never use the telephone, not even for discreet conversation.

2. Keep careful reserve in dealing with natives of the country [Brazil], who did not rate our complete confidence before this time, because they may now become very dangerous to the sacred cause of the Empire with the new change of the tide [Brazil's declaration of war].

3. Maintain the spirit of action, guiding it principally through the Portuguese feeling in opposition to the fluctuating Pan-Americanism. Beware of employing the terms Hispanidad and Hispanismo—words that may hurt the extreme sensitivities of these [Brazilian] people.

These are instructions received from the Consejo de Hispanidad, and should not be mentioned in any conversations. If others quote these instructions, you must affirm that it [the Consejo de Hispanidad] has been dissolved. . . .

6. Never forget the spirit of sacrifice of the Falange Española, nor the punishment that is reserved for all the traitors or cowards who might compromise in any way—such as answering police questions or exhibiting copies of this bulletin, which must be returned within three days of its receipt.

The slogan "Attack for Victory" is now changed to the new slogan, "Discretion for Victory." . . .

This circular is worth noting for the clear way in which it identifies the Spanish Embassy with the subversive activities of the Falange Exterior. Note, too, the reference to "International Jewry" as being the sole force opposed to the Axis in the war, and the line about avoiding the usual Falange meeting places "even if they remain open for purely commercial ends." Many Spanish business houses in Latin America act as headquarters for Falange cells, and the Spanish firms in Brazil were no exception.

Brazil's declaration of war on Germany and Italy not only forced the Brazilian Falange to retrench, but also made it inadvisable for Spanish Ambassador Cuesta to operate out of Rio. The Axis was afraid to risk having him interned if the United Nations ever widened their war front to take in all Axis nations, including Spain. One of the jobs assigned to the Aunos mission was making Cuesta's retreat from the Western Hemisphere an orderly one.

The center of Falange activities on the continent was shifted to Argentina. Shortly after Aunos completed his mission, Cuesta was recalled from Brazil and named Spanish Ambassador to Rome. In the general shifting of leaders and headquarters, one other significant change was made. Colonel Manuel de la Sierra, attached to the Spanish Embassy in Washington, was transferred to the legation at Buenos Aires. Sierra is one of the key figures in the Spanish Secret Service, and his new assignment was made as part of a broad master-plan for all of the American nations.

One of the most amazing parts of the dossier on the Falange in South America is the section dealing with Peru. A prominent Peruvian writer put his finger on the strange power of Falangismo recently.

Falangismo speaks for feudalism as an ideal. In Peru, where feudalism is not an ideal but a bitter reality, Falangismo therefore found fertile soil. On the Peruvian *hacienda*, the *hacendado* is All Powerful. Each *hacienda* represents, in spirit, a perfect Falangist state in miniature. It is therefore not surprising to find the Falange strongest among the great landowners and their spokesmen in the press and the government.

The power of Falangismo was felt in Peru very early during the course of the Spanish War. José Maria Arguedas and Manuel Moreno, two Peruvian writers, organized a meeting at the University in Lima and spoke up in favor of the Spanish Republic. They were immediately arrested and kept incommunicado for six months in prison before protests from all over Latin America forced the government to release them. After that, there were no open anti-Falange manifestations in Peru.

The country's "Two Hundred Families" vied among themselves to see who could do the most for the Axis cause during the Spanish War. When Eugenio Montes, one of the most important Falangist propagandists, visited Peru during this war, he had limousines and villas put at his disposal wherever he went. Montes returned to Peru to lecture after the Axis triumph. He was followed by José Maria Peman, the Falangist writer whose lectures were attended by Peru's President, Manuel Prado, and other leading Peruvian dignitaries.

The man generally credited with being the real leader of the Falange in Peru is José de la Riva Aguero, one of the country's wealthiest citizens. He likes to be known by his Spanish title, the Marqués de Aulestia—a title he had revalidated in Spain in 1934. Riva Aguero is one of Peru's leading intellectuals, and in both the press and on the public platform he is the most outspoken exponent of Falangismo and Hispanidad.

To the Peruvian Falange, whose slogan is, "Spiritual Unity between Spain and Peru," Riva Aguero has been an intellectual and financial tower of strength. He visited Spain in 1940, and on his return in 1941 was quoted in the magazine *Tourismo* as declaring that Falangismo "is necessary for the life of Peru . . . the movement in Spain is an inspiration for all of us."

Riva Aguero's ties with the Japanese in Peru—where they formed the most powerful Fifth Column in the country—were as close as were his ties with Franco.

When Peru, at the last minute, cast its diplomatic lot with the United Nations, the hysterically anti-United States organ of the Peruvian Falange, *Unidad*, was suspended by the government. This, however, was little more than a gesture—because the most powerful voice of the Falange also happens to be one of the largest papers in Peru, *El Comercio*.

There are many points of similarity between *El Comercio*, of Lima, and Havana's *Diario de la Marina*. Like the *Diario's* Pepin Rivero, *El Comercio's* guiding genius, Carlos Miro Quesada Laos, also won the Maria Moors Cabot Prize for Journalism in 1941—the prize awarded to the editor who does the most to cement North and South American friendship. Like the *Diario*, *El Comercio* also jumped on the Franco bandwagon with the first shots of the Spanish War. Like Pepin Rivero, Miro Quesada also enjoyed good relations with Axis diplomats other than those of Spain.

He was, in fact, violently opposed to Peru's diplomatic break with Japan. "There is no harm at all in the Japanese being in Peru," he told an American magazine writer about a week before Pearl Harbor. He also told this American that, "There is nothing like the progressive character of National Socialism. However, Falangismo is even a step higher than National Socialism."

During the Spanish War, Miro Quesada visited the Franco side as correspondent for his paper. *El Comercio* has long preached Hispanidad and Falangismo, and if Miro Quesada's detractors sometimes describe him as "Franco's Unofficial Goebbels," they can hardly be blamed or accused of exaggerating the role of *El Comercio*.

In addition to his journalistic writings, Miro Quesada also wrote a book based on his interviews with Hitler, Franco, Salazar, and Mussolini. Needless to say, this book—which bore an introduction written by Riva Aguero—had nothing but praise for these dictators. For Miro Quesada likes dictators as much as he hates Spanish Republicans, whom he calls by one name only: "Reds." He was the man most influential in keeping the Spanish Republican refugees out of Peru. His uncle is one of the intimate advisers of President Prado.

The Falange and its partisans in Peru abound in such colorful personalities as Riva Aguero and Miro Quesada. There is also, for example, Raoul Parras Barrenechea, who is noted both as a toreador and as an essayist. He served as an attaché in the Peruvian Legation in Franco Spain, where he spent a good deal of time doing research in the archives of the Council of the Indies, the historical predecessor of the Council of Hispanidad.

Upon his return to Peru, Barrenechea published a work based on "new material" he had found in the ancient archives—a book proving that Conquistador Pizarro was not a murderous looter but a shining and kindly knight of Christian brotherhood. The unique thesis of the book took hold in Peru's wealthy Spanish colony, but Peruvian democrats laughed and coined a nickname for the author: "Pizarro the Good."

Barrenechea now holds a post in the Ministry of Foreign Affairs. An intimate of Riva Aguero's, he is openly anti-United States and a fervent propagandist of Hispanidad.

Another important member of Riva Aguero's social set is Raoul Ferrero Rebagliatti, a Peruvian lawyer of Italian descent. An admirer of Mussolini, Rebagliatti once tried to found a "real" Fascist party in Peru. He praises Riva Aguero as a "master of Peruvian youth." In 1941 he delivered a famous pro-Franco lecture to the foreign students (most of them from the United States) at the summer school of the University of San Marcos in Lima.

Riva Aguero's close friend Hoyos Osores, editor of the daily *La Prensa* of Lima, is an outspoken pro-Falangist.

El Comercio and *La Prensa* are addressed to adults, but the Falange message is served to Peruvians from the moment they begin to read. An official textbook used in all Peruvian schools describes Franco as a savior of Christianity "against the assaults of Jewish Communism."

Now that Peru has broken diplomatic ties with the Axis nations, Spain has taken over all Axis representation. Franco's Ambassador, D. Pablo Churruca, is active in public functions day in and day out. His words and public activities are breathlessly recorded in the openly pro-Falangist press of the country, to whom he is a statesman of world importance.

Peru's own envoys to Spain have been as ardently for Franco and Hispanidad as Churruca. In 1940 Peru's Ambassador was Ex-President Benavides, who was decorated by Franco and given a banquet by Spanish military officers in Barcelona. He now represents Peru in Argentina. Pedro Irogoyen, who succeeded Benavides as Ambassador to Spain, made a Columbus Day address in 1941 in which he declared, "The Spanish movement should serve as an example for South America."

These personalities are a reflection of the strength of Falangismo in a country whose importance must never be underestimated. The Falange itself was never large in Peru —it never had to be. The Axis relied on the huge Japanese and Italian Fifth Columns for manpower there.

Since Spain took over the Axis diplomatic front in Peru, the Falange has increased in importance. Shortly after Pearl Harbor, Antonio Luis Escobar, a high-ranking officer in the Spanish Secret Service (SIM) arrived in Peru from Spain to serve the Axis in ways that need no description. He is still there.

Peru's impoverished neighbor, Ecuador, is no less afflicted with the Falange virus. As in Peru, the Falange did not become the dominant Axis front until after Pearl Harbor. The Italian Army had a contract to train the Ecuadorian officers. The largest school in Quito was the German Collegio Aleman. And the Japanese had a large hand in the economic destinies of the country.

Because of this all-Axis front, the most important organ of Falangismo, *El Debate*, was financed not only by Spain but also by Italy, Germany, and Japan. It was run by Mariano Suarez Veintemilla, now a deputy in the nation's Congress, and Senator Moises Luna—a statesman who denounced the Rotarian Congress held at the University in Quito as a "Masonic-Jewish" conspiracy against Ecuador. *El Debate*, like the Falangist organs *Hoja Popular* and *Crisol*, was finally banned in May 1942.

Since Ecuador's diplomatic break with the Axis powers, the Nazi Transocean News Service, which reached all Ecuadorean papers free of charge, has been replaced by the Franco news agency, EFE—which also furnishes a free service. The EFE wires go to all papers in Ecuador with the exception of anti-Fascist publications like *El Día* and *La Defensa*.

Before Pearl Harbor, the Nazis maintained a number of clandestine radio stations in Ecuador. Many of them are now operated by the Falange.

Ecuador's wealthy Spanish Colony is as fervently Falangist as that of Peru. Nevertheless, in 1940 the Falange worked with the Japanese and the Nazis to stir up still another war growing out of the century-old border controversy between Peru and Ecuador.

Little was said in the press of the world about this war. Described in most North American papers as a typical minor "border dispute," it was very much of a real modern war during the months that it raged. The von Faupel- and Japanese-trained Peruvian Army finally crushed the Italian-trained Ecuadoreans—but at a cost in human lives far beyond the space they won in the headlines. It was a war which saw Italian Caproni bombers in the hands of the Peruvians blot out whole villages, and such bombings spell death even in unpublicized wars. (Italy sold to both sides.)

When the shooting·was over, and the disputed territory securely in the hands of Peru, the Falange in Spain sent a delegation of prominent Falangistas to Peru to commemorate the 450th anniversary of Columbus. The most distinguished of the delegates, who came as guests of the Peruvian Government, was the Marquesa de la Conquista, descendant of Pizarro—a fitting note, since the prime purpose of the delegation from Spain was to lend moral authority to the Peruvian conquest. This feat they accomplished by citing ancient maps of the Council of the Indies which justified Peru's border claims.

More than Peru and Ecuador were involved in this war, however. It was nothing more than a well-timed dress rehearsal of the hell the Nazis are prepared to unleash in all of Latin America.

Border wars, military uprisings, civil wars, fake minority movements like that of Patagonia—all these are weapons, in Latin America, against the United Nations and particularly against the United States. The Axis aim in Latin America is to increase the war-borne hardships to acute misery, and then convert this misery to chaos—a chaos that will have a telling effect on the war effort of every American nation.

Spain became a Nazi colony as a result of a fake military uprising organized by the Germans. Today Spain is nearer to many Latin American countries than the United States. And the Nazi-run Spanish Falange is active and large in these countries. It will cost the Germans next to nothing in men and materials to stir up serious disturbances in Latin America through the Falange Española.

The all-over dossier on the Falange in Latin America gets very hot when it touches Colombia, the strategic land which flanks the Panama Canal on the South.

Here the Falange pattern seems like a carbon copy of Cuba's. As in Cuba, Falangismo came to Colombia's wealthy Spanish Colony and to one of the country's largest publishers long before the Falange could send an agent from Spain to Bogotá to formally organize the Falange Exterior branches.

The two dominant figures in the Franco camp in Colombia in 1936 were Laureano Gómez and Hilario Rajul. Gómez publishes the influential daily, *El Siglo,* one of the most violently anti-United States papers published anywhere in the world, including Falangist Madrid. He is also the leader of the Conservative Party of Colombia. Rajul, a Spanish citizen in his fifties, is a well-to-do Bogotá business man.

Aided by other Spaniards and wealthy Colombians, Gómez and Rajul kept the Franco fires burning brightly until the end of 1937, when the Falange in Spain sent Gines de Albareda to Bogotá (the Falangistas always used the ancient name of Sante Fé de Bogotá for the Colombian capital) to organize the Falange Exterior cells.

Laureano Gómez gave the visiting Falange agent a lavish banquet, at which the young men of the Caro Academy acted as Albareda's guard of honor. For weeks, Albareda sat as the guest of honor at a series of dinners and receptions. Special Masses were said in his honor at the San Ignacio and other Spanish Churches. Were Albareda a less cynical fellow, he might have imagined that Colombia was ripe for a Falangist uprising of its very own.

But the average Colombian, and even the average Spaniard in Colombia, was not at all like Laureano Gómez. Albareda sensed the anti-Falangist feeling of the Colombian majority and therefore, in setting up the Falange Exterior structure, he gave it the name of "Círculo Nacionalist Español."

When Albareda tried to speak at meetings to which the general public had been invited, he met with near disaster so often that he decided to confine his orations to more exclusive gatherings. At least, at closed meetings attended only by Falangistas and their sympathizers, he could make himself heard.

At one of these meetings, Albareda heard Laureano Gómez make a speech that brought the house down. It was an impassioned address which ended with these tingling words:

All Spain, coming forward as the solitary fighter for Christian culture, has taken the vanguard step of all nations of the occident in the reconstruction of the Empire of Hispanidad, in whose Falanges we inscribe our names with indescribable joy.

We bless God because he has allowed us to live through this epoch of unforeseen transformation and because we are able to exclaim with a cry that comes forth from our deepest feelings—*Arriba España*, Catholic and Imperial!

As he sounded this tocsin call, his face purple, sweat pouring into his tear-filled eyes, Laureano Goméz snapped to attention and flung his hand up in the stiff-arm Fascist salute—the *brazo en alto*.

Albareda led the applause which greeted this speech. It told him that the time had come to begin circulating among the wealthy Spaniards of Colombia to collect large sums for the cause of El Caudillo. He had little difficulty in raising a most respectable war chest. The Falange organized and the money collected, Gines de Albareda decided to take his leave.

Before sailing for Spain, Albareda appointed Antonio Valverde to the post of chief of the Colombian Falange.

His pockets heavy with the money he had raised in Colombia, Albareda said farewell to the leading Falangists of Bogotá with the classic *brazo en alto* and a manly embrace for each man. But according to an account published in Buenos Aires quoting *El Liberal* of Bogotá, the money proved to be more powerful than the ideology of Nueva España. Gines de Albareda was there accused of personally pocketing every penny of the moneys donated to El Caudillo by the Colombian Falangistas. He was never sent abroad on a confidential mission again.

Valverde tried to make the Falange over into an ascetic religious order. He soon gave up this tack. After the triumph of Franco, Valverde had a series of arguments over the work of the Falange with the first Franco Minister to Colombia. He resented this interference so much that he turned the affairs of the Colombian Falange over to his assistant, Luis Roldan, and went to Spain to seek justice. One of the results of this trip was a letter to Roldan (quoted in Chapter I) promising that the Minister would soon be placed under the orders of the Falange chief.

The letter was no idle boast. Shortly after Roldan received it, the Spanish Legation in Bogotá received a new secretary, one Ónos de Plandolit. Plandolit was new to the diplomatic business, but he had grown up with the Falange in Spain, and he had the implicit confidence of men like General von Faupel and the highest-ranking Spaniards in the Falange.

Plandolit became the absolute chief of the Legation, and it was he who restored order to the Falange in Colombia. He became, in effect, the actual chief of the Falange, and remained in Bogotá until his post-Pearl Harbor transfer to the Spanish Legation in Panama.

In Bogotá, Plandolit busied himself with more than merely Colombian affairs. During his tenure the Spanish Legation was taking advantage of the Pan-American Postal Convention franking privileges to send propaganda to the United States and other countries. The following excerpt, taken from a bulletin the Spanish Legation in Colombia sent to New York City via franked mail, is a fair sample of Plandolit's work.

. . . Roosevelt . . . will do all he can to aid in the defeat of Hitler and of the European people who are fighting for their liberty against Bolshevik barbarism and the sordid egoism of the democratic, Jewish, and Protestant plutocracies.

During the Spanish War, Valverde started a campaign to raise funds for the Axis forces. The campaign—which was announced as a "permanent" one—was assisted by a permanent announcement appearing daily in Gómez's *El Siglo*. This announcement, which bore the heading, in big capital letters, "VIVA FRANCO! ARRIBA ESPAÑA!" called for funds for Franco and published honor lists of those who contributed the money.

Gómez's fervor for Falangismo had very interesting, if

pathological, roots. He not only hated the Spanish Republic but, with equal venom, the Republic of Colombia as well. During the Spanish War, the Bogotá publisher found a way of addressing an impassioned plea to Franco personally, a plea for aid in overthrowing the government of Colombia. Franco answered this request with a definite promise of military aid—after the Spanish Republic was destroyed.

Franco's solemn promise made Gómez work all the harder for the triumph of the Falange in Spain. The zeal of the Colombian Falange's most fervent member did not diminish when Luis Roldan succeeded Valverde as chief of the Falange in 1940. Gómez gave Roldan the full support he had shown Valverde.

Roldan remained chief of the Colombian Falange until August 1941, when he was transferred to Panama—one of the most important Falange concentration points in the world. On December 18, 1941, he sailed from Panama to Havana on a Chilean liner, the *Imperial*. He was in Havana to await passage on board a C. T. E. steamer bound for Spain. But Roldan's movements in Havana Falange circles aroused the suspicions of the Cuban Secret Police, who were in possession of letters Roldan had sent to Alejandro Villa-nueva in 1940, when Villanueva was the Inspector General of the Falange in the Americas.

The Cuban police arrested Roldan on January 2, 1942. He was tried ten days later, but was acquitted—largely by his promise to take the next boat out of Cuba.

Roldan's arrest, however, led to the revelation of many of the secrets of the Colombian Falange, for he had been carrying a case of important documents and a file of his correspondence to Spain when the Cuban police arrested him.

The documents included copies of orders Roldan had sent to Dario Cuadrado, the landowner and textile magnate who succeeded him as chief of the Colombian Falange; orders received by Roldan from Spain; letters linking German and Italian diplomats with Falangist activities in Latin America; and assorted documents relating to Falangist activities in Bolivia, Costa Rica, Puerto Rico, El Salvador, and other Latin-American nations. There were official communications to Roldan from Valverde—then his Falange chief—sent from Venezuela, Panama, Germany, England, France, and Spain. Roldan had kept a complete file—including copies of every letter he sent as a Falangist officer.

Among these, as a starter, was the letter he had sent to Valverde in Barranquilla, Colombia, in December 1938, a letter which contained these sentences:

I already went to the Italian Legation to take leave in your name and to tell them to cable to Caracas your arrival there. The [legation] secretary promised to do so.

A later letter (the italics are mine) from Roldan to Valverde was mailed when the then-chief of the Colombian Falange was in Zaragoza, Spain. It said, in part:

. . . As I announced to you in my previous letter, I have completely organized the Auxilio Social and to that section I have dedicated number four and five of our *Review*. . . . I have distributed the girls in groups as well as the boys, and I have ordered them to make a collection among all the friends and businessmen of Bogotá who sympathize with our Movement. . . . Immediately after, that is, on the first Sunday of March, we will hold a grand bazaar, which surely will be held in the Plaza de los Martires. . . . I am giving a religious character to the organization of this Bazaar to collect funds for the reconstruction of the churches demolished in Spain. . . . In this manner I believe I will achieve a greater success, since I will have the collaboration of almost all the religious orders which I warned in advance, and will get the support of all the Colombian people who in their inner self are religious even though they take a liberal pose. . . . All this, as it is natural, I will manage, and I will distribute the women of the Auxilio Social in the various booths, *and the funds, I don't have to even tell you, will be exclusively for the Falange*. . . .

This letter speaks volumes for the sincerity of the Falange's noisy crusade for Catholicism, and for the real character of the Auxilio Social, the Falange's own "relief" society.

But the most sensational document of the Roldan collection was a copy of a report Roldan sent to the National Delegation of the Falange Exterior in Spain on February 15, 1939. This report said, in part (the italics are mine):

The circle of conferences that I initiated here I had to stop because of serious reasons which exist in this country [Colombia]. Here the political atmosphere is heavy now, for among the Conservatives themselves there have been splits because some, *among them Laureano Gómez, wish violent or revolutionary attitudes . . . these gentlemen have adddressed themselves to our victorious Caudillo [Franco] requesting help to accomplish in this country a revolution similar to ours [in Spain], and the Caudillo has answered them that they shall have everything they wish after our war finishes. . . .* Under these conditions the officials of the government here have thought that these activities are being carried on through the Falange and ordered a raid on our office by the Secret Police.

It was a bombshell in Colombia. Here was a signed admission from the former chief of the Colombian Falange that Laureano Gómez had petitioned Franco for aid in overthrowing democracy in Colombia!

El Liberal, the newspaper of Colombia's present President, Alfonso Lopez, published the Roldan-Valverde-Falange Exterior documents in full in February 1942. The nation was shocked—and the Colombian police began a series of raids on the homes and offices of Falangistas and Franco partisans.

The raids produced some amazing results. At the home of Dario Cuadrado, the Falange chief of Colombia, police found orders sent from Madrid and signed by José Gimenez Rosado, the Secretary General of the Falange Española. There were also copies of orders sent by Cuadrado to regional heads of the Falange in Colombia, and their reports to him. When questioned by the police, Cuadrado admitted that Laureano Gómez attended secret meetings of the Falange.

At the home of Hilario Rajul, the police were insulted by the Spanish Falangista's wife, who called them "Red Communists" and similar names. While the detectives were at Rajul's files, Irwin Goldtucker, the German chauffeur of the Spanish Legation, arrived at the Rajul household and cursed them out roundly. They were about to arrest him when he whipped out his Spanish diplomatic passport and flaunted it in their faces.

The raid produced one document that shook the country. It revealed that, prior to Pearl Harbor, the Falange and the Conservative Party had formed a working alliance, and that a Falangist official traveled throughout the Republic (with all expenses paid by publisher Gómez's party) and converted the Conservative Party into a replica of the Falange. The name of this Falangist agent was revealed to be Arturo Rajul—son of Hilario and Chancellor of the Spanish Legation.

Rajul's tour was followed by a circular letter sent to all chiefs of the Conservative Party in Colombia on December 20, 1941, announcing the start of a new drive for power.

The raids of February 1942 served only to make the Falangistas more discreet in Colombia. The Nazis have very good reasons to keep the Falange functioning at top efficiency in Colombia. The reason can be best expressed in two words—Panama Canal.

The Darien Mountains, between Colombia and Panama, are only sixty miles from the Canal. They are crawling with Axis agents, and are so important to the Nazis that the Ibero-American Institute in Berlin has a separate "Office of Darien Affairs" run by a staff of specialist officers.

While the Falange has been made illegal as such in Colombia, it continues under the name of the Acción Nacionalista Popular, and publishes a magazine called *Falanje*. It is still aided by the Spanish Legation, and it is still a menace to the Republic of Colombia and to the war effort of the entire Western Hemisphere.

Another fascinating section of the Falange Exterior dossier covers the Dominican Republic. When the Spanish War broke out, the Spanish Republic was one of the biggest customers for Dominican produce and cattle. Rafael Trujillo, the Dominican dictator, sympathized with Franco —but the Spanish Republicans paid their bills on time, and Trujillo had important private investments at home that depended on these bills.

Ninety per cent of the Spanish merchants were openly pro-Franco. Like their colleagues in Havana, they collected vast sums of money, coffee, tobacco, rum, and other supplies for the Axis forces in Spain. The pro-Nazi chief of Dominican Intelligence, Major Miguel Angel Paulino, had many supporters of the Spanish Republic arrested and imprisoned. Then, in 1937, the Spanish Falange sent Francisco Almodovar to Trujillo City to organize the local division of the Falange Exterior.

Almodovar visited Trujillo at his home, where he received funds and promises of other aid. When Almodovar left Santo Domingo, the Falange ordered another agent, Francisco Larcegui, to continue the organization job in Santo Domingo.

Larcegui was stationed in New York when he received these orders. A veteran Falangist, Larcegui entered the United States as the accredited correspondent of three Latin-American papers—Pepin Rivero's *Diario de la Marina*, Laureano Gómez's *El Siglo*, and the Falangist *Diario Español* of Montevideo, Uruguay. He, too, received some funds from Trujillo. He remained in Santo Domingo for some months, establishing a strong branch of the Falange.

In December 1937, after Larcegui had returned to New York, the Franco Junta in Burgos sent a Captain Torres to ask Trujillo to break off diplomatic relations with the Spanish Republic. The Captain's mission was unsuccessful, for

Trujillo was then in the process of selling a large order of cattle to the embattled but solvent Republic.

The Falange, however, made great headway among the Dominican Republic's upper crust. *Listin Diario,* one of the nation's leading newspapers, jumped on the Franco victory chariot. The paper ran a series of pro-Franco stories by Emilio S. Morel, President of the Superior Junta of the dominant Dominican Party. When Franco took power, Morel was named Dominican Minister to Madrid— where he placed a wreath on the tomb of José Antonio Primo de Rivera in Rafael Trujillo's name and then sank into obscurity.

Since Pearl Harbor, the Falange in Santo Domingo has been running a vigorous anti-American campaign and attempting to take up the tasks of the Nazis imprisoned or expelled by the *Realpolitik* fortunes of the war.

In June 1942 alert American Intelligence agents discovered that the Captain of a Spanish ship had deposited $300,000 in a Dominican bank, and that the money was to be used to meet the expenses of the Nazi agents in the Americas. News of the discovery of this cache leaked out to the newspapers of several Central American countries. Trújillo quickly announced that he was confiscating the $300,000—but until the news broke in the press, he had been attempting to convert the money into Cuban currency. His agent in this transaction had been Sanchez Arcilla, the former staff writer of the *Diario de la Marina* who was serving as Cuba's Minister to Santo Domingo. Arcilla was very close to the Falange.

The Spanish Legation in Trujillo City not only transmits orders from Madrid to the Falange of the Dominican Republic, but also certain confidential letters from Germany to pro-Nazi Dominican government officials. It also acts as a forwarding station in the information service the Axis maintains in the Caribbean.

When you learn that the Falange in Santo Domingo is today the front for one of the most powerful Fifth Columns the Nazis succeeded in establishing in the Americas before

Pearl Harbor, you understand why General von Faupel is held in such high esteem in Berlin. For the Caribbean is one of the graveyards of United Nations shipping in the Atlantic. Between Miami and Venezuela, the Axis—through the Falanges of Cuba, Santo Domingo, Puerto Rico, and the Vichysois of Martinique—maintains an almost unbroken chain of observation posts and secret radio stations in constant contact with Nazi submarine and surface raiders.

The northern coast of Venezuela is infested with hundreds of Falangist agents—many of whom have casually and without ecclesiastical authority donned the robes of priests—whose radio instructions lead Nazi submarines across the paths of United Nations oil tankers.

The dossier is endless. Wherever you turn in Latin America, whether in small but strategic Panama or in large and powerful Argentina, the Falange Exterior hits you between the eyes.

There is no mistaking the facts once they face you. Spain has taken over the diplomatic fronts behind which Axis Fifth Column work is carried out in Latin America. In every Latin-American country, the Falange Exterior has an active, well-trained, well-financed organization—either under its own name or under such false fronts as the Acción Nacionalista Popular of Colombia; the Fatherland, Order, and Liberty Society of Uruguay; or, as in Mexico, under both its own and the false banners of Sinarquismo.

Upwards of a million Falangistas and their dupes—acting on orders dictated by Nazi General Wilhelm von Faupel in Madrid—are actively engaged in warfare against the United Nations, for the Axis.

This warfare is waged on many fronts: political, economic, military. The fronts are endless. A recent confidential survey of Axis operations in the Americas revealed that the Spanish Secret Service, the SIM, has 14,763 operatives functioning between the Rio Grande and the wind-sheared pastures of Patagonia.

Wilhelm von Faupel makes few speeches, but when he

does mount the rostrum he never minces his words. In June 1939, during the Pan-American Conference in Lima, von Faupel delivered a lecture before the German Academy in Berlin. Pointing to Lima on the large map beside the lectern, von Faupel quietly declared:

A victory for Fascist Spain will cement our relations with Latin America and will be a rude shock to the Good Neighbor Policy of President Roosevelt.

Today, to make this shock even ruder, von Faupel maintains a special school in Barcelona for Latin-American Falangistas. The school is in the Barcelona Building of the Ibero-American Institute, and from it pour Latin-American Falangistas who know just how best to serve the Axis in their native lands.

The increasing tightness of the war situation is grist to the Falange mill. As the war continues, we can expect an increase of Falangist activities which will exploit the hardships and the sacrifices the war is forcing on all civilians in Latin America.

Granting that it is perhaps far-fetched to speak in terms of a German or an Italian or a Japanese invasion of Latin America, the fact remains that the Falange is with us in force in the Americas *now*. Hitler is not fooling—and the Falanges in Latin America are Hitler's.

One immediate step can cripple the Falanges of the entire Western Hemisphere, can make their objectives a thousand times more difficult to achieve than they are now. The Falangist diplomatic front must be eliminated: every legation of Axis Spain must be shut down and its officials sent back to Madrid. This will not end the Falange menace by any means, but it will certainly pull some of its sharpest teeth.

The initiative for this hemisphere-wide diplomatic move rests in only one place—Washington. As the United States moves, so move the nations of Latin America. They followed us into the war, and the average Latin-American is more than anxious to see the Franco legations driven from his country forever. Yet, until we make the initial move, the Latin-American nations are powerless to act.

CHAPTER TEN

The Falange in the United States

THE FRANK and revealing book *La Falange Exterior* which the Nazis tried so hard to destroy completely after it was published in Santander, Spain, contained a most interesting paragraph on page 20. In translation, this paragraph reads:

> In some countries there are but few Spanish colonies. But in those where it is convenient to assist the cause of Spain, in a sense of effective propaganda, groups of foreign sympathizers have been constituted, maintaining also a close and continuous relation with the [Spanish] compatriots residing there. Although their number might not be sufficient to create a formal organization of the Falange Española Tradicionalista de la J.O.N.S., delegates and representatives have been named that carry out a useful work for our Movement.

The United States is one of these countries where "there are but few Spanish colonies." But early in the Spanish war the United States became the home of the other type of Falange Exterior organizations described in the above paragraph. Never very large numerically, the Falangist organizations and their American off-shoots have nevertheless proved themselves to be one of the most effective of the Falange Exterior Fifth Columns in the world. When the history of the Second World War is written, the role the Falange Exterior played in the successful American campaign to prevent the lifting of the Arms Embargo on Loyalist Spain will fill some of the blackest pages in that tragic chronicle.

In January, 1937, a group of Franco partisans held a formal meeting in the Alhambra Coffee House, at 2 Stone Street, New York. Most of the men present were Spaniards living in the United States but retaining their Spanish citizenship. Some were powerful Puerto Ricans, others were Spanish-born American citizens.

The most powerful men in Spanish-American shipping, Marcelino Garcia and Manuel Diaz—owners of the firm of Garcia & Diaz—dominated the first meeting of this group. José Maria Torres Perona, personal representative in New York of Havana's Pepin Rivera, and Francisco Larcegui, the Spaniard carrying credentials from Rivera's *Diario de la Marina* and other papers, were among the others in the group. They shared ideas and delicacies with Dr. Ramon Castroviejo, Julio Rojo, a Puerto Rican Spaniard, Benito Collado, Felix Lopez, José Reyes, and other prominent members of the Spanish big-business set in New York.

Out of this meeting came the organization of the Casa de España (House of Spain), a club which set up headquarters in the Park Central Hotel. The manager of the Spanish department of the Park Central, a charter member of the Casa de España, was Tomas Collado. His brother Benito, also a charter member, owned El Chico, a Greenwich Village night club.

The Casa de España was the first American branch of the Falange Exterior. Like all foreign Falanges, it soon organized the local branch of the Auxilio Social of the Falange. In the United States the Auxilio Social took the form of two American committees—the Spanish Nationalist Relief Committee and the American Spanish Relief Fund, and one Spanish organization, the National Spanish Relief Association, Incorporated. The directors of the Spanish association included Emilio Gonzalez, Dr. Castroviejo, and Juan Gallego, a Spanish shipping man of New York.

Among the "foreign sympathizers" whom the handbook of the Falange Exterior sought were the American members of the Spanish Nationalist Relief Committee. These included Americans like W. Cameron Forbes, former American Ambassador to Japan; James W. Gerard, former Ambassador to Germany; Dennis Cardinal Dougherty, Archbishop of Philadelphia; Mrs. Harry Payne Whitney;

Anne Morgan; Mary Pickford; and Dr. A. Hamilton Rice. The literature of this committee stated that it was the "American representative for raising funds in the United States for the Auxilio Social—Social Help Service—which represents in a marvelous manner the spirit and unity of New Spain."

While the Auxilio Social organizations raised funds for the Axis in Spain, the Casa de España concentrated on making propaganda for the Fascist armies in the Spanish War. The Park Central Hotel became the scene of endless dinners, forums, dance and music recitals, and lectures on the Franco movement. On the tables of the Casa de España visitors and the seven hundred-odd members could always find Fascist propaganda pamphlets and magazines printed both here and abroad. A large painting of Francisco Franco hung on the wall of the club headquarters.

The feminine section of the Falange, run by Pilar Primo de Rivera in Spain, had its American representation in the feminine section of the Casa de España. Prominent in the leadership of this section was Mary Greevy Garcia, wife of Marcelino Garcia, and a native of the United States. The leader of the American feminine section was Mrs. Etelvina Lubiano of Yonkers, N. Y.

Francisco Larcegui, one of the founders of the Casa de España, was originally its closest link with the Falange in Spain. A veteran member of the Falange in Spain, Larcegui operated both in Central America and the United States. Always well supplied with funds—Larcegui loved to flash an impressive roll of big bills at the slightest provocation—he proved to be the American correspondent for the *Diario de la Marina* of Havana and the fervently anti-American *El Siglo* of Bogotá, Colombia. From time to time Larcegui went to Havana to have his visa renewed at the American Legation there. But these visits to Havana also saw Larcegui conferring with Falange Exterior leaders like Juan Adriensens, Alejandro Villanueva, and Miguel Espinos.

Although Larcegui's job was primarily of a propaganda

nature, he was—at least in the early days of the Casa de España—a contact man for the espionage network then being created by the German masters of the Falange.

Larcegui, however, was not as important to the Spanish Fascists as were Garcia and Diaz. The role of these two Spanish shipping men in New York was brought to the attention of the United States Senate as early as May 1937, when Senator Gerald P. Nye charged them with being Franco spies who "would look with favor upon the violation of the Monroe Doctrine."

The knowledge which caused this outburst by Senator Nye—whom even the most fervent American Fascists could not accuse of Communist bias—was contained in two letters taken from the files of Garcia & Diaz in New York. The letters were inserted into the Congressional Record. Both letters were written on the letterhead of Garcia & Diaz, 17 Battery Place, New York City.

The first, sent via air mail to Señor Don Federico Varela, Apartado 60, Vera Cruz, Mexico, was signed only by Manuel Diaz, and dated February 20, 1937. It said:

In accordance with your indication, and in order that you should know that we had received the code, I have just sent you the following cablegram:

"Just received your letter February 17. Many thanks." And when in the future we have to communicate with you by cable we will make good use of the words that you were so good to prepare.

I am very pleased to see that you so disinterestedly offer yourself to keep us posted about everything going on there; this, of course, encourages me to continue bothering you: but in the same manner I wish to offer myself to you for anything, in case I can be of any service, and without anything further for the moment, I am, yours truly,

Manuel Diaz

The full meaning of this letter was indicated in the second letter, dated March 5, 1937, and mailed to Juan Claudio Guell, Conde de Ruisenada, Hotel Fernando Isabel, Valladolid, Spain. The second letter said, in part (the italics are mine):

Here we live hour to hour pending news from Spain. The *press, in its majority Jewish*, is rather hostile to our cause and while it advances the lies of the Reds (they make enormous propaganda) it makes efforts to belittle the success of our glorious army.

The help from Russia is well known, as well as the enormous help from Mexico. *It is a pity that there is not a speedy armed ship in the strait of Yucatan. If there were, not one of the ships with armaments would get through.* The place could not be any more advantageous because for the provisioning of its needs the ship could be helped in Puerto Barrios, Guatemala, a friendly country.

Fond greeting from your good friends,

MANUEL DIAZ
MARCELINO GARCIA

Senator Nye minced few words in his denunciation of the two leaders of the Casa de España. (Garcia, in fact, was president of the club.)

It is plain to be seen from a study of the Garcia and Diaz correspondence that this firm is party to and aware of activities which violate and threaten American neutrality. It is evident as well [Nye declared], that these persons would look with favor upon violation of the Monroe Doctrine and encourage the presence of foreign warships in American waters to destroy shipping related to the present Spanish Government, which is recognized by our government.

Nye reminded the Senate of the fate of the *Mar Cantabrico*, a Spanish ship which sailed from New York in January 1937 with a cargo of food, medicines, and munitions (the last arms sold to the Republic before the Embargo was declared). The ship was torpedoed by a German submarine off the coast of Spain toward the end of the voyage.

During the entire time the ship was in American waters

[Nye told the Senate], it appears to have been spied upon by agents who were reporting to Garcia and Diaz in New York, who, in turn, were reporting to the higher-up agents of the General Franco forces.

The Senator had more than a complaint to lodge, however; he also had a suggestion. In the course of his investigation he discovered that, although both Garcia and Diaz had been in the United States for over thirty years, neither of them had become an American citizen. "They and their kind should be no part of us," Nye told his Senate colleagues. "It seems to me that Garcia and Diaz are engaged in activities that subject them most absolutely to deportation."

The Government took no action on this suggestion. But Garcia and Diaz did. On February 28, 1938, Manuel Diaz became an American citizen in the Federal Court of the Southern District of New York. On March 10, 1938, Marcelino Garcia was made an American citizen by the Eastern District Court of New York. Today, the Garcia and Diaz firm is the American agent for the notorious Compañía Transatlantica Española, Hitler's bridge of spies between occupied Europe and the Western Hemisphere.

About six months after the Casa de España was founded, the Nazis in Burgos sent José Gonzalez Marin to organize the Falange "shirt" cells in New York and Puerto Rico. The effeminate poetry reader, an "Old Shirt" of the Falange in Spain, gave several recitals at the Casa de España and then got down to the real business of his American tour.

Because of the widespread anti-Fascist sentiments of the American people, General von Faupel felt that it would be wiser to choose another name for the Falange in the United States. The name chosen was the Club Isabel y Fernando. Marin appointed José de Perignat, a Spaniard who lived at 500 West 144th St., Manhattan, chief of the New York Falange. Second and third in command were Antonio Gallego and Abelardo Campa. Most of the 700 members of the Casa de España signed up with the formal Falange organization, but an hysterical speech Marin delivered at a secret meeting of the Club Isabel y Fernando sent the majority of them scurrying for the nearest exits. Marin, in his speech, declared that all who joined the Falange would have to return to Spain to bear arms on the front lines—and the prosperous Spanish importers and shipping men who formed a majority in the Casa de España got cold feet.

Only a hundred-odd fanatics remained in the Club Isabel y Fernando after Marin left for Puerto Rico. Burgos then ordered Alejandro Villanueva, the ranking Falange official in the Americas, to visit New York to correct this state of affairs.

Villanueva reached New York early in 1938. He promptly purchased a Packard roadster with Falange funds and began touring the brothels of New York. After a month of high living, Villanueva visited the Casa de España, where he addressed a secret session of the Club Isabel y Fernando for something like ten minutes. He had seen enough of New York to learn that if he ever ordered his Falangists to don blue shirts and appear in public like the uniformed Falangistas of Latin America, mayhem would be the mildest of the results. "Camaradas," he said, "I must depart for Havana at once. But carry on for our glorious cause despite what the Jewish-controlled press of America says about us." And with these parting words, Villanueva skipped to Havana.

There just was no place in the United States for the type of Falange organization Gonzalez Marin had tried to organize, and the practical Villanueva was the first to see this. In his report to the Falange in Burgos, however, Villanueva did not underestimate the effective job the Casa de España and its subsidiaries were doing for the Axis cause in Spain. Charles Coughlin's *Social Justice* had become in many respects a house organ for the Falange, and both the members and the publications of many native American Fascist groups were spreading the Franco propaganda widely.

The Casa de España worked very closely with Juan F.

Cardenas, who had held diplomatic posts under both the Spanish monarchy and the Spanish Republic. At the start of the Spanish War, Cardenas set up headquarters in New York's Ritz Carlton Hotel as the official representative of Francisco Franco. He was made an honorary member of the Casa de España, and, via orders received through the Italian Consulate in New York, he was able to guide the organization's destinies effectively.

The Casa ran special affairs two and three times each week. At one of these, held in 1938 at the School of the Franciscan Fathers, 300 West 16th Street, New York, they offered as a speaker Magistrate Sylvester Sabbatino, an old-line Tammany politico. Sabbatino delivered a long speech attacking the American authorities for their "persecution" of the Spanish Fascists. The affair is recalled here because it was so typical of the Casa activities during those days. At such affairs, and at "patriotic celebrations" sponsored by Fascist groups like the Christian Front and featuring Casa speakers like Marcelino Garcia, the Casa de España brought its propaganda to large bodies of Americans.

Casa leaders like Garcia also enjoyed close relations with Americans of the stripe of Merwin K. Hart, intimate of native American Fascist leaders and himself a spokesman for all the hate-England, hate-Roosevelt, and other reactionary causes. Hart made a trip to Franco Spain in 1938 and wrote a book about his experiences which left no doubt about where he stood in the war between the Spanish Republic and the armies of Germany and Italy. Hart's usefulness to the Falange in America was limited, however, to that lunatic fringe of the American Fascist movements. Few Americans outside of this lunatic fringe ever took Hart's words very seriously.

In direct contrast to Merwin K. Hart was the middle-aged and somewhat dipsomaniac Marquesa de Cienfuegos. The Falange organizations in America imported the Marquesa in 1938—and turned her loose on reporters, radio audiences, and paying guests at various Fascist rallies. They sent her forth to modest duplex apartments on Park Avenue and to the most exclusive homes in the exclusive suburbs of many great American cities.

The Marquesa de Cienfuegos was everything that the local Falange could want in their dreams. She bore a noble name; fine for the Park Avenue trade. She was a native of Atlanta, Georgia, having been born plain Jane Anderson. This gave her story a neat American appeal. She had been jailed by the Spanish Republic in Madrid, and held there on charges of being a Franco agent. She won her freedom through the intervention of the American Embassy—and then went on tour to prove that the Spanish Government had not jailed her in error.

The Marquesa had rare oratorical talents. She clenched her fists, and closed her eyes, and sobbed with nearly every sentence. The effect, to detached observers who knew something of her past, was that of a small-time actress giving an imitation of Hitler and Eleanora Duse rolled into one. But to those who took her at her face value, the Marquesa de Cienfuegos was a sensation. Monsignor Fulton Sheehan of the Catholic University declared that the Marquesa was "one of the living martyrs" of history. The *Catholic Digest* described the Marquessa as "the world's greatest woman orator in the fight against communism."

The Marquesa regaled her listeners with blood curdling accounts of the doings of the Spanish Republicans—like her Falangist colleagues, she called them the Reds—and then went on to speak of the glories of Franco Spain. Millions of Americans read her words in their newspapers—the Marquesa got a good press—and the fact that she was just a simple Georgia girl added credibility to her claims. Thousands were swayed by her act on the public platforms, and hundreds of influential Americans who sat through informal dinner parties with her were completely sold on the Franco cause by the American-born noblewoman who had suffered so cruelly at the hands of the "Reds."

After the Spanish War, the Marquesa de Cienfuegos disappeared from the American scene. But her words were not to be lost to American ears. Shortly after the second phase of World War II started in Warsaw, the Marquesa turned up in the real capital of Spain—Berlin. Here, as plain Jane Anderson, the Georgia cracker gal, the tear-jerking Marquesa continued her career along logical lines. Seated before a microphone in the Nazi short-wave sending station, Jane Anderson started to make regular broadcasts to her native land in Georgia English.

These broadcasts continued after Pearl Harbor, but now they were made more often. During the first week of January 1942, Jane Anderson made four separate broadcasts to her native land. The broadcasts had a familiar ring to them. To her many friends in America, plain Jane Anderson shrieked that the entry of the United States into the war was part of a Jewish plot to save the necks of Joseph Stalin and the International Bankers. Her other broadcasts were all in this vein.

Jane Anderson's success as a Nazi short-wave radio speaker won her a new noble title—one she acquired without marrying another nobleman. The newspapers unanimously chose to call Jane Anderson Lady Haw-Haw. The Government of the United States, in January 1943, chose to indict Plain Jane de Cienfuegos Haw-Haw Anderson along with other "radio traitors" like Ezra Pound, Robert Best, and Fred Kaltenbach. If this "living martyr" ever does return to her own, her native land, it will be as a federal prisoner.

But in 1938, when Jane Anderson toured the United States for the Falange, she was able to play a highly important part in the Axis campaign to keep the State Department from lifting the embargo on arms to the Spanish Republic—a step that many Americans in all walks of life were demanding of their government. Perhaps, next to the versatile Garcia and Diaz, the future Lady Haw-Haw was the one person who accomplished the most for the Falange Exterior in the United States during the organization's first period. For in the United States, as in Latin America, General von Faupel had planned for the Falange to go through

three distinct periods: the organization and propaganda period ending with the triumph at Madrid, the period of
tightening and preparation between the victory at Madrid
and the bombing of Warsaw, and finally the period of
maximum effort.

The second period of the Falange in the United States
got off with a grand flourish. The battered body of the
Spanish Republic was still warm when the United States
recognized the Franco gang as the legal government of
Spain. Even as the victorious Fascists started organizing
firing-squad parties in Spain, the gates of the United States
were swung wide open by a considerate State Department
for a veritable army of Falange agents bearing diplomatic
passports.

Juan F. Cardenas was accepted as Spanish Ambassador
to the United States. The Falangistas in Madrid assigned
Miguel Echegaray to the Embassy in Washington to supervise the real work of the Spanish diplomatic corps in the
United States. Echegaray was given the nominal title of
Agricultural Attaché. Then to check on both Echegaray
and Cardenas, General von Faupel sent Colonel Sierra to
Washington as Military Attaché. Sierra's real job was Chief
of Spanish Military Intelligence for the United States.

Timid Daniel Danis, the new Minister Plenipotentiary in
Washington, was detailed to handle one of the most confidential jobs in the Legation. Danis was the contact man
between Cardenas and Augustin Ibañez Serrano, the Falange
Exterior Chief in Mexico. He worked out a system early
in his career of maintaining this liaison through the Portuguese Legation in Washington. It was Danis who arranged
for Ibañez Serrano to get an office in the Portuguese Embassy in Mexico City. Because of his extreme caution, Danis
decided to use third persons for most necessary trips between Ibañez Serrano and Washington. Most of these
couriers were girls, one of them being the daughter of a
Mexican general.

The Spanish Consulate in New York became an important Falange outpost in the Americas. Miguel Espinos, the current Consul General, is a completely pro-Axis Fascist who has previously worked for the Falange in Manila and in Havana. One of the friends he sees very often today is Andres Soriano, the powerful associate of the Philippine Falange who serves as Secretary of Treasury in the Philippine government-in-exile. Another intimate of Espinos's is José Maria Casabo, personal representative of Francisco Cambo. Señor Cambo heads Chade, the international public utilities corporation whose ties with corporations in Rome, Berlin, Lisbon, and Buenos Aires bulked so importantly during the Spanish War.

Under Espinos, the Consulate in New York started to work overtime for the Axis. Juan Adriensens, one of the earliest organizers of the Falange in Cuba, was brought to New York and installed as Vice-Consul. He and Antonio Mendez de Quiros, the new Counselor of the Consulate, were put in charge of direct contact with the Falange in the United States.

Adriensens tried to continue the organization of the "shirt" Falange where Gonzalez Marin had left off. He began holding regular clandestine meetings with Falange Chief José de Perignat.

The most efficient Falangista in the New York Consulate is Joaquin Sunyé. A protégé of the Count de Güell, Sunyé takes his orders directly from Echegaray in Washington. Sunyé helped organize much economic support for the Franco regime, assuming the post of secretary of the Spanish Chamber of Commerce to aid his efforts along these lines. His brothers are powerful officials of the Compañía Transatlantica in Spain.

On the Pacific Coast, the Consulate was staffed with men highly acceptable to General von Faupel. The Consul General in San Francisco is Francisco de Amat, a cousin of the Philippine Resident Commissioner in Washington, Octavio Elizalde. His Vice-Consul, Captain José Martin, played a major share in the organization of the Falange fronts on the Pacific Coast. The confidential liaison work between de Amat and the Embassy in Washington is handled by Maria Arrillaga, who carries messages that can not be entrusted to the mails.

Before the Republic fell to the Axis troops, the Falange maintained a formal propaganda service in the United States. The Cardenas "Junta" published an elaborate magazine in English, *Spain*, and operated a bureau known as the Peninsular News Service.

Sunyé converted the magazine into the official publication of the Spanish Government, and made Larcegui head of Peninsular News Service. But this was not in line with von Faupel's more ambitious plans. Larcegui's amorous life made him a bit unreliable for the major job of running all Falangist propaganda in the United States. Before many months had passed, Madrid sent Gaytan de Ayala, a rotund and heavy-drinking "Old Shirt," to Sunyé.

The newly arrived de Ayala was given diplomatic standing as an attaché of the Embassy. Under Sunyé's immediate supervision, de Ayala opened a separate office in New York called the Spanish Library of Information. This new bureau took over the duties of the Peninsular News Service, the publication of *Spain*, and the other propaganda tasks of the Falange Exterior in the United States.

The Falange had an existing mailing list for its propapanda when Ayala reached the United States. It had been compiled by the Casa de España and its various offshoots. Agents of General von Faupel immediately arranged for this list to be amplified by a still larger list—that of the German Library of Information in New York. Subscribers— paid and free—to the publications George Sylvester Viereck was putting out for the German propaganda office began to receive *Spain* and other publications of the Spanish propaganda bureau. Further to cement the friendship between Madrid and Berlin, people on the old Falange propaganda lists began to receive publications of the German Library of Information.

Larcegui, who was retained as assistant to de Ayala, started a new service devoted to Central American affairs.

He established independent headquarters in the Hotel Lincoln in New York and operated the Inter-American News Service—a convenient blind for his real activities.

Under Ayala's supervision, the Falange published or subsidized the following organs:

Spain. This was a most expensively printed monthly magazine, crammed with pictures, and devoted mainly to propaganda about the marvels Franco was accomplishing in Falangist Spain. It was written in English.

Cara al Sol (Face to the Sun). The name is taken from the anthem of the Falange. A Spanish-language weekly, it was listed in the official handbooks of the Falange in Madrid as the official organ of the Falange in the United States.

España Nueva (New Spain). A Spanish language monthly, edited by A. F. Arguelles. Mailing address P. O. Box 84, Station W., New York City. Violently pro-Axis, anti-Semitic, anti-British. Although on the surface a private venture, it was supported by advertisements from the Spanish Consulate, Spanish banks, and other enterprises of the Spanish Government.

Epoca. Another Spanish magazine, published at 1775 Broadway, New York City, by Rafael O. Galvan. *Epoca* received similar subsidies through de Ayala.

In addition to these periodicals, the Spanish Library of Information published hundreds of pamphlets and brochures which received wide distribution both through the mailing lists at De Ayala's disposal and through the schools and colleges of the land.

Under the Cardenas unofficial Junta, *Spain* had employed a bombastic adventurer named John Eoghan Kelly as a writer on military and historical subjects. Kelly, who held a captain's commission in the United States Army Reserves, cut quite a swath in the lunatic fringe of the native American fascist movements.

Son of a German mother and an Irish nationalist father, Kelly was trained as an engineer. During the last World War, he was in Mexico, he claims, as a "civilian attached to Military Intelligence," but his former wife has a less charitable version of why Kelly spent the war in Mexico as a civilian.

Early in the Spanish War, Kelly popped up in New York as one of the glamour boys of the Franco camp. With Merwin K. Hart and Allen Zoll, he served on the board of the American Union for Nationalist Spain. Kelly, in fact, was the secretary of this Franco group.

Before this, he had maintained an engineering office at 17 Battery Place, New York. Here he had met a German named Buelow, who introduced him to the Steuben Society. Kelly started to move in circles which included native American Fascists like George Deatherage, Van Horn Mosely, and James Campbell. He became a Lieutenant in the United States Army Reserves, and subsequently won two promotions in rank. When the charter papers of the Christian Front were filed with the New York State Supreme Court, the name of John Eoghan Kelly was registered as one of the organizers.

During the three years of the Spanish War, Kelly made a number of trips to Spain and Germany. On May 22, 1939, Kelly was introduced at a Brooklyn Christian Front meeting as a "representative of the Spanish Government."

When Merwin K. Hart wanted to go to the Franco zone during the Spanish War, he found himself halted by the fact that his passport had been stamped "not valid in Spain." Hart managed to get to Spain and even wrote a book about his trip. Not included in the book was a certain letter written on his behalf to the Passport Division of the State Department. The letter explained that Hart wanted to go to Franco territory and concluded:

I would greatly appreciate any help that you can give Mr. Hart and have asked him to convey my personal regards.

This letter was signed by John Eoghan Kelly.

In 1938 Kelly started to write for the Peninsular News Service, the propaganda agency of the Franco *Junta* in New

York. He spoke at scores of Fascist rallies, and became a leader in the Falangist campaign to keep the United States from lifting the arms embargo applied against the Spanish Republic. He wrote for *Spain*, and, after the triumph of the Nazis in Spain, received a fee from the Spanish Library of Information of twenty-five dollars for every Franco meeting he attended. Although the Spanish Library and its chief, Gaytan de Ayala, were registered with the State Department as paid agents of foreign powers, Kelly never registered.

Kelly's activities led to his being dropped from the Army Reserves in 1941, after he had attained the rank of major. On March 1, 1943, John Eoghan Kelly was arrested by the F. B. I. in California following a federal grand jury indictment in Washington. The jury charged that Kelly had failed to register as an agent of the Fascist Spanish Government. In announcing Kelly's arrest, Special Agent Nat J. L. Perrin said that Kelly had made "defeatist" statements in California—where he had operated a mine—and had tried to talk two young Americans out of joining the Army.

The Fascist character of *Spain* and other Falangist publications in the United States was never disguised. Openly, firmly, at times arrogantly, the Falangist organs in the United States attacked democracy, American institutions, and our defense outposts.

On the subject of fascism, *Spain* has printed some very explicit statements.

Fascism is at least theistic and it respects and promotes the values of religious institutions. . . . The Fascist dictatorship, which respects individual liberty and dignity, private property and savings, the family and the nation, morals and religion, inserts itself in an ordered civilization.

In still another issue, *Spain* carried these words:

Authentic fascism establishes order, invokes unity of destiny and gathers together all the vital forces of a people.

Only a few months before Pearl Harbor, *Spain*, like all Falangist publications in Spain and Latin America, sneered at American influences in the Philippines. The issue of September 1941 carried a story on the Philippines which said, among other things:

It is a seat of Hispanicism and as such should receive the attention of our greatest intellectuals. Today the entire University [Santo Tomás] has come under the spiritual and symbolic rectorate of the Caudillo of Spain. By having rescued culture from barbarism, he made a peace with his sword for the continued flowering of the sciences, letters, and the arts.

At the time this was written, Caudillo Franco's chief representative in the Philippines was José del Castano—who was then very busily engaged in preparing the way for the Japanese allies of the Caudillo.

The weekly publication of the Spanish Library of Information, *Cara al Sol*, was openly acknowledged to be the official organ of the Falange in the United States. Each issue bore the yoke and arrows emblem of the Falange, and the official orders of the Falange Exterior were always carried in this magazine.

An editorial in *Cara al Sol* which typifies all of the editorials the magazine carried was the lead editorial of the February 25, 1939, issue. This began with these words:

Our movement is not democratic; it is rather the greatest opposition that can be raised up against democracy. The democracies need, in order to "fulfill" the will of the people, to bother them with continuous calls to drop papers in voting urns. . . .

Shortly after this editorial ran, *Cara al Sol* ran an article by Rafael Sanchez Mazas, then chief of the Falange Exterior. This article ran not only in *Cara al Sol*, but in every other official organ of the Falange Exterior from *Avance* in Puerto Rico to *Arriba* in Argentina. (The italics are mine.)

The Falange from its center, from its heart, is born and grows like the spiral of the Empire. *At least a third of the great work, the total work, of the Falange lies with you of the foreign service.*

This appeared shortly after *Cara al Sol* editorialized:

It is indispensable that the good Spaniards who live outside of Spain, without class distinctions, impose on themselves the obligation of aiding in the aggrandizement of Spain.

The significance of the "third of the total work" Mazas mentioned and the "aggrandizement of Spain" was further amplified by *Cara al Sol* in a subsequent issue.

Our missionary labor has begun. Spanish America again turns its eyes to us and again on the other side of the Atlantic there are bent knees for the triumph of Franco. The race has heard once more the voice of God, and Hispanidad, aware of its historic mission, is again on the march behind the proud banners of national-syndicalism. . . . It is now the work of the Falange to unify the desires of those millions of Spaniards who, far from the Motherland, feel . . . in their souls the pride of our old glory; and to . . . shout to the world that our jurisprudence, our industry, and our spiritual influence have the right of hegemony over a third of the earth. . . . Hundreds of thousands of Blue Shirts scattered over the continents demand this with their arms raised in salute, their faces to the sun, and in each corner a flag with the Yoke and Arrows . . . speaks of the imperial mission of Spain. This is the essential function of the Foreign Service of Falange, and this is our arduous missionary task.

Such editorials never affected the security of the United States proper. But *Cara al Sol* reached many Spaniards in America who took it to heart. What such sentiments, once accepted by their readers, meant to our security when the "imperial mission of Spain" clashed with the armed forces of the United States in Manila after Pearl Harbor is something else again.

The sentiments expressed in *Spain* and in *Cara al Sol* were, however, very mild beside the fiery words flung by *España Nueva*, the privately owned monthly supported by paid advertising from the Spanish Consulate, the Spanish Library of Information, Spanish banks, the National Spanish Relief Association, and similar clients.

From *España Nueva* its readers learned that Pan-Americanism is "of Jewish and Protestant origin." Speaking of the war, *España Nueva* declared:

If among the results of the present war we can count the appearance of a world free from the Jewish press in place of the perpetuation of the Jewish free press, European blood will not have been shed in vain.

The Jewish problem, in fact, has long been one of *España Nueva's* greatest worries. Like the Nazis, the men behind this New York magazine feel it incumbent upon themselves to protect all Americans from the Jews. *España Nueva* makes its reasons for fearing the press quite clear. In no uncertain terms, it wrote—and these writings were carried through the United States mails and distributed free of charge by the Spanish Library of Information to thousands of American high school students—editorials like the following:

The Jewish press, whose mission is none other than Marxist and Bolshevik propaganda, personifies the international clique which applauds or hisses at Moscow's command. The champions of Stalin, those who conferred Zionist honors on Roosevelt, those who take tea with Mrs. Roosevelt, those who applauded the robbers of the Spanish treasury and the assassins of the Spanish people must logically attack and defame Franco and the ideals he personifies.

This particular outburst was brought on by an article in that organ of international Marxism and Bolshevism known as "the New York *Times*."

España Nueva, however, also carried messages of cheer

for its readers. If it exposed the nefarious plots of the Jews, it also pointed the solution to these plots. In the March 1940 issue, A. Sanchez Saavedra wrote:

The Jewish chain, in order to shackle with efficiency and to continue deceiving the universe, needs to maintain intact all its links. Fortunately, the appearance of Hitler on the political and diplomatic scene has pulverized the Jewish-German link and whatever may be the outcome of the present war, the world is witnessing the last act of the great Jewish farce.

This and other issues of *España Nueva* were among the thousands of pieces of Falangist propaganda the Spanish Library of Information sent, without charge, to hundreds of Spanish teachers in American high schools. On such tidbits of the language, thousands of American high-school students learned Spanish.

Although all of these publications reached Falangist sympathizers on the Pacific coast, they were supplemented by a Los Angeles publication—*Boletin de la Casa de España*. It was published by an organization larger than the New York Casa de España.

California's Casa de España was founded in 1937 by Gregorio del Amo, a wealthy Spaniard who had long been an intimate of Francisco de Amat, Franco's Consul General in San Francisco. The Casa worked very closely with local native fascist organizations, and its thousand-odd members were guided by instructions emanating from the Casa de España of New York, the Spanish Library of Information, and the Spanish Legation. Their Bulletin, whose editors were never named, was one of the most violently anti-British and anti-Democratic organs in the United States.

The other groups of Falangistas in the United States had no publications of their own. These included the Club Isabel y Fernando, of Boston; the Renovación Española, organized and led by Marcos Garcia in San Francisco; and small centers in Tampa, Houston, Philadelphia, Baltimore, and other ports touched by Spanish ships. Falangistas in these cities were kept informed largely through the publications of the Spanish Library of Information.

The propaganda of the Falange in America has been aided no little by David Rubio, Curator of the Hispanic Foundation of the Library of Congress. Rubio wrote often for *Spain,* and his official position lent great weight to his articles. He is no stranger at the Spanish Embassy. In fact, he was one of the speakers at the ceremonies held in Washington when Juan Cardenas formally took over the Legation's building. Wrote *Cara al Sol* at the time:

Then Father Rubio spoke, praising the Motherland and its civilizing work, with which the spiritual Empire of our race was founded—the Empire that caused the material and spiritual reconquest of Spain itself, center of Hispanidad, by the glorious troops of the Generalissimo and Caudillo of Spain.

If *Cara al Sol's* rhapsodic phrases are an accurate reflection of Rubio's remarks on that day, his appointment to the Library of Congress post raises some interesting questions. The Hispanic Foundation was organized to spearhead the American effort to establish closer cultural relations with Latin America. It must, of necessity, combat the efforts of the Falangist propagandists who have been painting the United States as the enemy of culture in the Spanish-speaking countries of the Western Hemisphere. It must, by virtue of its sponsorship, uphold the banners of democracy in the war against fascism. The standard bearers of fascism in Latin America are led by the Falange Española. And Rubio was an open and acknowledged Falange partisan. *Qué passe?*

While Falange propaganda poured from all of its many outlets in the United States, other Franco activities attracted little attention. Lopez Ferrer and Captain Julio de la Torre, who made tours for the Falange in the early days of the Spanish War, visited the Casa de España in New York in 1937. They had little difficulty in getting visas.

Later, Carlos Montoya, a guitarist who had served as secretary of the Falange in Paris, transferred his activities to the Casa de España in New York. The dancer Manuel del Rio—now in Berlin with his entire troupe—joined Montoya in the New York club.

Many Casa members often enjoyed outings at the Alpine, New Jersey, estate of Manuel Rionda.

But the activities of Dr. Ramon Castroviejo, Vice-President of the Casa de España, were the most interesting of all. An excellent ophthalmologist, Castroviejo was one of the charter members of the Casa. He made many trips to Latin America, combining medical with political business quite neatly. The Falange of Puerto Rico turned out en masse to honor him at a dinner in San Juan in 1938. In each Latin-American country Castroviejo visited, he was always feted by the local Falange.

In 1941 Castroviejo started a new magazine, *América Clinica*. Written in Spanish, distributed mainly in Latin America, the magazine had the backing of Laboratorios Andromaco of Barcelona—a German-owned chemical firm.

The editor of *América Clinica* was an up and coming young man named Enrique Cervantes. During the Spanish War, the Republicans caught and jailed Cervantes for espionage. Upon his release from prison, Cervantes made his way to the United States. Despite his record, he had no difficulty in gaining admission to the country. The Falange in New York welcomed him to its bosom as a hero of the war.

New York's Park Central Hotel, headquarters for the Casa de España, became the stopping place for all Falange agents in transit from Spain to Latin America. To the Park Central, in November 1941, came the Number One man of Falange espionage in the Atlantic—the notorious Miguel Barcelo Martinez. Traveling as usual as the chief radio operator of a Spanish C. T. E. liner, the much-hunted "Camarada Martinez" reached New York on the *Marqués de Comillas*.

In Martinez's party was a delegation of important Spanish Falange officials en route to Peru for the Falange-inspired celebration of the 400th anniversary of the conquests of Pizarro. The delegation was led by the chief of the National Council of the Falange in Spain, José Maria Areliza, and also included three official representatives of the Spanish Army, the Spanish Navy and the Spanish Air Force—the Duke of San Lorenzo, Captain Francisco Regalado and Colonel Francisco Iglesias Brage.

Although Martinez's presence was kept quiet, the presence of the official delegation was made known to the press. Alarmed Spanish Republicans, patriotic Protestant laymen like H. Rutledge Southworth, and publications like the newspaper PM correctly saw the delegation as a danger signal to the progress of Pan-Americanism and the Good Neighbor Policy.

PM, which revealed that the delegation consisted principally of members of the Council of Hispanidad, quoted *Arriba*, official organ of the Falange in Madrid to the effect that:

The Council represents the ambitious foreign policy of Spain in its most vital sense.

And then PM went on to say: "Why the State Department should have given them permission to enter this country, even in transit, is one of those diplomatic mysteries that ought not to remain unsolved until it is too late."

Warnings like these fell on seemingly deaf ears. Even the publication (by PM) of the official orders naming José del Castano as Regional Chief of the Philippine Falange Exterior caused hardly a ripple in the Washington calm—although this warning was published less than a month before Pearl Harbor.

The Japanese bombs which fell on Pearl Harbor on December 7, 1941, had their immediate effect on the Falange and its branches in the United States.

In Washington, a new sign went up on the white gates of

the Spanish Embassy. It read: "SPANISH EMBASSY: IN CHARGE OF JAPANESE INTERESTS." Few signs have ever revealed more truths in fewer words.

Before Pearl Harbor, Miguel Echegaray, the "Agricultural Attaché" of the Spanish Embassy, took a trip to the Pacific coast. He left for the West immediately after Ambassador Cardenas returned from an emergency trip to Madrid.

Echegaray's visit was described, officially, as a pleasure trip. Actually, his trip was made in connection with one of the most important aspects of the Axis espionage network in the United States. Prior to America's entry into the war, confidential Axis correspondence reached Europe via the Spanish diplomatic pouches. With the bombing of Pearl Harbor, the Nazi masters of Spain feared that the Spanish diplomatic pouches would lose some of their immunity— particularly when cleared through the British censorship station at Bermuda. The Nazis, therefore, arranged for new routes for confidential papers clearing through the Spanish Legation. Echegaray's job was to establish these new routes.

Before Pearl Harbor, confidential communications from the military chief of the Spanish espionage network in Central America—Colonel Sanz Agero, Spanish Minister to Guatemala—cleared through Washington via the Spanish Consulate in San Francisco. After Echegaray's visit to San Francisco, Sanz Agero's reports were sent to General von Faupel via Sangroniz, the Spanish Minister to Venezuela.

The most important communications of the Spanish network were placed on this same route. They now leave Washington via courier to San Francisco, and then find their way to Madrid and Berlin via Guatemala and Venezuela. When greater speed is needed, the Falange communicates with Nazi Europe via the diplomatic pouches of Finland and Portugal. The Spanish pouches which still go from Washington to Madrid via the old pre-Pearl Harbor routes contain little material of vital importance.

While these arrangements were being made by the Falange legations, the Casas de España of Los Angeles and

New York were suddenly dissolved. Just as the Falange
of Puerto Rico—frightened by the prospects of United
States participation in the war against the Axis—quietly
and officially folded its tents, the main Falange groups in
the United States mistook Pearl Harbor for the handwriting
on the wall. Franco's Spanish Blue Legions in Russia, the
speeches of Franco and all of the Falange leaders in Madrid,
and the open Fascist line the Falangist publications had
followed in the United States up to Pearl Harbor led most
Casa members to presume logically that within weeks of
the Pearl Harbor attack Axis Spain would make its war on
the United Nations an official one.

The Club Isabel y Fernando—most fanatical of the
Falange cells in New York—did not disband. This group
continued to hold meetings on Thursday nights at the
Reno Café, 154 West 145th Street, New York. Headed by
José de Perignat, Jr., these shirted Falangistas (their uniform, incidentally, is confined to blue undershirts) have
continued their activities to this day.

As in Manila and Puerto Rico, the Falangistas and their
closest collaborators rushed into every type of Civilian
Defense and civilians' military service organization.

Benito Collado, charter member of the Casa de España
and one of the leaders of the Franco movement in America,
became a member of the New York City Recreation Committee. He joined the Red Cross, along with Casa members
like Lucrezia Bori and with Falangist Spaniards like Ramon
Salo Munoz, personal representative of Count Vallellano,
head of the Spanish Red Cross. Collado's night club, El
Chico, began giving free tickets to service men through
the U.S.O.—and service men are still relaxing and drinking
in this hangout for local and visiting Falangists from Spain.

The Condesa Santa Cruz de los Manueles, former wife
of del Amo, and herself a member of the Casa de España,
wormed her regal way into the Asociación Cultural Inter-
Americana, which has been raising money to buy am-
bulances for American armed forces. Gaspar Mediavilla, an-

other Casa member, is active in the Comité Hispano Pro Defensa Nacional.

Not all Casa de España members in defense work are volunteers, however. Many outspoken partisans of Axis Spain today hold important civilian war jobs. There is, for instance, Alberto Cugat, a native of Catalonia. A member of Casa de España, Cugat got himself a job as chief of the Spanish Branch, Political and International Division, Postal Censorship. Cugat, who is stationed in New York, supervises the work of a whole section of censors.

Other Casa de España members employed as censors in the New York Post Office include Bernabe Solis, a native of the Philippines; Ricardo Mendoza; and Roberto Forbes. Mendoza was the editor of *Cara al Sol*, official organ of the Falange Exterior in the United States. Forbes, a Spanish-born American citizen, also owns the Eagle Travel Agency, of New York. Through this Agency, he is always well informed about various ship movements.

The official English organ of the Spanish Library of Information, *Spain*, ceased publication in February 1942. It was replaced by a mimeographed weekly news bulletin which lasted about three months. Then this bulletin ceased publication, and Gaytan de Ayala started to make preparations to close his office and transfer its activities to Washington.

This retrenchment, however, was not one of cadres. In fact, shortly after Pearl Harbor, the Falange dispatched one of the most important of its propagandists from Madrid to New York. This man, Francisco de Lucientes, was the chief editorial writer of *Arriba*, the official organ of the Falange in Madrid. In Spain, the official papers often called Lucientes the "Virginio Gayda of Spain."

Suddenly, in December 1941, Lucientes appeared in New York Harbor as a passenger on an incoming liner. Although his papers were in order—his credentials, incidentally, showed him to be the new American correspondent of EFE, Franco Spain's official news agency—he was taken to Ellis Island and held for deportation.

Lucientes's deportation had immediate diplomatic repercussions. The Spanish Government threatened to expel every American correspondent from Spain if Lucientes were not admitted to the United States. Juan Cardenas, the Spanish Ambassador, had to make a special plea to the State Department to get the Falangist editor admitted.

Once allowed to enter the country, Lucientes began to divide his time between New York and Washington. He made Francisco Larcegui his chief assistant, and they started to send daily one thousand word cables to Madrid. Why so important a Falange writer holds so minor a post is a question that time alone will answer—perhaps the clue to his real role in the United States lies in the communications he exchanges regularly with José Ignacio Ramos, press attaché of the Spanish Embassy in Buenos Aires.

These moves were in line with the post-Pearl Harbor reorganization of the Falange on an active, belligerent war basis. A confidential report submitted by a responsible source to our government early in 1942 described the Falange organization in the United States in these words:

The Falangists act by the cell system. They are also divided into First, Second, and Third Line. Each of these lines have their work marked out. Each of these lines are split into groups of five men, of whom one is the leader. The orders are received by the Regional Chief, who in turn transmits them to the local chiefs. . . . In the Spanish Consulates, there is a Falangist responsible for transmitting orders to the local and the Regional chiefs. In New York, this person is Juan Adriensens, the Vice-Consul; he is sometimes replaced by the Chancellor, Mendez Quiros. In the Spanish Embassy in Washington, there are many men with this mission. There is Miguel Echegaray, Mr. Gortaza, Mr. Nunez, and Colonel Sierra, who is also in charge of the Secret Service. Gortaza is in charge of direct relations with the Japanese. Gortaza and Nunez are connected with the Falange groups in Mexico. They use young ladies for liaison work with the Mexican Falange cells.

This reorganization was accompanied by the establishment of a complete espionage network covering all ports in the United States. Falange agents on water-front assignments make their reports either to their Falange chiefs or to officers of visiting Spanish vessels who take their orders from Miguel Barcelo Martinez.

Among the Falange agents now in our ports permanently are men like José Gómez and Julio Torres. Gómez (alias Conacha) was a spy for Franco in Spain during the Spanish War. He now works out of New York with Torres, a former sailor who lives in the Puerto Rican section of Harlem. Both Torres and Gomez, who have no visible means of support, are always well dressed and well supplied with funds. They frequent bars used by seamen of all nations in the New York area. One of their regular hangouts is the International Bar on South Street, opposite the New York and Cuba Mail Pier. They mingle regularly with Italian longshoremen in Brooklyn and with known members of the Christian Front on the New York water front. At least once a week they tour the bars frequented by sailors on tankers plying out of Bayonne, New Jersey—the Standard Oil refining and shipping center.

Other Falangistas in American ports are occupied primarily with the task of smuggling vital and embargoed war materials to Spain. On at least two occasions, the United States Government has had to arrest Franco partisans for illegally sending aid to the Axis via Spanish ships.

The Spanish freighter *Isla de Teneriffe*, operated by a Spanish company, was seized in New York on December 15, 1941, by federal agents as it was about to sail with a cargo of lubricating oil, airplane silk, and enough radio parts to build fifty powerful short-wave transmitting stations. These war materials were being taken out of the country in violation of the export-control provisions of the Neutrality Act.

José Alberti and Eduardo Fernando, captain and radio operator of the ship, were arrested. Marcelino Garcia and Manuel Diaz, representatives of the shiping line, and José Mayorga, a shipping broker, were placed under bond.

The materials had been listed in the manifest as "ship's

stores." Garcia and Diaz were cleared of the charges when the Federal Attorney admitted that the government had no evidence to prove that they were directly implicated. Mayorga and the two ship's officers were fined $1000 each, the shipping line had to pay fines and penalties totalling $22,000, and the war materials were confiscated.

Less than a year later, the F. B. I. announced that the captain of the Spanish liner *Motomar* and four other men in Baltimore and New York had been arrested on charges of smuggling platinum out of the United States. In addition to the captain and the first mate of the C. T. E. liner, the F. B. I. arrested three Spaniards in New York—Dr. Juan Tomas Bareno, Manuel Rodriguez, headwaiter at the Park Central Hotel and member of the Casa de España, and Juan Gallego, a shipping man and leader of the Franco forces in New York.

What Gallego never knew was that some of his Casa de España *camaradas* who also happened to be his business rivals had had more than a little to do with his arrest.

Early in 1943, the F. B. I. ended the American career of Francisco Larcegui, dean of the Falange agents in the United States. Without consulting the State Department, the F. B. I. quietly saw to it that Larcegui departed for Madrid. The Falangista left behind a mistress employed by a government bureau and a host of fellow Spanish Falangistas still enjoying the hospitality of the United States. But he left with the certain knowledge that if he tries to return to the United States during the war he will wind up in a federal prison. He is now believed to be in Argentina. But his old superior, Francisco Lucientes, is still functioning in Washington.

The Falange in the United States, at this writing, is still an effective organization—doing Hitler's work with what amounts to immunity, and doing it well. Its chief strength lies in the diplomatic immunity the Falange legations continue to enjoy. Outside of Larcegui, none of the other key Falangist agents has been molested. Against the diplomatic immunity the leading Falangistas enjoy, the excellent work of the F. B. I. and of Army and Navy Intelligence is almost completely wasted. Only the end of diplomatic relations with Hitler Spain can seriously affect the machinations of the Falange Exterior in the United States.

Yet even the breach of diplomatic relations with Franco might be somewhat nullified in a strange manner.

Early in 1941 an individual named Augustin Guitierrez de Balbontin, or the Marqués de Aguiar, arrived in Washington on a British passport. The Marqués registered with the State Department as the official representative of the Catholic and the Royalist parties of Spain. His mission, he told reporters, was to win American aid in a movement to throw Franco out of power. To replace Franco, the Marqués proposed to restore the old Spanish monarchy.

To reporters, the Marqués conveyed information which had long been known to all governments. He revealed that the Falange, directed by Berlin, was working actively in Latin America. He revealed that, since November 1940, there had been at least twelve German divisions in Spain. He even described the Nazi military installations in the Canary Islands and in Spanish Morocco.

The Marqués sounded like a man who meant business. Spanish Republicans, however, refused to throw their hats into the air and cheer. Guided primarily by the knowledge that Republican opponents of Franco had less chance of getting United States visas than lepers, they began a quiet investigation of the Marqués.

A slight probe revealed that the royal title claimed by the distinguished visitor was not Spanish but Portuguese. It further disclosed that the last person to hold the title of Marqués de Aguiar in the twentieth century was Prince Dom Luis de Portugal. Dom Luis married Donna Maria de Mendoza. They had one son, who died while very young—thereby extinguishing the title.

On closer investigation, the claims of the gentleman in Washington began to seem as dubious as his title.

About the only thing that could be learned about the

man in Washington was that he was the probable owner of a large estate in Rapallo, Italy. In 1942 he visited Mexico accompanied by an officer of the British Intelligence Service. In Washington he joins the Falangistas in damning the Spanish Republic and talks about recruiting a legion of Spanish Royalists to fight against the Axis.

The Marqués, and his agent in Mexico—"the Marqués de Castéllon" born Luis Sevilla—seem to have won acceptance as the official opposition to Franco. In the light of events like the Darlan deal in North Africa, there would seem to be a real danger that in such "opposition forces" we can see the germ of a new appeasement scheme being devised by the State Department.

On paper, the anti-Franco statements of men like the Marqués de Aguiar sound good. But it must never be forgotten that the parties the Marqués says he represents formed the Spanish part of the Axis armies in the Spanish War. It was they who plotted with the Nazis to overthrow the Republic, and it is they who enjoy all the privileges of trusted Quislings in Spain today. They live well, they eat surpassingly well, and they have regained each of the privileges they had lost under the Republic. There is no reason why they should rise against Franco—unless Hitler orders such a rising.

Remember always that Hitler's chief use of Spain in this war is a source of oil and other supplies, and as a base of operations for spies and agents. To maintain these values, Hitler will not hesitate for one moment to sacrifice Franco for another puppet government which will perform the same services for him in Spain.

Reviving the Spanish monarchy might well turn out to be one of Hitler's trump cards in Spain. The Spanish Monarchists themselves—the huge landowners and industrialists —could continue to serve the Axis, and the Falangistas could simply change their uniforms. They know the art of changing uniforms well. In fact, José Maria Alfaro—who arrived in Washington as a member of Marqués de Aguiar's "official" Monarchist mission in 1941—subsequently turned up at a Nazi congress in Weimar, Germany, in November 1942. Alfaro and Ernesto Gimenez Caballero spoke as official representatives of the Spanish Falange at this congress.

The Marqués and his Mexican agent spread many stories about dissension in the Spanish Army. They are the source of endless rumors about Spanish generals becoming dissatisfied with Franco, angry at the Nazis, and anxious to assume the mantles of the Spanish Girauds and Peyroutons. These stories would sound better if Spanish generals were not now commanding Axis troops on the Russian front and doing Hitler's police work in Spain. They would sound still better if they did not come on the heels of similar rumors from Germany.

During the first World War, we heard similar tales about the German generals turning on the Kaiser. But after that war, the German generals destroyed the Weimar Republic and organized Hitler's armies. Even before the beginning of World War II, the Nazis were starting whispering campaigns abroad about dissension between the generals of the old *Reichswehr* and the Nazis. These whispers rise to a shrill crescendo every time the Allies slap another German army around. But somehow the Nazi legions never seem to lack for Junker generals.

On the heels of these rumors, the stories about the dissatisfaction of Franco's generals have an all too familiar *Reichswehr* ring. But then, it is a *Reichswehr* general who runs Spain today. His name, lest we ever forget it, is General Wilhelm von Faupel.

The Marqués de Aguiar, despite the dubiousness of his title, might be perfectly sincere. But he is admittedly the representative of those Spanish parties which joined with Hitler to destroy the Spanish Republic and bring Spain into the Axis. He is admittedly still an enemy of the only Spaniards who stood up and fought the Axis invasion of the Spanish Republic. His toleration by the State Department must therefore be classed as one of the most disturbing aspects of the Spanish picture today. If he does succeed in winning the support of London and Washington, we will find ourselves backing the creation of a Spanish government composed of just those Spaniards who have made the Falange a menace to our security as a nation.

CHAPTER ELEVEN

Womb of Postwar Fascism

THE FALANGE EXTERIOR is the "Auslands division" of Hitler's Spanish-speaking offensive against the United Nations. In this book we have seen the way the Falange Exterior operates in the Latin-American lands closest to our own borders, in the United States itself, in the Philippines, and—briefly—on the continent of South America. We have seen the Falange Exterior for what it is—a vast, organized, and highly dangerous Axis Fifth Column poised to strike in full force at the first word from the German High Command.

But what of Falangist Spain itself? Does Spain hold the same degree of menace for the United Nations? Or is Hitler's chief concern in Latin America?

On December 7, 1942, the first anniversary of the bombing of Pearl Harbor, Generalissimo Francisco Franco y Bahamonde, the nominal chief (by courtesy of the Third Reich) of the Spanish State, acknowledged Hitler's birthday greetings with a gracious thank-you telegram. "Many thanks to you and the German peoples," Franco wired Hitler. "May your arms triumph in the glorious undertaking of freeing Europe from the Bolshevik terror."

What Franco meant by "Bolshevik terror," of course, is known in the non-Axis world as the United Nations. Lest this be misunderstood, Franco, on the day following his wire to Hitler, delivered a long speech to the National Council of the Falange Española Tradicionalista de la J. O. N. S. in Madrid. The speech was broadcast to the entire nation. Among the honored guests of the Falange, at this meeting, were the German Ambassador; Sir Samuel Hoare, the British Ambassador; Carlton J. H. Hayes, the American Ambassador; the Papal Nuncio; and other top-ranking diplomats.

Franco spoke at length about Spain's role in the world at war, spoke in the weird mystic sentences so typical of

Falingismo. The war, he declared, was one which confronted the world with only one choice: fascism or communism. And Spain, he said, chose fascism.

In his speech Franco praised Mussolini as the founder of "the Fascist revolution—a social urge and a national idea. Later," Franco continued, "Germany found a new solution for the popular yearnings in national socialism, which unites the national and social idea for the second time in Europe with the special peculiarities of a race thirsting for international justice.

"Those are not isolated movements," Franco told the Falangistas and diplomats present to hear his speech, "but rather aspects of one and the same general movement and mass rebellion throughout the world. On the face, a new, useful consciousness emerged, which reacts against the hypocrisy and inefficiency of the old systems."

Franco pulled few punches in his address. "The moment of disillusionment is not far distant," he continued. "When the war ends and demobilization begins, the moment will arrive to settle accounts and to fulfill promises.

"Then, whatever projects there may exist now, the historic destiny of our era will be settled, either according to the barbarous formula of Bolshevist totalitarianism, or according to the spiritual, patriotic formula Spain offers us, or according to any other formula of the Fascist nations.

"Those are mistaken," Franco said, "who dream of the establishment of democratic liberal systems in Western Europe, bordering on Russian communism. Those err who speculate on liberal peace agreements or a bourgeois solution."

The speech of Francisco Franco, like his wire to Adolf Hitler, was clear as crystal to everyone but government officials in Washington and London. Both the White House and the State Department refused to comment on the speech at all. A United Press survey of official circles in London came up with the news that British leaders saw the speech as "mere lip service" to the Axis. The U. P. quoted one "London commentator" as saying: "Lip service to the Axis can be expected from the present Spanish leaders up to Germany's final defeat. This does not alter the fact that Spain wants to remain neutral and Franco knows it."

Berlin, to be sure, saw the speech in a more realistic light. The diplomatic correspondent of the Nazi Transocean News Agency reported that Berlin felt it was a "great speech championing the European cause and as a spiritual declaration of war against liberalism, democracy, and Bolshevism."

Eight days after the speech was delivered in Madrid, Foreign Secretary Anthony Eden blandly refused to heed the demands of many members of the House of Commons, that Britain send Franco a stiff note for his utterances. Eden declared that he could sense "no value" in such an action.

At the moment Hitler was chuckling over Eden's answer to the House of Commons requests, Franco called up the third military class to be conscripted since November 1942. And the Spanish Blue Legions, 100,000 strong, went on firing their guns from the Nazi front-line positions in the Soviet Union.

On January 15, 1943, American Ambassador Carlton Hayes delivered a speech of his own in Madrid—this time to a group of diplomats and Spanish officials. The topic of his talk was "American War Aims." Ambassador Hayes attacked Germany, Japan, and Italy, praised the Atlantic Charter, and then attacked what he chose to define as Axis-inspired murmurs that Falangist Spain could not survive a United Nations victory.

"If the political and social institutions of this country (Spain) undergo change or modification in future years," Hayes declared, "it will be the work of Spaniards within Spain—not of the United States or of Spanish émigrés."

Less than a week after this speech was delivered, I had dinner with a group of Latin-American diplomats in Washington—all of them individuals in close touch with their countries. To a man, they swore (and not too pleasantly) that with these few ill-chosen words, Hayes had set the United States back at least fifty years in Latin America, and all but destroyed our prestige with that vast majority of

Spaniards *within Spain* who live only for that day they can strike a mortal blow at their Nazi overlords. The Hayes speech was instantly interpreted as an American guarantee that Falangist Spain will not be held to account for its open, if undeclared, war on the United Nations.

The remarks Hayes made about the "Spanish émigrés" were particularly painful reading to all enemies of the Axis. For these émigrés include those whole companies of Spanish Republican soldiers who were among the first to instruct and fight with the British Commandos; those regiments of émigré Spanish Republicans who joined the French Foreign Legion to continue their armed struggle against Hitler's troops and who were interned in North African prison camps by Pétain and Laval after the fall of France; those thousands of émigré Spanish Republicans who risk their lives daily in their unceasing campaign against Falangist spies and agents in the New World. In effect, Ambassador Hayes said that those Spaniards who have been waging war against the Axis since July 1936 are undesirables; that the only Spaniards worthy of American support are those Latin Quislings who hold empty offices merely by the good graces of Adolf Hitler and General Wilhelm von Faupel.

The Hayes speech came at a time when American troops in North Africa were exposing their flanks to the Nazi-armed and Nazi-led troops of Spanish Morocco. This Spanish colony itself was the seat of all anti-American Fifth Column activities in North Africa. Here Falangist chiefs were and are working with all elements who can add to the toll of American lives in the African theater of this war. Among the men who are working so closely with the Falange in Spanish Morocco are Merebi Rebbo, the Hitler-blessed "Blue Sultan" and the former chief of the pro-Axis Iraq government, Rashid Ali El-Gailani. (In Spanish Morocco, while Spain was still a republic in 1936, the government had a garrison of 1683 officers and 40,383 men. The Fascists increased this garrison, in 1939, to two complete army corps—a force of over 200,000 soldiers. By

1943, this 200,000 strong army had been more than doubled in size.)

Were the Hayes speech the isolated remarks of a not-too-intelligent American citizen, it could be overlooked. It is no secret that, during the Spanish War, Carlton Hayes was one of Franco's most outspoken partisans in American university circles. As an individual who attacked today's Spanish émigrés when they started to fight Hitler's legions, Hayes has a perfect right to retain his animosity for the Spanish Republicans. But when Hayes spoke in Madrid on January 15, 1942, he no longer spoke as a medieval-minded professor in a private university. He spoke as the United States Ambassador to a Spain which at that moment held a minimum of 16 divisions of Nazi troops within its borders —Nazi troops poised to take Gibraltar and kill American soldiers in North Africa.

For obvious reasons, the Hayes speech is a warning signal to all Americans that something has gone wrong somewhere. It is a sign that the full significance of Axis Spain must be examined—and at once.

The time has come for all whose destinies are bound up with victory for the United Nations in this war to turn the spotlight on the menace Spain holds for just this victory. We must examine and evaluate and act—lest our delay add at least another million lives to the cost of ultimate victory. We must begin to see Falangist Spain in its true colors— Hitler Spain with its networks of spies and hidden war bases in the Western Hemisphere, its Blue Legion of 100,000 troops fighting against our allies in Russia, and its terrifying "neutrality."

This neutrality of Falangist Spain is one of Hitler's richest Iberian bonanzas. It pays enormous dividends daily. To thousands of United Nations seamen, one of the dividends Hitler gets from Spanish neutrality has never been a secret. This dividend is oil.

Since the summer of 1939, a fleet of nearly eighty tankers and merchant ships flying the crimson and gold flag of

Franco Spain has been carrying oil and gasoline from Curacao and other ports in the Caribbean to the Canary Islands, Tangiers, Vigo, Barcelona, Ceuta, Cadiz, and other neutral Spanish ports. These ships were often supplemented by the tankers of other nations—including the United States —which maintained diplomatic relations with Franco Spain.

None of the Spanish tankers are painted wartime gray or otherwise camouflaged. Not one of them has been deliberately torpedoed or attacked by air since the war began, although United Nations freighters bound for United Nations ports have been sunk regularly in these waters since September 1939.

At Teneriffe the fuel carried by these neutral Spanish ships is transferred to the storage tanks of the great submarine base the German Navy started to construct in 1937. This Canary Islands depot not only fuels Nazi submarines but also transfers vast quantities of oil to Italian and German tankers which visit the port regularly.

A newer German submarine base is serviced by the Spanish tankers which call at Vigo, in Galicia, an important port near the Portuguese border. Vigo is more than a German submarine base, however. It is also the city which harbors the chief southern European headquarters of German Intelligence.

The Nazis maintain naval fueling stations at Ceuta, Melilla, Cadiz, and Tangiers, as well as emergency air bases for all Axis aircraft. These bases, too, are serviced by the tankers which ply blithely between the Caribbean and Spain.

When gasoline rationing began to affect thousands of American motorists, the Nazis in Madrid made political capital out of the Hitler oil line to Spain. They released a story, shortly before Christmas 1942, to the effect that a new pact with the United States had eased the restrictions on gasoline for private automobile owners in Spain. Washington authorities issued quick denials. The Associated Press quoted one anonymous official who denied that gasoline supplies were flowing from the United States to Spain, but affirmed that Spanish tankers were loading up at Caribbean ports.

To date, no American official has seen fit to comment on the ultimate consumers of this oil. The Nazi bases which get this oil are not imaginary. Hundreds of American seamen have seen them. Nevertheless, the newspapers and radio commentators periodically repeat the Nazi-propaganda story about Franco's latest refusal to cede these bases to the Nazis. With each repetition of this fairy tale, the myth of Franco's independence has grown. The fact that all of these stories have originated from such obvious sources of Nazi propaganda as Switzerland, Turkey, and Stockholm has been generally overlooked.

The quest for oil has long been one of Hitler's principal war aims. He has, to date, received probably more oil via Spanish neutrality than he has through European conquest. The Nazi efforts to preserve this Spanish oil line have also proved far less costly in men and material since September 1939 than the drives for the oil of Roumania, Trans-Caucasia, and the fields of Maikop. For the preservation of this Spanish oil line, then, if for no other reason, Hitler can ill afford to sacrifice Spanish neutrality for the sake of a few redundant headlines in the German press.

Hitler's anxiety to preserve Spanish neutrality is therefore much easier to comprehend than the frantic official anxiety over this specious neutrality that crops up on Mondays and Thursdays in London and Washington. Apologists and official spokesmen for the Foreign Office and the State Department explain our continued appeasement of Franco Spain in only one way: United Nations appeasement of Spain is preserving Spanish neutrality.

These apologists for appeasement present a case that would be impregnable if it had the remotest relation to the ugly realities of the world of 1943. The case is based largely on the map of southern Europe and North Africa, a map which includes Gibraltar and the Mediterranean. Pointing to this map, the spokesmen for appeasement point to Spanish Morocco and the 500,000 troops it harbors. They point to

Spain's strategic position, its proximity to Gibraltar and France.

"Here then is the map," runs a typical appeasement argument. "If we offend Franco, he will send his 500,000 troops in Spanish Morocco against our troops in North Africa. Moreover, Spanish troops will attack Gibraltar. Therefore, we must remain on good terms with the Spanish leader. Moreover, if we get Franco angry, he will turn over the Canary Islands and the Balearics to Hitler for use as submarine and air bases against us. Moreover, Hitler will then overrun Spain itself."

The commanders of the Nazi submarine and air bases in Spanish Morocco, the Canaries, and the Belearics, like the officers of the minimum of sixteen divisions of German troops in Spain itself, find this argument comforting reading when British and American papers fall into their hands. They are even more amused by the argument put forth in London and Washington, and repeated frequently in the British and American press, that Hitler represents the greatest threat to the neutrality Franco is trying valiantly to preserve.

The Nazis are far from loath to spread this story. Nazi propaganda mills in Berlin, Bern, Ankara, Stockholm, and Madrid have been keeping this story alive since 1939. From the very start of the war, Nazi-planted stories have kept the press of Britain and America speculating at great length about Franco's chances of making a firm stand against the rapacious Nazis. This propaganda has been so successful that all newspaper war maps of Europe always show Spain as a neutral nation—in contrast to Axis-Germany and Italy and Axis-dominated France and Holland and other Axis-occupied countries.

This Nazi plan to paint Francisco Franco as the Great Neutral has, in many instances, followed certain proved Nazi formulae. One of these has been the creation of an *Ersatz* set of Axis foes within the portals of an Axis government. Since 1933 the Nazis found that this stunt worked quite well in Germany: starry-eyed statesmen and correspondents accepted at face value Nazi fictions which diverted their attention from Nazi realities. Chief among these fictions has been the once-well-believed story that Herman Goering was really a moderate conservative who joined the Nazis only to stamp out communism, but was really a friend of the Western Democracies. The Goering myth still lingers, as does the other hardy Nazi lie about the *Reichswehr* generals who always hated Hitler.

In Spain, the Nazis created a neat little straw man to play Hitler to Franco's Goering. This straw man was Serrano Suner, Franco's brother-in-law and, before July 1936, a nonentity of minute proportions. Carefully the Nazis built Suner up as the very symbol of Spain-Axis collaboration. Suner was made Foreign Minister of the puppet Spanish State. His visits to Berlin and Rome were broadcast to the world by the Nazis. His violent pro-Nazi speeches were conceived and edited by no less a personality than General Wilhelm von Faupel himself.

When Suner was sufficiently tarred by the Nazi brush, the Nazi rumor mills in Turkey and Switzerland began to put out wild stories of dissension within Spain. The wilder the stories, the more credence they gained in our press. The gist of these stories was that Franco and Suner were quarreling over Spain's neutrality: Suner was demanding that Spain go in on the side of the Axis, whereas Franco, the anti-Nazi, was holding out for neutrality.

These rumors were reaching their peak in the summer of 1942. By that time, the German High Command started to realize that the Soviet oil fields were not going to fall into Nazi hands for at least another year—if ever. Anxious eyes in Berlin looked toward the Spanish oil line from the Western Hemisphere to Nazi Europe. Nazi leaders locked heads over the problem and started to work out a means of making this Spanish oil field more secure.

A plan was devised in Berlin, with the assistance of von Faupel in Madrid. It called for Falangist leaders in Latin America to start weeping for the art treasures of old Spain in the presence of American diplomats and good-will missions. When the dewy-eyed Americans handed the weeping Falangistas their handkerchiefs, the Latin-American art lovers were then to hint broadly that if the United States would only do something about restoring the ruined paintings and churches of Spain, Franco would surely do something to please the Jew-Protestant-Masonic dogs of Yankees.

The plan worked like a charm. Toward the end of August 1942 President Roosevelt announced that, in co-operation with Latin-American leaders, the United States would set up a project to restore Spain's churches, roads, and art treasures after the war. The pro-Axis press in Latin America picked this up and played it as a Roosevelt endorsement of Franco. The astringent-tongued Clare Booth Luce, then running for Congress, quickly painted this move as "our old friend appeasement under a new name." While the Nazis gloated, Mrs. Luce went on to say:

The insidious thing about the proposed art project in Spain is that it implies that Franco will be there after the war. If any Fascist dictator is there after the war, we will already have lost the peace.

But Mrs. Luce's all-too-rational words were buried in the mountains of columns the press devoted to the Spanish event which followed the President's announcement. For on September 3, 1942, the appeasement gesture brought forth a redundant dividend: Suner was dismissed as both Foreign Minister and Chief of the Falange.

Typical of the headlines on this story was the one appearing in the N. Y. *Post* on that day: "FRANCO KICKS OUT SUNER, NAZI STOOGE." Said the United Press:

Serrano Suner was the foremost advocate of all-out collaboration with Hitler and chief backer of the totalitarian Falange Party. For many months there have been repeated reports of a split between Serrano Suner and General Franco over the question of complete Spanish collaboration with the Axis. . . .

The Spanish censorship prevented correspondents from indicating what factors lay behind General Franco's sudden move. However, it was noted that only last week President Roosevelt advanced a program of American aid in restoring Spanish art treasures and cultural monuments damaged in Spain's bitter civil war. . . . The upheaval indicates at least the possibility of a Spanish swing away from the Axis orbit and toward that of the Allies.

In Washington, State Department appeasers pointed proudly to Suner's dismissal as a positive achievement of master diplomacy. No one bothered to look into the records of the "moderates" who entered the Spanish Government in this "anti-Nazi shake-up." Had the new Ministers been investigated, the appeasers might have been forced to sing another tune.

To replace Suner as head of the Falange, Franco "chose" Manuel Mora Figueroa—who had to return from the Soviet Front, where he was a leader of the Nazi Army's Spanish Blue Divisions, to accept the job. Figueroa, who was also made Minister of Industry and Commerce, is a veteran Falange leader whose pro-Nazi views were never kept secret. General Carlos Asensio Cabinallas, who became War Minister in the purge which pushed Suner out of the government, is another old Falange leader who proved his worth to von Faupel by strengthening the Nazi grip on the Spanish Army long before the "Suner Crisis." Blas Perez Gonzalez, the prominent "moderate" who became Minister of Government in this shake-up, previously served as the Attorney-General of the Supreme Court—where he was responsible for the legal veneer given to the Nazi terror waged on all anti-Nazis in Spain.

Within the Falange itself, those Falangistas who had been closest to Suner were promoted to more important posts after Suner was dropped.

These realities, however, seem to have been overlooked in London and Washington. Franco's move, although plainly dictated by the oil-hungry Nazis, was fervently accepted at its face value. The Spanish oil line remained untouched.

By the time Francisco Franco made his December 8 speech to the Grand Council of the Falange, Serrano Suner had long since been restored to his position on the Falange National Council. Suner was sitting on the dais as big as life when the American and the British ambassadors heard Franco call for an Axis victory over the United Nations. But despite Suner, despite Franco's words, our own appeasers were still making bright sayings about the anti-Axis importance of Spanish neutrality even after the Russian Army increased Hitler's dependence on the Spanish oil lines by retaking the Maikop oil fields in the January 1943 offensive.

General Wilhelm von Faupel, architect of Falangist Spain and its actual ruler, is no fool. He knows exactly how popular Adolf Hitler is in the non-Axis world, and he knows precisely what the consequences would be if Spanish neutrality were ended by an overt move on the part of the Spanish and German armies in Spain or Spanish Morocco.

The Nazi *Gauleiter* of Spain knows full well that appeasement, which bore such a heavy responsibility for the triumph of Nazi arms in Spain, is still the key to the defenses of Hitler's Spanish outpost. The thunderous reverses the Nazis have suffered on the Russian and African fronts—which have decimated German reserves of both men and materials—have made Axis Spain more dependent than ever upon appeasement as a prerequisite of Fascist power.

Any overt military move would, by sheer weight of military logic (which is generally closer to earth than diplomatic logic), force the end of appeasement in Spain. An analysis of the certain consequences of what would follow if what the appeasers claim they fear most materializes, explains why. The appeasers justify their action by making dire prophecies that Spain will attack Gibraltar from the Spanish mainland and our own troops in Africa from Spanish Morocco unless we give in to Franco at every turn.

But von Faupel could and probably has drawn a blueprint of what would follow if Spanish neutrality ended in this manner. In essence, this blueprint would run something like this:

As soon as the attacks were launched, the American and British military chiefs would counter with force. This counter-move would bring with it a declaration of war on the part of the United Nations against Spain. War would end Spanish neutrality, and with the end of this neutrality would come the end of the Spanish oil line which supplies Hitler's armed forces with oil from the New World.

The immediate effect of this open attack, then—even if Hitler's Spanish puppets raze Gibraltar and kill thousands of American soldiers in North Africa—would be the total loss of a vital oil supply for the oil-starved Nazi war machine.

The Nazi submarine bases in the Canaries and the Balearics would be bombed incessantly by American planes and, probably, captured by combined American and British naval and aerial forces.

The fleet of C. T. E. liners which today deliver hundreds of Axis spies and agents to all of the Western Hemisphere and transport vital food and war necessities from the New World to Nazi Germany would no longer be free to cross the oceans. The end of this vital link with the Americas, plus the closing of the Falange-controlled legations in every North and South American country except Argentina, would cripple the effectiveness of the Falange Exterior.

Within Spain itself, our armies would discover a population which will receive them as long-waited liberators. The hundreds of unsung Spanish Republican guerrilla bands who are making Nazi lives miserable in Spain today would seek out the American troops and join forces with them. In the hills of the Asturias alone, there is a guerrilla army of some 50,000 trained men who have been waging unceasing war on the Nazis since 1939. This and similar existing armies would fight alongside of our troops in Spain. Our military leaders would quickly discover that Spain has over 500,000 trained veterans of the three-year war against Hitler—a half-million tested soldiers ready to pick up American guns and use them for the extermination of Nazis.

The development of the American counter-offensive in Spain would quickly create the kind of second European front Hitler has successfully avoided since the start of the war. Under the combined weight of American troops and Spaniards armed with American guns, Spain would not remain in Axis hands for more than six months. The liquidation of fascism in Spain would hasten the United Nations drive on France—perhaps from both Spain and England at the same time. The United Nations drive on France would certainly cause the Russians to intensify their own drive on Germany.

This entire prospect is enough to give the Nazi leaders nightmares—and to guarantee against their allowing it to happen of their own free will. Spain's neutrality, like von Faupel's Hispanidad, is carefully utilized and protected by the Nazis as a war instrument of the Third Reich.

The fruits of this neutrality must never be ignored. Oil from the Americas. Phosphates—without which soils lose their fertility—from Spanish Morocco. Oranges and olive oil from Spain. Wheat, cattle, leather, wool. Copper, zinc, mercury, silver. The riches of Spain and the fruits of Spanish commerce. Only the neutrality of Spain can keep these necessities flowing into the increasingly hungry German maw. The last figures released by the Spanish Ministry of Commerce tell the story in their own way: Spanish exports to Germany rose from 14 million *pesetas* in 1940 to 161 million *pesetas* in 1941, placing Germany squarely at the top of the list of Spain's export customers. Little wonder that the 1942 figures were not revealed! (Nor, in citing these figures, must we overlook the aid given to the Axis by Portugal, that other Fascist state of the Iberian Peninsula. Portuguese exports to Germany rose from 29,000,000 *escudos* in 1940 to 565,000,000 *escudos* in 1941—quite a tidy little boom for a neutral nation.)

Despite the claims of our appeasers, it is painfully clear

that the *only* beneficiaries of Spanish neutrality are the Nazi masters of Spain. Similarly, it is also evident that for the sake of victory in this war, the United Nations must take immediate steps to end this Nazi-devised pseudo-neutrality. Even if this myth is ended by a formal declaration of war, the benefits to be gained by this act will far outweigh the costs.

Advocates of the continuing appeasement of Falangist Spain have one last-ditch argument: the effect of a United Nations stand against Franco on Latin America. Their claim, as stated, seems formidable. "The nations of Latin America are all firmly Catholic nations," runs this argument; "and Franco is a leader blessed by the Pope himself. As Catholics, Latin Americans support Falangist Spain. But more than religion binds the average Latin American to Falangist Spain. There are also the ties of race and blood with the mother country. These ties explain the widespread sympathy Franco has found in Latin America."

Like most appeasement theses, this one simply fails to stand up against the truth. The political power and the size of the Catholic Church in Latin America are grossly overrated. In most countries of Latin America, the political influence of the Church has been on the decline for the last four decades. Whatever support native Fascists and Spanish Fascists won from the Church Hierarchies during the past few decades has speeded the decline of the Church's political influence with the common people of the Latin countries. For just as the power of the Church has been consistently overrated, so, too, have the inherent intelligence and instinct for democracy of the average Latin-American Catholic been vastly underrated.

The average Catholic, like the average Protestant or atheist, in Latin America is not a person of means. He is a person who has to work for a meager living, who suffers under tyranny, who benefits from even the slightest vestige of democracy. When he is forced to choose between fascism and democracy, the average Latin-American Catholic will choose democracy—whether or not his Church backs fascism. In Latin America, when the Church has become adamant and demanded that communicants choose fascism or suffer excommunication, such ultimatums have generally seen the Church losing members in droves.

The 1942 Uruguayan general elections are a fairly good reflection of the actual power of political clericalism. The candidate of the pro-United States and liberal Colorado (Red) Party, Juan José Amezaga, won the Presidency by a vote of more than twice that given his Blanco (White) Party opponent—who ran on an isolationist, hate-Uncle Sam platform. The Colorados elected eighteen senators, the Blancos seven, the Independent Nationalists three, and the Catholic Party—exactly one senator. The Chamber of Deputies, Uruguay's lower house, was formed of sixty-one Colorados, twenty-two Blancos, ten Independent Nationalists, three Catholics, two Communists, and one Socialist.

These figures show that Latin-American Catholics—Uruguay is an almost completely Catholic country—are as independent in their political thinking as are North American Protestants. Every candidate elected in the Uruguayan elections—from the Colorados who stood for the democratic liberalism and the Communists who stood for the Marxism Franco has chosen to designate as the twin evils of the modern world—was put into office by the ballots of Latin American Catholics. In the light of these figures, it is, therefore easy to understand why, in 1943, Uruguay declared April 14—the twelfth anniversary of the founding of the Spanish Republic—a legal holiday. The Governments of Cuba, Chile, and Mexico sent official delegations to Montevideo to join in the initial celebration of this "Day of the Motherland."

The racial ties which bind Latin Americans to Franco Spain are misunderstood. Every Latin American country has a comparative handful of Spaniards and sons of Spaniards of great wealth—men whose funds are in large or small measure tied up in Spanish investments. This element backed the Fascists against the Spanish Republic because they felt that this was best for their investments. Now that Hitler has frozen all Spanish funds, these investments no longer pay dividends. Most of the wealthy Spaniards in Latin America are convinced that their Spanish funds will be unfrozen if the Axis wins the war. Consequently, to guarantee their Spanish investments, they back Hitler and Hitler-Spain.

But these Franco supporters represent a slim minority. The majority of the Spaniards and sons of Spaniards in Latin America are poor people who were driven to Latin America by the poverty of old Spain. A not inconsiderable number of them were Republicans and Freemasons and radicals who held the monarchy responsible for their misery. Their only stake in Franco Spain is their families—poor people, like themselves. Most poor people in Spain were and are Republicans, and, as such, are persecuted by the Falange in Spain.

These people outnumber the Franco supporters in Latin America by about a hundred to one. During the Spanish War they fervently supported the Republic against the Fascists.

Those Latin Americans who back the United Nations in this war—and they constitute the vast majority of the population of every country in Latin America, including Argentina—are against Franco as much as they are against Hitler. Precisely because of their racial, cultural, and often family ties with Spain, they were aware of the menace of Spain and the Falange long before Pearl Harbor.

Beginning in July 1936, the people of the Latin-American countries have watched the spectacle of their own native Fascists, their own powerful enemies of democracy, line up solidly behind the Axis in Spain. Next to Spaniards today living under the iron heel of the Nazis in Spain itself or Spanish Republican émigrés, our simple, average, hardworking Latin-American neighbors understand the real issues of Spain better than any other peoples in this world.

If they actually seem a little anxious for the United Nations to invade Franco Spain, their anxiety can be traced to more than ideological tenets. Talk to a democratic United Nations statesman off the record, and the chances are that one phrase will crop up in the discussion. "To us Latin

Americans," he will say, "a long war is as bad as a lost war."

What he means, of course, is that the war had just about completely cut off nonindustrial Latin America from its necessary quota of manufactured goods. In former years these necessities came largely from the United States and England—and to a lesser but considerable extent from the Axis nations. Unable to import manufactured goods, unable to export their agricultural produce, the Latin-American nations are feeling the war more drastically than the United States.

An example of how this pinch feels—and this case is chosen at random—is a typical Mexican town. This is a small but important town whose one sugar refining mill employs some 18,000 workers. The whole town draws its water from a central artesian well equipped with an American pump. Less than a year after Pearl Harbor, the pump began to break down. Engineers who examined it pronounced it beyond repair, and a hurry call was sent to the United States for a new pump and a new electric motor. After six months of agonizing negotiation, the town was able to secure a second-hand motor and a slightly used pump. During these six months, the pump broke down often. But the town was lucky. Many towns in Latin America have not been able to get needed pumps, or sewing machines, or even shoes, in time.

Such hardships have been fuel for the Fascist fires burning all over Latin America. Falangistas—who control the press of so many Latin-American countries—play up these wartime hardships for all they are worth. The war will bring still wider misery to Latin America. In the wake of these hardships, the Falange Exterior—kept at top efficiency by its diplomatic network and the immunity of Spanish ships on the high seas—will pour Nazi oil on the war fires of Latin-American nations.

"A long war is as bad as a lost war for us," the Latin-American democrats repeat. "Therefore any step that will shorten the war is one we will back. If this step is the invasion of Falangist Spain, which most of us hate, so much the better."

The appeasement sets of London and Washington suffered a shock when President Fulgencio Batista of Cuba visited the United States in January 1943 and frankly discussed Spain with the reporters in New York.

One reporter asked Batista: "What would be the effect in South America if the Allies should invade Spain?"

Without hesitating Batista replied: "Everyone would love it!" He went on to explain in very graphic terms that such a move would meet with total support in all of Latin America.

Perhaps President Batista was not speaking for all of the statesmen or the newspaper publishers of Latin America. But everyone who knows Latin America knows that Fulgencio Batista was voicing the sentiments of the overwhelming majority of the people of the Latin-American nations.

The facts, then, boil down to one military possibility: thousands upon thousands of Latin Americans in belligerent and non-belligerent countries will be among the first to volunteer for overseas duty if Falangist Spain becomes a fighting front in this war.

On January 3, 1943, the American State Department issued a White Book on United States Foreign Policy during the decade 1931—1941. Like the Carlton Hayes speech in Madrid, it was eloquent evidence that our State Department still persists in the disastrous belief that the international issues raised in July 1936—when Germany and Italy invaded Spain—were liquidated by the triumph of Axis arms in April 1939.

The very thesis of the White Paper, stated on its opening page, exposes the fantastic blindness of the men responsible for our present costly policy toward Falangist Spain. The opening section of this important document is, correctly, entitled "The Fateful Decade." It starts with these words:

The fateful decade, 1931-1941, began and ended with acts

of violence by Japan. It was marked by the ruthless development of a determined policy of world domination on the part of Japan, Germany, and Italy.

In 1931 Japan seized Manchuria. Two years later Germany withdrew from the Disarmament Conference and began rearming. In 1934 Japan gave notice of termination of the Washington Treaty for the Limitation of Naval Armament.

In 1935 Italy invaded Ethiopia. In 1936 Hitler tore up the Treaty of Locarno and fortified the demilitarized Rhineland Zone. In 1937 Japan again attacked China. In 1938 Hitler occupied Austria and dismembered Czechoslovakia. During the first half of 1939 Hitler completed the destruction of Czechoslovakia and seized Memel, while Italy invaded Albania.

In September 1939 Hitler struck at Poland, and during the two years that followed almost all of the countries of Europe were plunged or dragged into war. In 1940 Japan with threats of force entered French Indo-China. Finally, on December 7, 1941, Japan launched an armed attack on the United States, followed immediately by declarations of war against the United States on the part of Japan, of Germany, of Italy, and of their satellites.

During the decade described in these paragraphs, Italy and Germany invaded a sovereign republic about thirty times the size of Albania and subdued it after nearly three years of bloody warfare. It was the first major European battle of the World War which finally hit us at Pearl Harbor in 1941. The world will never forget what happened in Spain. But the State Department evidently does not even know it happened.

The White Book contains 144 pages of fairly small type. The chapter called "Civil Conflict in Spain" takes up just slightly less than one page. This page says, in part:

Another threat to peace occurred in July 1936 with the outbreak of a civil conflict in Spain. The attitude of this Government toward the conflict was based squarely upon the consistent policy of the United States of promoting peace and at the same time avoiding involvement in war situations. . . .

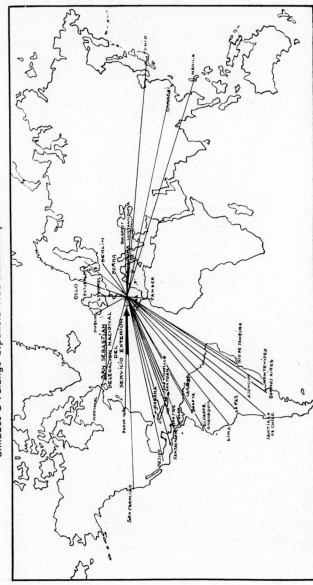

afiliados a Falange Española Tradicionalista y de las J. O. N. S.

¡ARRIBA ESPAÑA!

THIS MAP OF GENERAL VON FAUPEL'S IN-
TERNATIONAL Fifth Column, the Falange Exterior, is taken from the book, *La Falange Exterior*,
printed by the Spanish Falangistas in Santander, Spain,
in October, 1938. San Sebastian was then the main
Falange headquarters. The frankness of this map and
of the book's pictures (*see* pages 14 and 15 of this section) led the Nazis to suppress the publication immediately. Note that the Falange made no secret of its
Manila branch.

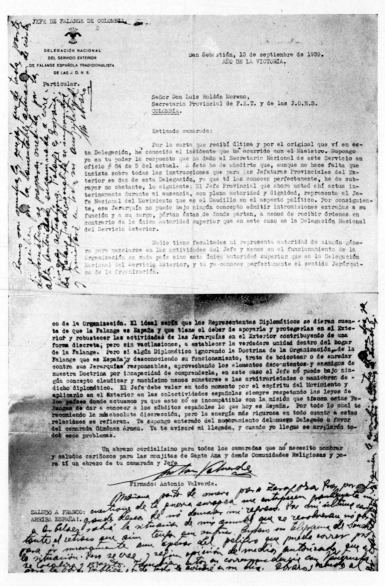

JEFE DE FALANGE DE COLOMBIA

DELEGACIÓN NACIONAL
DEL SERVICIO EXTERIOR
DE FALANGE ESPAÑOLA TRADICIONALISTA
DE LAS J. O. N. S.

Particular.

San Sebastián, 13 de septiembre de 1939.
AÑO DE LA VICTORIA.

Señor Don Luis Roldán Moreno,
Secretario Provincial de F.E.T. y de las J.O.N.S.
COLOMBIA.

Estimado camarada:

Por la carta que recibí última y por el original que ví en esta Delegación, he conocido el incidente que ha ocurrido con el Ministro. Supongo ya en tu poder la respuesta que ha dado el Secretario Nacional de este Servicio en oficio # 84 de 5 del actual. A ésto he de añadirte que, aunque no hace falta que insista sobre todas las instrucciones que para las Jefaturas Provinciales del Exterior se dan de esta Delegación, ya que tú las conoces perfectamente, he de subrayar no obstante, lo siguiente: El Jefe Provincial que ahora usted ahí actua interinamente durante mi ausencia, con plena autoridad y dignidad, representa al Jefe Nacional del Movimiento que es el Caudillo en el aspecto político. Por consiguiente, esa Jerarquía no puede bajo ningún concepto admitir intromisiones extrañas a su función y a su cargo, pártan éstas de donde partan, a menos de recibir órdenes en contrario de la única Autoridad superior que en este caso es la Delegación Nacional del Servicio Exterior.

Nadie tiene facultades ni representa autoridad de ningún género para mezclarse en las actividades del Jefe y menos en el funcionamiento de la Organización en cada país sino esta única autoridad superior que es la Delegación Nacional del Servicio Exterior, y tu ya conoces perfectamente el sentido Jerárquico de la Organización.

co de la Organización. El ideal sería que los Representantes Diplomáticos se dieran cuenta de que la Falange es España y que tienen el deber de apoyarla y protegerla en el Exterior y robustecer las actividades de las Jerarquías en el Exterior contribuyendo de una forma discreta, pero sin vacilaciones, a establecer la verdadera unidad dentro del hogar de la Falange. Pero si algún Diplomático ignorando la Doctrina de la Organización, de la Falange que es España y desconociendo su funcionamiento, trata de boicotear o de enredar contra sus Jerarquías responsables, aprovechando los elementos descontentos y enemigos de nuestra Doctrina por incapacidad de comprenderla, en este caso el Jefe no puede bajo ningún concepto claudicar y muchísimo menos someterse a las arbitrariedades o maniobras de dicho Diplomático. El Jefe debe velar en todo momento por el espíritu del Movimiento y aplicarlo en el Exterior en las colectividades españolas siempre respetando las leyes de los países donde actuamos ya que esto no es incompatible con la misión que tienen estas Falanges de dar a conocer a los súbditos españoles lo que hoy es España. Por todo lo cual te recomiendo la más absoluta discreción, pero la energía más rigurosa en todo cuanto a estas relaciones se refieran. Te supongo enterado del nombramiento del nuevo Delegado a favor del camarada Giménez Arnau. Ya te avisaré mi llegada, y cuando yo llegue se arreglarán todos esos problemas.

Un abrazo cordialísimo para todos los camaradas que no necesito nombrar y saludos cariñosos para las monjitas de Santa Ana y demás Comunidades Religiosas y para tí un abrazo de tu camarada y Jefe

Firmado: Antonio Valverde.

SALUDO A FRANCO:
ARRIBA ESPAÑA!.

PROOF THAT SPANISH DIPLOMATS TAKE ORDERS from the Falange Chiefs in Latin-American countries. This letter, sent by the Chief of the Colombian Falange, Valverde, was passed by the Spanish Censors. (The important paragraphs are translated on page 29.) Luis Roldan Moreno, recipient of this letter, later succeeded Valverde as Chief.

ONE DAY AFTER José del Castano (above) was appointed Spain's Consul-General in Manila, *Arriba* of Madrid published official notice (right) of his also being made Chief of the Falange in the Philippines.

Servicio Exterior

NOMBRAMIENTO

En uso de las atribuciones que me están conferidas. vengo en nombrar Jefe de F. E. T. y de las JONS en Filipinas al camarada Jose del Castaño y Cardona.

Por Dios, España y su Revolución Nacional-Sindicalista.

Madrid, 4 de noviembre de 1940

El Delegado Nacional,

P. D.,

El Secretario Nacional,
José Jiménez Rosado

IN MANILA, BEFORE PEARL HARBOR, the Falange did not hide its light beneath any bushel. Scenes like this were quite common. In the above picture, published in *La Democracia*, of Manila, in July 7, 1941, the men in the front row are (left to right) Antonio Porta, Falange Chief Martin Pou, Andres Soriano, and Enrique Zobel. Soriano is now Secretary of The Treasury in the Philippine Government-in-Exile.

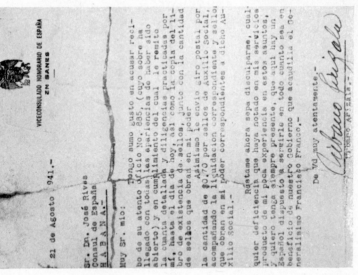

THE FALANGE USES SPANISH LEGA-
TIONS for even the most minor of Axis Fifth
Column tasks in the Western Hemisphere. Thus
men like Vice-Consul Arizala of Banes, Cuba, even
collect pittances for Falangist cells and front

ALTHOUGH ILLEGAL IN CUBA when this letter
was written, the Falange maintained excellent relations with many powerful groups—in this case a college. (*See* page 68.) Spanish Consul-General Riestra,
letter's recipient, was later expelled from Cuba for Fa-

THE FALANGE EXTERIOR'S MYSTERIOUS "CAMARADA MAR-
TINEZ" (wearing uniform) visits North and South American ports regularly as a wireless operator on Spanish ships. (*See* Chapter Six.) With him
(above) are Sergio Cifuentes, Francisco Alvarez Garcia, and Miguel Baguer.
(*See* Chapter Three.)

CUBAN SECRET POLICE SEIZED THESE GUNS in home of just one
Falange member in Havana during the raids of 1941 (*see* Chapter Three.)
Franco's framed portrait was hidden with the rifles. Similar arsenals were
found in countless Falangist homes during the Cuban raids.

DIARIO DE LA MARINA
DIRECTOR

La Habana, 29 de Febrero de 1940.

Sr. Jesús M. Marinas,
Jefe Legionario Nacional,
Legión Nacional Revolucionaria Sindicalista,
Manzana de Gómez 311,
Habana.

Muy señor mío:

Me es grato acusar recibo de su atta. 27 de los corrientes, por la que me envía su felicitación por el discurso que hube de pronunciar en el acto de afirmación patriótico-religioso, celebrado el día 24 del actual en el Teatro "Nacional".

Créame muy agradecido por sus atentas líneas, y reciba un cordial saludo de su atento y s. s.

José I. Rivero

DIARIO DE LA MARINA
DIRECTOR

La Habana, 18 de Marzo de 1940.

Sr. Jesús M. Marinas,
Jefe Legionario Nacional,
Legión Nacional Revolucionaria Sindicalista,
Manzana de Gómez 311,
Habana.

Mi distinguido amigo:

He recibido su atenta fecha 5, en la que me hace recordar su amable visita en unión de los Miembros del Consejo Supremo de la valiente Legión Nacional Revolucionaria Sindicalista.

El cúmulo enorme de responsabilidades que pesan sobre mí en estos tiempos me ha obligado a cancelar entrevistas por un mes. Es por ello que le envío esta corta respondiéndole se entrevista con el Secretario de la Redacción, Dr. Oscar Cicero, quien ya tiene órdenes mías de atenderlo como usted merece y poner las páginas del "Diario" a disposición de los buenos legionarios cubanos.

Espero avisarle dentro de breve tiempo, concediéndole una entrevista que será para mí de sincero placer.

Le saluda con afecto, brazo en alto,

su afmo. amigo,

José I. Rivero

HAVANA PUBLISHER RIVERO lent his aid and advice to the Gray Shirts, a Falange subsidiary. These letters to Gray Shirt Chief Marinas begin with an exchange of compliments. (See

THREE WEEKS LATER, Rivero lets Marinas know that he has ordered his aide to throw the columns of his paper open to the "brave" Gray Shirts, and ends with *Brazo en Alto*, the

¡ARRIBA ESPAÑA!

POR LA PATRIA, EL PAN
Y LA JUSTICIA

REVISTA MENSUAL ILUSTRADA

Acogida a la franquicia postal e inscripta como correspondencia de segunda clase en la Administración de Correos de la Habana.

AÑO DE LA VICTORIA

TERCER ANIVERSARIO DE LA REVOLUCION NACIONAL SINDICALISTA

La Habana, 18 de Noviembre de 1939

Director: MIGUEL BAGUER

Administrador: SERGIO CIFUENTES

Redacción y Administración:

LEALTAD No. 120, Apartado 2484. — : — HABANA

No. 31   AÑO III

EL SECRETARIO PARTICULAR
DEL DIRECTOR DEL DIARIO DE LA MARINA

La Habana, 5 de Octubre de 1940.

Sr. Jesús M. Marinas,
Jefe Legionario Nacional,
Legión Nacional Revolucionaria Sindicalista,
Manzana de Gómez,
Habana.

Distinguido amigo:

El Subdirector ha recibido su atenta carta en la que solicita usted una entrevista en compañía de algunos integrantes del Consejo Supremo de la Legión.

El Dr. Maestri tendrá verdadero gusto en recibir su visita y la de sus compañeros, el martes próximo, a las 12:00 a. m.

De Ud. atentamente,

Miguel Baguer
Miguel Baguer

RIVERO ALSO GAVE PERSONAL advice to the Gray Shirt leader. When he was too busy, his secretary, Miguel Baguer, arranged for Rivero's aide, Raoul Maestri, to receive Marinas. Masthead of Falange organ (right) listed Baguer as editorial director.

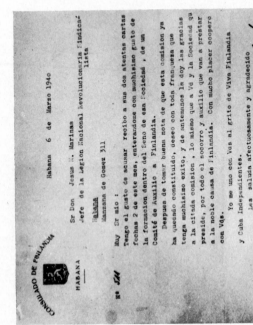

THE FINNISH CONSUL sent Gray Shirt leader this letter (*see* pages 84-85) during Finnish-Soviet War. Note use of the violently anti-American Gray Shirt slogan—*Cuba Independientes.*

SPIRITUAL ADVICE came to the Gray Shirts through a Counselor appointed by the Archbishop of Havana shortly after this letter (translation on page 86) reached Marinas.

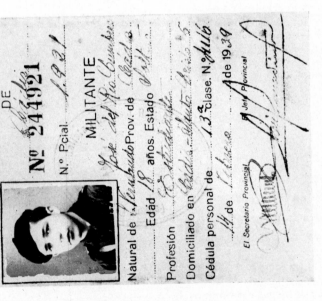

FALANGE SECRET AGENT, José del Rio Cumbreras, attempted to slip into Cuba from a Spanish liner in 1941. (*See* page 93.) Caught by the Cuban Secret Police, his Falange card (above) was taken, and he was held incommunicado pending further developments.

THE LONG ARM OF AXIS diplomacy handed the Cuban-Cuban authorities a signed contract Panama had made with the Falangist through its Havana Consulate. Arnulfo Cumbreras was released, went to Panama. Arnulfo Arias, then dictator of Panama, had close ties with the Falange.

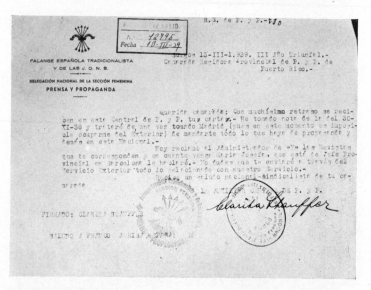

SECRET COURIERS have long carried special correspondence between Spain and Falangist officials in the New World. Above is a letter from Burgos (then capital of Franco Spain) to Puerto Rico, and the envelope in which it arrived. Such letters—this one is addressed to the Chief of Press and Propaganda of the Feminine Section of the Falange and promises to send certain requested materials—arrive on Spanish ships. They are stamped "Franked Mail" but are carried by secret agents.

HEILS ACROSS THE BORDER was the order of the day when the Nazi cruiser *Meteor* visited San Juan, Puerto Rico in 1938. The pro-Falange Casa de Espana threw a party for the Nazi ship's officers. The Nazis assembled under Franco's portrait, toasted the Falange, posed for this picture. And the Captain made a pro-Franco speech.

IN THE SAME ROOM, at the same time, members and sympathizers of the Falange of Puerto Rico posed under this picture of Hitler. The first three men (left to right), José Maria del Valle, Dionisio Trigo Jr., and Tomas Rodriguez were members of the Falange. Leopoldo Martinez Ochoa, right, was Chief of the Puerto Rican Falange.

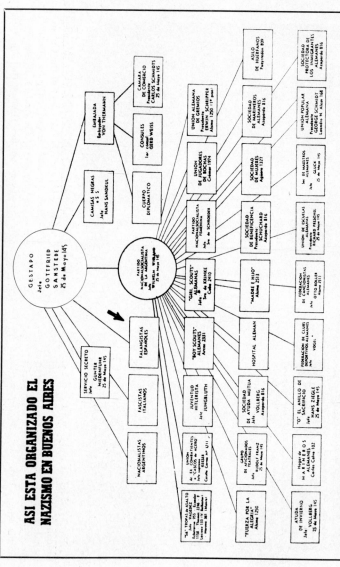

SUPPRESSED BY THE CASTILLO GOVERNMENT, the famous report on Nazi activities in the Argentine, prepared by Deputy Raoul Damonte Taborda for the Argentine Congress, exposed the Falange as a Nazi tool. In the above chart, taken from the Taborda Report, arrow points to the Argentine Falange as part of the Nazi network. In Latin-American countries which have broken with Germany, Falange-run Spanish legations act as diplomatic fronts for German, Italian, and Japanese subversive groups. (*See* pages 179-181.)

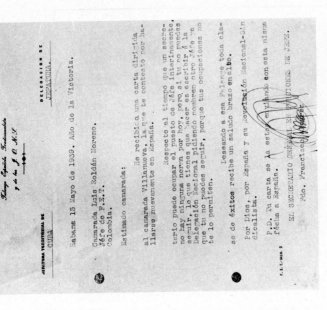

CUBAN AUTHORITIES INTERCEPTED this letter from Francisco Alvarez Garcia, Chief of the Cuban Falange, to Roldan. Alvarez Garcia, acting for Alejandro Villanueva—the Inspector General of all the Falanges in the Americas—notifies Roldan that his request for a ruling has been sent to Spain.

THE CONFIDENTIAL FILE of Luis Roldan, Chief of the Colombia Falange, included reports he made to his predecessor Valverde on mines and topography. In this letter, Valverde asks for further reports and a new code. (See page 201.)

COLOMBIA

CUBA

FRANCO PROMISED ARMS to these blue-shirted Colombian Falangistas when they attempted to stage a Fascist revolt.

THE NAZIS SUPPRESSED the book, *La Falange Exterior*, from which these eight pictures are taken. Augustin Parla (without uniform) was Inspector of Cuban Airports.

GUATEMALAN FALANGISTAS had cause to celebrate early in the Spanish War when their government became one of the first non-Axis powers to recognize

THE FALANGE IN CHILE no longer dares to appear in public wearing Fascist uniforms as they did when this picture was taken in 1938. The temper of the Chilean

WHEN JAPAN DECORATED the Philippine Falange for its role in the fall of Manila, it paid tribute to the skill with which Tokyo's Spanish friends played every card in the deck.

SWASTIKAS ARE ALWAYS PRESENT (*see arrows*) at Falange banquets, meetings, and other public celebrations in the Argentine. But most Spaniards in Argentina oppose the Falange.

FILIPINAS

THE PHILIPPINES were an early target of the Falange leaders and their Nazi masters. The Philippine Falange organizations (*see Chapter Two*) included even tiny pre-school toddlers.

Argentina

LIKE THEIR NAZI TUTORS, the Falange of Argentina went in for mystic and military ritual, anti-Semitic mass meetings, and excursions into street brawling and disorder.

LA FALANGE ESPAÑOLA

CON Franco triunfó la Falange Española en la madre patria, y con la Falange Española triunfó el Instituto Iberoamericano de Berlín. En términos justos: el nazismo.

La Falange es un calco del Partido Nacionalsocialista, a tal punto que tradujo literalmente apropiándoselos los marbetes con que el pardofascismo esparce a todos los ámbitos las semillas de su propaganda. Técnicos nazis forman en sus cuadros orientándolos políticamente. Su labor de penetración en los países latinoamericanos se orienta hacia la agrupamiento en sólidos bloques de las grandes masas españolas, procurando conseguir lo que lograron los nazis con los "alemanes de sangre". Es la fuerza de choque del iberoamericanismo practicado desde Berlín.

La simple lectura del programa de Falange nos previene contra ella. En el capítulo tercero declara: "Tenemos voluntad de Imperio. Afirmamos que la plenitud histórica de España es el Imperio. Reclamamos para España un puesto preeminente en Europa. No soportamos ni el aislamiento internacional ni la mediatización extranjera. Respecto de los países de Hispanoamérica, tendemos a la unificación de la cultura, de intereses económicos y de poder. España alega su condición del eje espiritual del mundo hispánico como título de preeminencia en las empresas universales". En el IV. "Nuestras fuerzas armadas —en tierra, en el mar y en el aire— habrán de ser tan capaces y numerosas como sea preciso para asegurar a España en todo instante la completa in-

dependencia y la jerarquía mundial q...
Y en el V: "España volverá a bu...
za por las rutas del mar. Es...
potencia marítima, pa...
Serrano Suñe...
ni, jefe abso...
fundó la pró...
x... español en Latinoamé...
...a a conocer con un manifiesto en...
...ona la "Confederación Fas...
...do a adherirse a todos los fascistas
am... ambos sexos, y poco más tarde crea el "Consejo... panidad" para "redescubrir el nuevo mundo"
Ante... palabras del mismo Suñer (mayo 14 de 1940) huelga todo comentario: "España sabe ya por experiencia cuanto cuesta descubrir un mundo. Para redescubrirlo el Consejo de Hispanidad no será menos generosa y desprendida. Todo cuanto somos y valemos pondremos en la empresa; pero, bien entendido, que esta vez España no está dispuesta a que otros pueblos se aprovechen del descubrimiento en beneficio de ella y las naciones de hispanidad. El Consejo de Hispanidad restaurará la conciencia unitaria de todos los pueblos que forman la comunidad hispánica". En pocas palabras, es la resurrección del viejo Consejo de Indias que

"IN EXACT TERMS—NAZISM," says the famous Taborda Report in describing the Falange. The Report adds: "With the Spanish Falange, the Ibero-American Institute triumphed in Berlin ... The Falange is a copy of the Nazi Party. ... Nazi technicians take part in their plans, directing them politically. ... It is a strong Ibero-Americanism practiced from Berlin. The simplest reading of the Falange program tells us to beware of it." (See pages 179-181.)

The White Paper goes on to describe the Neutrality Legislation and the arms embargo imposed on the Republic to further this policy. It continues with a paragraph that will be long remembered as a classic of understatement:

Shortly after the beginning of the conflict in Spain it became evident that several of the principal powers of Europe were projecting themselves into the struggle through the furnishing of arms and war materials and other aid to the contending sides, thus creating real danger of the spread of the conflict into a European war. In an effort to remedy this menacing situation, a committee was set up in London, by agreement of the European governments, to carry out a concerted policy of nonintervention and to put an end to export of arms to Spain.

Why, at this late date, the authors of the White Paper carefully neglected to mention the names of these "principal powers" who furnished "arms and . . . other aid" is a question that should not be left unanswered.

The brief section on the Italo-German conquest of Spain winds up with another paragraph which admits that "there was a feeling in some quarters that our policy should be changed"; but was nevertheless not changed for two reasons: "growing complications" and the "thoroughly unsatisfactory experience during 1935 in endeavoring to preserve peace in the Italo-Ethiopian situation."

The war has produced no greater confession of intellectual and diplomatic bankruptcy than those sections of this White Book which deal with the Spanish War either directly or by significant omission as on Page 1. It explains perfectly why ships flying the Falange flag have continued to carry fuel from the New World to the Nazi planes raining death on American and British troops in North Africa and the troops of our allies in Russia. It explains with sickening clarity why Falange agents like José del Castano were able to disrupt the civilian defenses of Manila when the Japanese attacked. It explains why, in every Western Hemisphere country with the exception of Mexico, Falangist

Spain maintains legations which are field headquarters for the largest organized Axis Fifth Column in the Americas.

This White Paper makes bitter reading when stacked up along the writings and speeches of those world statesmen who saw the issue of Spain more realistically during the Spanish War. This handful of statesmen saw the Spanish War not as a "civil conflict," but as the first of the battles of the present war. Men like Maxim Litvinov and Pierre Cot, and Georges Mandel, and Jan Masaryk gave ample warning that if Hitler won the Spanish War he would then move on to further European conquests. History—if not the American White Book—records that less than six months after General Wilhelm von Faupel entered Madrid, Nazi bombers were pulverizing Warsaw.

Liberal Pierre Cot and Conservative George Mandel knew, in 1936, that the Spanish Republicans were talking sense when the Spaniards said: "If Madrid falls, Paris is next." They did what they could to prevent the Hitler triumph in Spain. But their efforts were undermined in London. Mandel, now a Nazi prisoner at Riom, is credited with remarking, after the fall of France, that the French goose was cooked in Madrid and served in Munich.

Visionary Lazaro Cardenas, then President of Mexico, sent what aid he could to the embattled Republic. He never recognized the Franco Government, and opened Mexico's doors to the Spanish Republican émigrés of whom Carlton Hayes speaks with such disdain.

In our country, we did not lack for statesmen who saw the issues of the Spanish War in their true colors. Outstanding among their number was Henry L. Stimson.

As Secretary of State in the Hoover Cabinet, Mr. Stimson tried to apply the only measures which would have halted Japan in Manchuria in 1931. The appeasement-minded British Foreign Office wrecked the Stimson plan at the time—and gave him an unforgettable inkling of what the history of the next decade would be if appeasement persisted. On December 7, 1941, history tragically affirmed the correctness of Mr. Stimson's Manchurian position a decade earlier. His stand on Spain, during the bloody years of the Spanish War, was no less correct.

Early in the course of that war, Mr. Stimson became convinced that the Arms Embargo the government had applied against the Spanish Republic was not only illegal but, more important, also unwise. In a statement submitted to the State Department on January 23, 1939, the former Secretary of State made a brilliant appeal for the end of this embargo.

The Spanish Republic [he wrote], has for many months been putting up a most surprising and gallant defense against opponents who have had every advantage in the way of land and naval organization and who are illegally aided by powerful organized forces from Italy and Germany.

Unlike the State Department, Mr. Stimson knew how to spell the names of the Axis powers who had invaded Spain. His memorandum continued to say:

If this Loyalist Government is overthrown, it is evident now that the defeat will be solely due to the fact that it has been deprived of its right to buy from us and other friendly nations the munitions necessary for its defense. I cannot believe that our government or our country would wish to assume such a responsibility.

Mr. Stimson's long statement concluded with a passage which, if heeded, might have changed the history of the world.

In short, I have come to the conclusion that the embargo imposed under the resolution of May 1, 1937, should be lifted by the President. . . . The embargo, which by terms of the law authorizing it was intended as a protection against conditions which would endanger the peace of the United States, is now shown by the events of the past two years to be itself a source of danger to that peace. Any danger that may come to the people of the United States from the situation in Spain would arise not from any lawful sale of munitions in our markets to the [Republican] Government of Spain, but from assistance which our embargo has given to the enemies of Spain. It is the success of the lawless precedents created by those enemies which would constitute our real danger. There is no reason why we should ourselves facilitate and accentuate that danger. There is still less reason why we should violate our own historic policy to do so. The prestige and safety of our country will not be protected by abandoning its self-respecting traditions, in order to avoid the hostility of reckless violators of international law in Europe.

But when he wrote the brief from which these passages are taken, Mr. Stimson was merely a private citizen. The Secretary of State—who should have written such a brief himself—was Cordell Hull, whose epic and fiery denunciation of Japanese deception was not made until *after* Pearl Harbor.

Hull had also made a strong statement on the Arms Embargo during the Spanish War. It was in 1937, shortly after the Nazi battleship *Deutschland* had shelled the defenseless Spanish town of Almeria in reprisal for an attack on the battleship by a Republican plane which got away. The entire world was shocked, and a delegation of Congressmen—O'Connell of Montana, Coffee of Washington, and Scott of California—visited Hull with the request that the Arms Embargo be applied against Germany and Italy for their belligerency in the Spanish War. At that time the Spanish Republic was the only nation against which the embargo was applied.

The Secretary of State was appalled by the suggestion made by the Congressmen. "No, no," he told them. "We can't do that. We must not do anything to offend Hitler at this moment."

The Embargo was never to be applied against the Axis nations during the entire Spanish War.

We have now "offended" Hitler to the extent of declaring war on Germany. Anxious Americans have the right to ask if fear of offending Hitler is still the motive behind our continuing and increasing appeasement of Falangist Spain—an appeasement so complete that even in 1943 our State Department gingerly refrains from mentioning the role of Germany and Italy in what it delicately still chooses to designate as the "Spanish civil conflict." United Nations citizens have a right to ask whether the life of one United Nations seaman who met death at the hands of Nazi-Falange agents like Heinz August Luning and Ricardo Dotres is worth less than the sensitivities of the Axis statesmen and puppets who are struggling to destroy us.

In the light of the harsh realities of our times, the "Spanish White Paper" issued by the National Maritime Union in New York on March 11, 1943, is couched in terms that all Americans can applaud. The seamen, who had by March 11 seen close to 5000 of their number perish as war victims of the Axis, passed a resolution pledging to refuse to serve on any ship carrying supplies to Hitler Spain. The resolution notified the State Department that they would have "to hire Japanese, Germans, and Italians" to replace American seamen on all ships bound for Spanish ports.

The National Maritime Union's resolution, framed in simple language, was a perfect answer to the Spanish theses of the State Department's White Paper. Among other things, the resolution proclaimed:

Some sections of the State Department have been flirting with notorious Fascists and seem intent upon losing the peace while thousands of seamen are dying to win the war against fascism.

The old policy of appeasing Japan with scrap iron and oil while sympathizing with China brought death not only to millions of Chinese, but also to thousands of our soldiers, sailors, Marines and Merchant Seamen.

A similar policy of suicide is being pursued in our dealings with Franco Spain.

This, in spite of the fact that high government officials belatedly have agreed that a mistake was made by Britain and the United States in not supporting Loyalist Spain in its fight against Franco and his Fascist allies.

It is well known that Franco Spain is stooging for Nazi Germany.

We feel that diverting valuable ships for Franco Spain is the same as diverting them for Hitler Germany.

We therefore condemn this appeasement policy of the State Department as inimical to the best interests of the American people and the United Nations.

Unhappy Spain, in 1936, became the battleground of Hitler's first major military offensive against the democracies of the world. We had it in our power, then, to make Madrid the tomb of fascism. Had the democracies drawn the line in Spain, had they simply recognized the tenets of international law, Hitler Germany would have been crushed forever.

In 1936 Hitler had had a mere three years in which to prepare for war. The Soviet Army was then more than a match for the *Reichswehr*. The French Army was then a well-trained, anti-German force of genuine effectiveness. Czechoslovakia was an independent little fortress of democracy, with an efficient and tough army and a tremendous arms-production capacity. The British, if weak in numbers, had a greater potential in 1936 than they had in 1940 after Dunkirk. And Spain's millions lacked only arms.

Arms to Spain alone might have turned the trick. But had this observance of international law and plain common sense—self preservation was the wrong law of nature to ignore in 1936—led to the spread of war that the appeasers professed to fear at the time, the resulting European war could only have spelled disaster for Germany and Italy— disaster that would have come so quickly that the United States would have escaped involvement as a physical participant in the war. Then, with Germany crushed, Japan would never have moved against us for fear of a strong Anglo-American-Soviet alliance.

Instead of firmness, the democracies met Hitler's challenge by neatly abandoning the Spanish Republic to the tender mercies of the Axis. Madrid became the inspiration of the common people of Europe—particularly in France. But when the heroic stand of Madrid led only to the shameful betrayal at Munich, the common French soldier lost his heart for war, and the Czech fortress became Hitler's. The continuation of appeasement in Europe gave Japan more time to prepare, more time to purchase oil and scrap metals and machinery from the United States.

In the fullest sense, the bombs that fell on Pearl Harbor on December 7, 1941, were machined in Madrid and filled in Munich by the appeasement policies of London, Paris, *and* Washington.

This is not hindsight for the sake of hindsight.

Nothing is gained by merely sighing and repeating that far-seeing statesmen like Henry L. Stimson were right in their judgments of the significance of the Spanish War while Hitler was still being frustrated at the gates of Madrid.

What is important is that we remember that the logic of their position in 1936-1939 still prevails. Truths never die; time merely makes them tougher.

If it was dangerous to appease fascism in Spain in 1936, it is a thousand times more perilous today. For the Fascist cancer has more than merely brought death to Spain itself: it has, in the form of Falangismo, spread to Manila, to Latin America, to the United States of America. Spain has become the base headquarters of the greatest Axis Fifth Column in the Western Hemisphere, a Fifth Column that will not be smashed until fascism is destroyed on the entire Iberian Peninsula.

The realities of Falangist Spain versus the United Nations in 1943 point in only one direction: in Spain, where the democracies of the world suffered the bitter first defeats of World War II, the same democracies can lose the peace of this war.

Fascism—and this includes Axis Spain—is waging a total war against the democracies today. As long as we permit the myth of Spanish neutrality to exist, our war of defense remains less than total—and it nurtures the seeds of World War III.

The entire background of World War II is tragic guarantee that if the Iberian Peninsula emerges from this war as the Fascist bastion that it is at this hour, then all our dead will have died in vain.

INDEX